How Your Chakras Interact

The Personal Integration of the Chakras from an Astrological Perspective

BY

Tom Sheeley

2010 Acausal Publishing
Minneapolis, Minnesota

First Edition, designed by Acausal Publishing 2010

ISBN: 978-0-9844880-0-1

To contact Mr. Sheeley e-mail
chakricastologer@hotmail.com

Table of Contents

Why Understand the Chakras?

What can knowing about the chakras do for us? Well, we can use how our chakras feel within our own body to understand our psychological state. For example, suppose that when we first go to work in the morning our stomach starts to tie up into knots. Knowing that the solar plexus chakra connects to our social identity, we can deduce that our workplace is hard on our ego. Then we can think about our job using our sense of social identity as the starting point. If we also understand how our own chakras interact, we can trace our solar plexus's underlying issues. We can see the larger chakric context in which we personally place our solar plexus.

Suppose we are talking with our father and we notice that our throat feels tight and constricted. Are we having trouble telling our father what we really think? Are we unable to put ourselves into words? This may be because we feel that he will not truly listen to us. Again, we can look at how our throat fits into our overall chakric picture and try to understand our throat's reaction. The point of physical stress gives us the immediate chakric focus. We need to examine ourselves a bit more to uncover the details. The place of chakric sensitivity alerts us that a particular part of our psyche is distressed. It gives us a starting point for our inquiry.

We will look at the chakras in some detail and we will also see how we can use astrology, of all things, to quickly grasp how a person's chakras work together. You may be wondering what is the value of chakric astrology? Why would you bother using such a system? Simply put, chakric astrology provides a quick method of seeing how a particular person's chakras most naturally interact.

While everyone has the same seven chakras, not everyone's chakras interconnect in the same way. One person's throat chakra may be dominant in their awareness. Another person's heart chakra may be the center of their attention. How each person's chakras interact describes their unique personality.

Of course, simply having a general grasp of the chakras can be very useful. While they are somewhat elusive, almost everyone has had "butterflies in the stomach," or "a lump in the throat," or some other physical feeling that can be linked psychologically to a chakra.

Hopefully the astrological parts of this discussion aren't too theoretical. Ultimately, astrology is just another tool for helping us to see who we are. While astrology is helpful as a short cut to seeing how our chakras interact, our own experience is our best guide. Astrology provides the theory, it is our lives that provide the facts.

The concept behind astrology is simple: our consciousness tends to echo itself on many levels and in many ways. Therefore, our personality's reflection can be seen in the location of the planets at the time of our birth. The planetary placements reflect our consciousness, if only symbolically. This means that we can use astrology to quickly grasp how a person's chakras work together.

In house-based astrology, our external circumstances are described by a circular wheel of twelve houses, or twelve different facets of our lives. House based astrology keys on external events. Our inner state of being is deduced from our outer situation. Our inner consciousness itself is never directly seen.

Chakric astrology has the opposite slant. It is wholly psychological. Within chakric astrology there is no description of any actual physical circumstance. There is no direct reference to anything that exists outside the individual's awareness. That an external world beyond the individual actually exists is assumed. Yet the details of that outer world are not the direct concern of chakric astrology. Chakric astrology focuses on how we internally create and sustain our own conscious awareness.

This highly subjective emphasis makes chakric astrology miserable at predicting actual events. What chakric astrology does do quite well is to describe a person's manner of understanding those events. It describes the perspectives they use when they interact with their environment. It reveals what a person uses as their inner anchor. It describes how they absorb their outer experiences into themselves. It also shows how their internal reality presses outward and how they seek to externally express their inner being.

In short, chakric astrology is completely psychological. So, why bother with something that has no direct connection to 'real life'? What's the point?

Our consciousness holds an even greater key to our happiness than our physical circumstances. Our spiritual journey occurs largely within our own understanding. How we relate to ourselves and the world around us is the crux of our journey.

This system, by describing the structure and nature of our consciousness, gives us a way to understand how our inner reality works. We will see how each of us takes the universal structure of human consciousness and personalizes it. How we each take the seven chakras and put them together in our own unique way.

But this system is not meant to put us into a psychological straight jacket. We are not finding out our chakric fate. Rather, we are seeing how we unthinkingly put our awareness together. This can help us to decide whether or not we wish to float along or to try to consciously choose to do something else. Self-knowledge gives us greater freedom.

As the underlying structure of our consciousness becomes more familiar, we may notice things that are normally hidden from our view. This is of real value to people who wish to know the 'whys' behind their internal awareness. Hopefully we will discover personality mechanisms that weren't visible earlier. For example, it can help someone to see that they tend to emotionally feel according to how they think. That is, if they think they should emotionally feel a certain way, then they will try to make themselves feel that way. Another person might find that they physically express how they emotionally feel. For example, they might cough when they get embarrassed. Yet another person may tend to emotionally feel the way their culture expects them to feel. They will not allow themselves to feel emotions that are socially unacceptable, or feel them in ways that are unusual.

Chakric awareness enables us to smooth out the rough spots in our character. Just as the outer world can be changed, so can our inner world. Our chakric awareness is actually rather pliable. We are not condemned from birth to enact our consciousness in a particular way. The chakric birth diagram merely shows our automatic tendencies.

It is best to see the chakric diagram as an accurate mirror. A mirror can only reflect how a person looks. It will not cause them to look a certain way. If you have brown eyes, then the mirror cannot make you have blue eyes. It is the same way the chakric diagram. It can only reflect what you are. It merely reveals tendencies. We can choose to do something other than our unthinking tendencies. Although, because the chakras are based on our conditioning and habits, it does require effort to make such changes.

We will learn about the chakras. We will look at their structure and notice the impact it has on our awareness. We will understand the impact of various chakras on how and what we feel. Understanding the structure of our chakras will also help us to grasp why the intuitive and mystical states of consciousness are so slippery and elusive.

Our chakras are the lens through which we experience and understand the world. Each of the seven chakras has a unique outlook. Together they create the richly textured world that we live in. The world changes a great deal with each different chakra's perspective.

We will learn how to diagram a person's chakric awareness. Each person's chakric diagram reflects the way that they internally process their reality. This is more a matter of style than of substance, as all of us contain the same seven chakras and interact with the same external world. Still, each of us emphasizes different aspects of our shared core humanness.

It cannot be emphasized enough that one person's chakric diagram is no better than another person's chakric diagram. There is no way to use this system to prove that one person is more evolved or more spiritual than someone else. It is impossible to accurately know what the chakric diagrams of, say, Jesus Christ, or Gautama Buddha, look like. And even if we knew what their diagrams look like, it is unlikely that these chakric diagrams would prove to be ideal for anyone other than them. Each person creates their own blend of experiences, reactions and understanding.

By the way, the chakras are only one of the seven 'vehicles' of awareness that we possess. Just as we have seven chakras, we also have seven vehicles. The vehicles are large scale perspectives. Seen in the context of the larger vehicle structure, the chakras are the etheric vehicle. The etheric vehicle acts as a kind of reservoir of responses to our environment. Eventually the etheric vehicle becomes a set of expectations and conditioned responses to the world around us. It is also termed the 'habit' body.

The overall structure of the chakras is the same as the vehicles, only on a smaller scale. Each one of the chakras echoes one of the seven vehicles. The root chakra is equivalent, in smaller scale, to the 'root' (or microcosmic) vehicle. The genital chakra is the smaller scale version of the larger corresponding organic (experiential) vehicle. The solar plexus chakra echoes the etheric (social) vehicle. The heart chakra mirrors the astral (emotional) vehicle. The throat chakra is equivalent to the mental (intellectual) vehicle and the designations of the upper two chakras depends on your theology. They both describe a sense of relationship and order that is extremely abstract, fluid and integrated. (See the Appendixes at the end for the structure of the Seven Vehicles.)

While from one point of view the chakras are merely part of a larger whole, from another point of view they are the larger whole, only stepped down into smaller form. They contain the whole within them. This means that the chakras can be taken as a completely self-sufficient field of awareness. Actually, each of the seven vehicles can be seen as a self-contained whole. But keep in mind that as the seven chakras together form a whole, so do the seven vehicles. Just as we are normally unaware of our chakra's activity, the vast majority of the seven vehicles work behind the scenes unconsciously.

Introduction to the Chakras

The term chakra comes from the Sanskrit word for wheel. The chakras can be described as spinning wheels of energy that run along our spine. These vortexes interact with our environment. They are also reservoirs of subtle consciousness that are the result of our personal experiences. Usually we are not aware of our chakra's activity. On those rare occasions when we do notice our chakras, it is usually in a moment of stress. We notice our solar plexus chakra when we are very nervous and have "butterflies in our stomach." Similarly, our throat chakra is felt when we cannot figure out what to say and we feel a "lump in our throat."

Each of the seven chakras deals with a distinct facet of our awareness. Knowing about our chakras can help us to understand how we feel. We can use our body's chakric sensations to more fully understand how we respond to certain situations. For example, suppose someone we love tells us just how inadequate we really are. If our stomach starts to hurt, then our sense of social identity is reacting. Who we are socially feels undermined. If our throat feels tight, then we feel misunderstood and that we have not been able to clearly speak our minds. We feel our ideas are being judged and attacked. If we feel tight around the chest, then we feel unloved and emotionally oppressed. We feel a sense of emotional pressure and feel emotionally disconnected from them. If we get a headache, then we are having trouble visualizing what they're saying and dealing with what it could mean. We may intuit that there is an underlying issue. Perhaps the issue is more complex than they're presenting.

From these simple examples you can see how having a basic understanding of our chakras, where they are and what they mean, can help us understand our day-to-day lives. As we mentioned earlier, the chakras run up along the spine and into our head. They are loosely connected to our autonomic nervous system. They can be seen as a seven-story building, like so:

Crown
Brow
Throat
Heart
Solar Plexus
Genital
Root

At the base of the spine we find the root chakra. This chakra is concerned with the broad foundations of our existence. In our normal day to day experience the root chakra is the source of very simple instinctual responses. This is why it is sometimes called the "fight or flight" level. At the same time it is the source of our amazingly complex physical being. The root chakra operates below our conscious awareness. For example, we are not aware of our body as it figures out all the details required when we do the very ordinary, yet extremely complex, task of walking's step by step motion. The root chakra automatically takes care of these things.

The root chakra creates and defines the structure that we live within. The scope of its awareness is greater than any individual, and yet it unconsciously exists within each of us. The root chakra is our personal connection to a collective human racial awareness. The root's physical reality impacts our underlying social structure. The root is where we stand on the physical foundations which were given to us by the human race. These foundations were created over a vast amount of time, changing and evolving slowly.

We unconsciously enact the root. In our personal awareness the root is usually experienced as instinctive responses, as an underlying sense of trust or mistrust, or a sense of the flow of large scale social forces around and through us.

Next up the spine is the genital chakra. It deals with our awareness of physical sensation. It is the only chakra where something actually happens. It is our first purely personal level of awareness and it is fairly naive. Here we either like or dislike an experience. We find ourselves either attracted to, or repulsed by, something. This chakra's experiences become the basis of what we expect to feel. Familiar situations are assumed to lead to familiar experiences.

At the genital chakra we are directly involved in our world. We develop some simple habits, but at this level we are pretty much wrapped up in what is happening right in front of us. The genital is very focused on what it is directly feeling at the present moment. The genital chakra's awareness is fairly simple and it doesn't really deal well with anything remote.

Occasionally our experiences at the genital level can be rather overwhelming. We seem to lose our sense of ourselves in the experience of what we are feeling. At the genital chakra our sense of being an individual self is still new and this makes it both tentative and invigorating. One minute we are totally immersed in an experience and suddenly all we feel is ourselves in the act of experiencing.

The third level is the solar plexus chakra. The solar plexus is the center of our outer social identity. This chakra is often considered the basis of the ego, or our social sense of self. While the solar plexus is more complex than the genital chakra, at this level our thinking is still fairly simple. Here we seek to anchor our sense of self securely through personal and cultural self definitions. We create a well defined world that is securely enclosed by what we presume is true. We find objects and events that disrupt our definitions disturbing and offensive.

It is through this somewhat naive chakric level that we create our social sense of self, our social identity. The solar plexus deals with our place in a cultural hierarchy. Struggles for social dominance are a large part of this level's reality. When the solar plexus experiences a situation that it cannot understand, we become unsure of who we are and how we fit into the scheme of things. Often as a result of this social identity stress our stomach becomes queasy. The huge sales of stomach acid relief products shows how common solar plexus issues are.

The fourth chakra, at the center, is the heart. It is the emotional level and it is the seat of the soul. It has emotionally charged reactions to objects and events which become our purely personal symbols. The heart is the core of our sense of inner personal identity. It is the first chakra to live both in tangible and abstract domains. Here we use our actual experiences to create fantasy realities which we use to understand and interpret the underlying meaning of our lives. The heart is the level of sleep's dream imagery. We use the heart to create how we feel and what we desire.

The heart is the level of personal desire and fulfillment. It is the underlying source of physical illness and health. We are exactly as we feel and desire in our hearts. The heart guides our personal choices. It adds depth and meaning to our lives. It connects our inner being, who we feel we are, to our outer reality. It dominates who we feel ourselves to be. The heart is where we take the bare facts of life and lift them up into abstract ideals. We come to desire more than social possessions and prestige, we desire personal emotional connection and fulfillment. The real also begins to give way to the ideal.

The fifth chakra is the throat. At the throat we are slightly above the physical world. It is also the home of our abstract sense of self, where the little voice in our head lives. It is where we assign symbols to reality which we then use to communicate with each other (language), and to manipulate relationships (mathematics). The throat is highly social and is extremely concerned with understanding, manipulating and creating various kinds of relationships.

The throat is associated with the mind. It creates rational structures that define relationships. In turn, these relationships define what we think things are. The throat is the seat of true, structured logic and intellect. The throat chakra is the abstract echo of the concrete solar plexus. It is our abstract inner identity in counterpoint to the solar plexus's concrete outer identity. Just as the solar plexus defines who we are physically (through genetics, social position, geography), the throat defines who we are according to our ideas (through the concepts associated with religious, social, and intellectual beliefs).

The throat is the first completely abstract chakra. It exists without any direct experience of physical time and space. The throat uses symbols, such as language, to represent actual things. It is far easier to juggle ideas than it is to juggle physical reality. This means that the throat can quickly look at concepts and see if they can work in the 'real world'. When an idea 'actually works' it is because our mental abstractions are detailed and accurate enough.

The sixth chakra is the brow. Also called the Third Eye, it is where we intuitively see what something is on deeper levels, which helps us know what it could become. The brow mirrors the genital chakra for it is also a form of direct knowing. The genital chakra perceives physical sensations, while the brow chakra perceives abstract sensations. Both of these chakras are nonrational: they experience something and therefore they know it. The brow, despite having a much broader perspective than the genital chakra, uses a similar perceptual mechanism. The brow uses the same 'like or dislike' reaction to makes choices about what it 'sees' in much the same way as the genital chakra. We either move toward a visualized potential at the brow, or move away from it. We like what we see, or we don't like what we see.

The brow chakra has a totally abstract awareness. Like the throat it is above time and space. This makes it very fluid and capable of seeing many different things very quickly. The brow also sees relationships that exist beneath the surface. The potentials that the brow sees are often quite fluid and so they may or may not happen. Some situations are more likely to happen than others. How like they are depends on the force and depth of the momentums involved and how strongly the various parts involved adhere together.

The seventh and topmost chakra is the crown. The crown perceives abstract patterns of relationship. This is the broadest perspective we have. At the crown we tap into a larger abstract structure. This can be a social conceptual framework, a group mind, God, or whatever pattern is working behind the scenes, above and beyond the scope of any individual perspective. We perceive order at the crown that goes beyond our personal creation. This is sometimes experienced as touching God. The crown chakra is the home of the mystical. The crown's perspective is above our ability to consciously understand. Often we experience the crown's awareness in a sudden flash of understanding. We have an intuition of the way things fit together, or of what we should do, in response to some larger reality.

The crown is the partner of the root. The crown can change the structure of the root. The abstract ideal at the crown precipitates the tangible reality of the root. This is how we evolve at the trans-personal human racial level. The crown mirrors the root, except it creates abstract patterns of relationship while the root creates tangible patterns of relationship. Sometimes these patterns are simple, such as the socially agreed upon rules for which side of the highway to drive on. Sometimes they are complex, such as an astonishing coincidence, whose odds are so great that it borders on the miraculous.

To the crown chakra reality is the result of abstract patterns of relationship. To the crown the physical world is created by converging patterns of formless energy. Things cohere by force of Will. Change the Will and you change the reality.

The crown sees reality as incredibly fluid. It perceives time and space, physical reality, as the stable motion of pure energy. The crown looks up and sees pure spirit, in the guise of formless energy, moving down into tangible form. Pure formless being exists above the crown.

As we have seen, structurally the chakras mirror each other. The top three echo the bottom three. The crown is the abstract equivalent of the tangible root chakra. The brow is the abstract equivalent of the tangible genital chakra. The throat is the abstract equivalent of the tangible solar plexus chakra.

The brow and the genital chakra are both concerned with gathering information. They react directly to what they perceive. Both the brow and the genital chakras use a "like or dislike" response. For both the throat and the solar plexus chakras the crux of their awareness is in making sense of the relationships they perceive. To do this, both of them manipulate facts and create the 'whys', or reasons, behind relationships. The solar plexus is not so much concerned with gathering information as it is with manipulating it for it's own ends. The throat is a bit less pragmatic and it believes in an ideal of truth and pure knowing. Both chakras define who we are according to the relationships that they perceive and believe in.

Each of the middle five chakras evolves into ever greater complexity as we rise up them. (The root and the crown chakras are both special trans-personal chakras.) With each step up the middle five chakras we increase our scope of awareness. This enables a higher chakra to use its broader perspective to understand the narrower awareness of a lower chakra. The lower chakra becomes data for the understanding of the higher chakra.

The genital chakra is the most basic of our personal chakras. Its scope of awareness is limited to our body. It feels and knows things through physical sensation. It is extremely specific. It feels, therefore it knows. It is our primary chakra. The rest of the chakras ramify our genital chakra's experiences. The next chakra up, the solar plexus, contains a somewhat broader perspective than the genital chakra. It takes the awareness of the genital chakra and places it into more complex patterns relationship. It adds cultural nuances to our personal experiences. The heart chakra, again, has a broader frame of understanding than either the genital or the solar plexus. It gives emotional depth and symbolic meaning to our experiences. The throat chakra, once again, has a broader perspective than any of the three chakras below it. It uses rational structures to cognitively organize, investigate and understand and build beyond our physical experiences. Lastly, the brow chakra gives us our largest personal framework of understanding. It takes our experiences and intuitively judges how they fit into the life that we are trying to create. It decides what to build on and what to ignore. The brow is our largest personal perspective and also the least consciously integrated of the five personal chakras.

A More Detailed Look at the Chakras

Root Chakra

The root contains a broad knowledge that is beyond the scope of our personal comprehension. The physical foundations of our own body, the heritage of humanity and our own personal place within that heritage, are all larger than we can consciously perceive. This is the realm of the root. On one level it is a transpersonal awareness of pure physical order and chemical relationships, while on another level it is the pure flow of personal and collective progress. The root becomes our sense of personal connection to the surging flow of humanity as it grows out of its experience. It is also our connection to our own personal large scale momentums.

We may taste a sense of destiny when our awareness goes into the root chakra. The root connects us to such vast momentums that we often get swept up in what we feel is the progress of humanity. But what we know at the root, and how we know it, is often rather vague. Dealing with the root is like seeing the above-the-surface tip of an iceberg. We see something's there, but there is much beneath the surface that we do not see. All we can consciously sense is that a great amount of activity is going on below the surface.

At the root the human race lives in us, while we also we live in the human race. The root chakra anchors us in the larger foundations that underlie our existence. The root helps us to place ourselves into a larger context. Even if we are not actively helping to shape it's course, through the root chakra we feel connected to humanity as a whole, to where it has been and to where it is going. We feel that we are a part of the human race. At times this can feel like an imposition on our individuality. It can also feel like the reason we were born. At the root we see the flow of destiny. The impact of the root on our psyches can be profound.

The root chakra is ultimately grounded in physical reality. It is where our body is formed. Our body follows the blueprint given to us by humanity. At the root we find the genetic coding of our existence. It gives us our particular body as a specific representation of the human race.

The root also contains our instinctive responses. The instinctual drives of the root are not our individual creation. We often personally experience the root as a fight or flight mechanism. This leaves us with the impression that the root is simplistic and mainly concerned with our survival. In purely personal terms this is largely true. At the root chakra we have a core sense of trust or mistrust. We either accept a situation and feel safe within it or we feel unsafe.

Our root also contains the personal momentum behind our own existence. The root is our connection to our reasons for incarnate physical being. It is where our personal reasons for being born into this particular body at this particular moment in human history is found. We can either trust or mistrust this reason, and thereby trust or mistrust our own existence.

The root chakra is slow to change because it is so large in scope. It must be extremely thorough. But this makes it very sure of what it knows and does. Because of its broad base of awareness, the root is highly sensitive to structure and context.

The foundation determines the size and shape of a building. The root is aware of the impact foundations have on what can be built. This sensitivity to structure is the root's special genius. The root looks at a given situation's structure and knows its inherent potentials and limitations.

Within the root there is a core human structure on which we build our individuality. At its center, the root is not overly concerned with the things that our purely individual levels of personality worry about. The root does not really care about our individual neurotic problems.

Within the root chakra dwells the kundalini. There is a great deal of glamorizing of the kundalini, giving it a great deal of magical allure. It is the creative energy/awareness that resides in our body. It is the raw fire of the spirit (the crown) ensouled in our flesh.

The kundalini is sometimes experienced as a white-hot fire that rises up through the spinal column out of the base of the spine. It burns away any personal blockages of consciousness that it finds in its path. When it goes through a blocked chakra there is often an abrupt sound associated with the kundalini's passage. The "thunderclap from Heaven" at the Baptism of Jesus Christ could be interpreted as the passage of the kundalini through one or all of Jesus' chakras. There are also tales of a loud thunderclap sound at the moment of the Enlightenment of Gautama Buddha. The root chakra transcends petty concerns and brings the individual into greater alignment with the whole.

There are stories of the kundalini spontaneously flowing through a person's body. A woman was talking with some friends when suddenly she felt a heat to go up her spine and her friends heard a distinct clapping sound at the moment she felt the warmth reach her throat. Another account tells of a woman whose big toenails turned blackish purple and fell off after the kundalini had spontaneously jumped up through her body. Afterward, she was astonished by how often people don't really say what they feel. There was such a large shift in her perspective after the kundalini jumped up her spine that she was actually afraid she might be placed in a mental hospital.

It is not unusual for people who have had the spontaneous arising of the kundalini to feel that people aren't very honest. The superficial niceties of social interaction, such as saying "How nice to see you." can seem deceitful. The clarity of perception that the kundalini gives enables us to know that they don't really feel it is "nice to see you".

It is generally considered to be unwise to try to consciously raise the kundalini up the spine. If nothing else, this is because it can be extremely disorienting. And that is ignoring all of the magical hype that the kundalini receives in whispered conversation. The kundalini is a very powerful connective awareness whose honesty can be just as naive as it is wise, even as it sees very subtle levels of interactivity.

The emergence of the root into consciousness can feel oppressive. It can feel demanding, unyielding, and unkind. It is largely a question of our relationship to the human racial structure that we live within. Do we embrace it and see it as a foundation for our personal fulfillment, or do we see it as an oppressive barrier to our individual wishes? Do we suffer our fate or do we feel fulfilled by what we see as our destiny? Obviously, the root is of greater concern to some people than to others. For some people, the foundations given to us by the root are simply assumed and never given a second thought. For others, the concerns of the root must be consciously investigated.

The root connects us to a vast, powerful, transpersonal awareness. If an individual personality is unable to integrate the root's collective awareness, they are in for a rough ride. Part of what our individual ego structure does for us is it blocks out information that we either do not need, or that we cannot deal with. This means that normally our root chakra runs on autopilot, taking us along for the human racial ride.

Chakric astrology can be used to help us understand how prominent the root is in someone's awareness. The problem is that the root is basically an unconscious awareness. Even if we know the root matters to a particular person, it is difficult to know exactly what their root chakra's concerns are. We usually have to speak in generalities when dealing with the root. The questions become "What is their destiny? What is the destiny of the human race? How personally connected are they to such matters?" Aside from these questions, the root can normally be taken in biological terms. It simply becomes our underlying physical mechanism.

It is difficult for most of us to view the root in personal terms. It is like we are in first grade and we are trying to understand how our going to school and learning all that boring stuff is part of the progression of humanity. It is the rare first grader that can comprehend this. Most of us react in very narrow personal terms to our experience of the first grade. When we were young, our going to school was something we were told to do by our parents. It was required of us by our culture. It is usually only much later that we understand how our cultural and individual needs fit together.

For the individual, the root chakra can be a source of stability. At the same time, as the foundation behind our own existence, it can be challenging. On the more mystical side, an assimilated root awareness enables us to personally stand as an equal to the whole human race. We identify ourselves with the human race. This is not megalomania, nor is it self aggrandizement. It is a simple realization of how we live through the human race and the human race lives through us.

The larger human racial consciousness has more force than an individual consciousness does. But when an individual becomes immersed within the root chakra, that person can take on the weight of our collective consciousness. They may become personally entwined with an archetype. Their lives may feel like they have grand mythic qualities. They may see themselves as similar to a character from mythology, a religious figure, or some other symbol of our collective human experience.

In Freudian terms the root chakra could be considered an unconscious component of the superego. We find ourselves striving to satisfy the demands of humanity as a whole. If we are unable to make our peace with the human race then we may become bitter and mistrustful. Or we may delude ourselves into thinking that we have a mythic role and have capacities that we do not actually possess, which can lead to folly.

There is a need to balance the collective and individual realities when we go into the root chakra. There is a need to retain our sense of personal identity even as we immerse ourselves in the vastness of humanity's collective awareness. Just as when the kundalini rises up the spine and burns away all personal knots of awareness, the collective awareness has so much momentum that it is unable to stop or turn for a particular individual's life. If you stand in the way of a fast-moving train, it will hit you. You want to get on the train and ride it, not become its victim. Just be sure before you get on a train that it is going where you wish to travel.

Genital Chakra

The genital chakra is the ground floor of our personal awareness. It is the realm of sensate experience. It is the only chakra where anything actually happens. In a way, the rest of the chakras are various perspectives of what they feel really happened at the genital chakra's sensate level of experiential awareness. Our physical sensations are the main entryway of the outer world into our personal awareness. The genital chakra's reality gives us a reliable awareness of a particular actual world. Our physical sensations enable us to directly know our environment. We use our genital chakra's awareness to make our physical actions fit into our tangible environment. For example, we quickly learn not to walk into solid objects because it hurts. We learn how to move through our physical world. We learn what we physically like and dislike. This knowledge enables us to respond to our environment in a way that is personally satisfying. Our genital chakra becomes a means of self fulfillment.

The genital chakra is our first fully personal conscious level of awareness. It is very naive and simple. We physically feel things. We experience through sensation. We either like an experience, or we don't like an experience. To illustrate this, suppose we are invited to a friend's house for dinner. On the table is a green vegetable we have never seen before. We take some because we both trust our host and we wish to be polite. We ask what it is. We're told it is steamed okra. When we taste the okra, we find that it has a texture that just makes us gag. We are barely able to finish the small portion on our plate. Later, for dessert, they offer us a caramel custard we've never had before called flan. After the okra experience, we are suspicious of the flan. Being polite, we try a bit of the flan and are surprised that it is very good. It reminds us a bit of a drink called egg nog, which we know and like very much.

The genital chakra uses very simple dichotomies such as 'I and not-I', 'experiencer and experienced', 'like or dislike', and so on. Essentially, physical experiences at the genital chakra either attract us or repulse us. We want more of a particular experience, or we want less of it. We want more flan and less okra. Our sensate preferences reflect our personal taste and become a way of defining who we are.

This use of contrasting polarities is the foundation of our personal conscious awareness. Our entire awareness is based on dichotomies. This seems impossible until we realize that all the complex calculations of a computer are ultimately based on an electric current either being on or off within a part of a processing chip. This simple foundational dichotomy is the basis of the computer's intelligence. Our human intelligence is also based on a few core dichotomies taken to extreme lengths.

Now, at the root we were given a body that follows the blueprint of the human race. We were also given a sense of personal connection to the larger context of the human race. Physical mechanisms for keeping us alive were handed down to us. Racial memory was transmitted to us in the form of DNA, instincts, and more subtle kinds of awareness. The root basically remains unconscious in its activity. It operates behind the scenes and sustains each of us almost invisibly. Our sense of individual identity at the root is formed and sustained by a larger context. At the genital chakra we are here as an individual. We are consciously self-aware and create our own sense of who we are. When "I" eat vanilla ice cream "I" either like how it tastes or "I" dislike how it tastes. This preference becomes part of how "I" create my sense of who "I" am.

The genital chakra is very personal and individual. While the heritage of the human race underlies our body's capacity to feel sensations, our personal individual body and what it feels is ours and ours alone. We can easily ignore what humanity as a whole may like or dislike. While everyone else may love vanilla ice cream, we may personally dislike it. Our own reality is experienced as a series of unique, personal events.

At the genital level we are only concerned with how we feel about our own experiences. It is true that what we sensately feel is shaped by the physical body that the human race has given us, but the immediacy of the genital chakra's experiences are very personal. At the genital chakra we go 'I feel the wind against my face.' (Genital perspective), not 'Humanity feels the wind against its' face through me.' (Root perspective). Both observations are equally true from their own chakric perspectives.

At the genital chakra we have a very narrow sense of time. We are mostly concerned with what we are experiencing right here, right now. While the genital chakra remembers prior experiences, these experiences only matter as they relate to the present moment.

At the genital level we use our prior experiences to determine how we will probably feel about another similar situation. We develop simple reflex responses to simple situations. For example, whenever we have eaten flan we've liked it, so at an unfamiliar restaurant we expect to like their version of flan as well.

The genital chakra is usually so busy dealing with the detailed richness of what it is experiencing that it cannot become too complex in its understanding. Because the genital chakra is extremely involved in what it is doing or feeling, it does not handle boredom well. Stimulation of some kind is always necessary for the genital chakra.

The genital chakra's sensations can be so enveloping, so overwhelming, that our sense of self blinks out. Its involvement with an experience can be so total that we sometimes lose the distinction between ourselves and what we are experiencing. This means that our sense of personal identity is very direct and also is not very stable at the genital chakra. Occasionally an experience may overwhelm our sense of self. Sometimes we may find this loss of self frightening, at other times we may find it exhilarating and refreshing.

There is a term "petite mort," or "small death," for sexual orgasm. This describes the idea. At orgasm the physical sensation can be so strong that our sense of self is overwhelmed and 'dies' for a moment. Intense physical sensations can overwhelm our personal distinctions of identity.

The genital chakra is almost incapable of an abstract, theoretical awareness. It does not conceptualize. It experiences. At the genital chakra we use a trial and error method of learning as our basis of knowledge. This gives its awareness a directness that is normally very trustworthy. We believe our eyes, we believe our ears, we believe our five senses. It is one of the most trusted levels of our awareness. We very rarely question whether or not we have experienced something. We may not know the full significance of an experience, or perhaps even if we actually liked it, but we usually know what our experiences are.

There are various ways that the genital chakra can get lost: it can become so pleased with an experience that it seeks it all the time. This can become physical addiction to a drug such as heroin, or to a pleasurable taste, such as vanilla ice cream. Also, it may not quite know how it feels about an experience. In which case it would either want to have the experience again so as to find out for sure if it likes it or not, or it may try to avoid repeating the experience so as to avoid the uncertainty. It can also be overwhelmed by an experience. This can be something that is so extremely pleasurable or unpleasant that we cannot contain it or deal with it. The desire to escape a confining sense of self can lead to an indulgence in physical sensations. We may use alcohol or drugs to try to change or enhance our physical sensations. The problem is that we quickly become used to a physical stimulus and have to increase its strength to provide the same stimulating effect.

The genital chakra is bluntly self involved. It is not very sophisticated and so it is not good at deceit. It is usually honest about its own self-interest. At the same time it presumes the same self-interest in everyone else. The genital chakra assumes that other people also react to things in much the same way that we do. The genital chakra is passionate about how it feels, about it's likes and dislikes. It will share this passionate involvement with other people quite easily. It's enthusiasm is infectious. It is not as concerned with establishing its own sense of social position as it is in seeking to reinforce its own experiential awareness.

The direct immediacy of the genital chakra makes it naive. It accepts whatever is presented to it on face value. At times this can lead to some amazing blunders. However, the genital chakra's genuine involvement in its experience and its surroundings enables it to know things, including itself, clearly enough so that most problems are either quickly solved, or quickly forgotten. There is a strong out of sight out of mind quality to the genital chakra. It finds whatever is in front of it fascinating. If something new wanders in front of its view then that new object will become the new, current source of fascination.

This can appear confusing to perspectives that have a larger time frame. The extreme present-moment focus of the genital chakra makes it honestly feel that everything it encounters is completely intriguing. The genital chakra is not lying when it claims that some romantic interest they just met is totally amazing. It is not lying when it similarly says that a person they met a week ago is also totally amazing. For the genital chakra they are both equally and uniquely fascinating. Beyond either liking and disliking something, the genital chakra doesn't make many value judgments. Well, it might really like something (such as chocolate) or really dislike something (such as toothaches). It also might think that something, such as vanilla is all right, but it does not really have a strong opinion. That is about as complex as the genital chakra gets.

The genital chakra does have a sense of memory. There is some degree of expectation at the genital chakra, but it is fairly simple and straightforward. This creates a low level of conditioning at the genital chakra. These habitual responses are not very complex, as they rarely involve more than a couple of steps. The genital chakra can only be aware of a few aspects of a situation at a time.

This means that the genital chakra gets by on innocence and directness. It can share enthusiasm easily and becomes passionately involved in the moment, but in a complex situation the genital chakra will become confused and shut down. For example, the genital chakra, glancing at a grove of trees and wondering how many trees are there, would be comfortable with the either the idea that "there are a lot of them" or else going out and physically counting each tree and getting a precise number. If someone told us that there were two hundred and twelve trees, at the genital level we'd presume the truthfulness of that figure.

The strength of the genital chakra is that it is very direct and honest. The genital chakra has a sense of camaraderie with what it feels, so it interacts with its environment fairly cleanly. It deals with physical facts. It trusts what it knows completely. The genital chakra may or may not enjoy something, but it doesn't question its own awareness. It rarely doubts the accuracy of what it feels.

The weakness of the genital chakra is that it can get lost in detail. It has trouble with complex relationships. Confusion will cause it to become unsure of itself and it may withdraw from complex situations.

Because the genital chakra can easily be overwhelmed, it tries to keep things simple. It is also quick to make decisions, as it's world isn't very complicated, but sometimes its decisions are inadequate because it hasn't paid enough attention to all the ramifications. For example, if the genital chakra is dominant in a person's love life, then that person may quickly decide to enter a relationship. They don't see the situation as all that complicated. They enjoy their beloved and want to be with them. It is as simple is that. All the problems of where they will live and how they will organize their lives together are not major concerns. Nor is it a big concern that their knowledge of their beloved is slight. All those problems will be taken care of as they come up.

The genital chakra can also be deceived by its own simplicity. If the outer world has a hidden agenda, the genital chakra is slow to become aware of it. The genital chakra will accept surface reality and think it is all that is happening. Hidden relationships are difficult for the genital chakra to see and understand. If a lie is told to the genital chakra and there is no direct evidence contradicting what it has been told, it will believe the lie. If your romantic partner tells you that they are not seeing anyone else and you only use your sensate awareness to judge the truth of their claim, you will believe them, unless you find physical evidence that they are lying. Only if you see lipstick stains on his neck, or find a love letter in her purse, would you confront them and tell them that they have deceived you.

The actual experiences of the genital chakra are stored within our bodies. Anything that shakes up the body, particularly the joints, may release these physical memories. This is part of the way deep massage is both stimulating and relaxing. Experiences are released from physical storage and dissipated. Usually we cannot recall specific experiences, we are only aware of the moods and feelings associated with the events that emerge. For example, after an intensive body work over, one woman cried for three days and never could quite understand why. There were no specific experiences that she could remember that made her sad, she was just flooded by an overwhelming sorrow.

Another weakness of the genital chakra is that if we have an experience often enough, our reactions will become automatic. Our reactions become fixed. For example, Pavlov took some dogs and after ringing a bell, he immediately fed them some food. After a while merely ringing the bell would cause the dogs to salivate. This habit mechanism can skew our awareness and make it difficult for us to experience a situation outside the boundaries of our expectations.

At the genital chakra our individually conditioned responses are not linked together into a larger, more complex whole. Such complex conditioning is found at the solar plexus chakra. At the genital chakra the conditioning remains simple. Each situation and our automatic reaction to them acts as a separate unit.

Although the genital chakra is located near the genitals, it is only loosely associated with sex. It is sexual only in terms of our purely physical attractions and sensations. The subtler psychological or social aspects of sexuality involve higher chakras. As we discussed earlier, with the petite mort, the sensate qualities of sex can be used to transcend personal ego boundaries. Physical sex combines a strong sensate impact with the instinctual force of the root chakra. This can create what feels like a self transcendent awareness. We touch an awareness that is beyond our personal being. The sheer depth and force of the root chakra can have a self transcending impact that can reassure us of our deeper anchorage.

The problem with using sexuality to descend into the root chakra in order to evoke self transcendence is maintaining the cohesion our personal identity. Our ego structure already has trouble maintaining a cohesive sense of "I" when dealing with strong sensations. The experience of the collective consciousness living within us can be overwhelming. We may feel lost in the vastness of the root chakra. Our sense of self, rather than becoming invigorated, may feel dwarfed and confused. We might feel like a drop of water that has lost itself in a huge sea. The root chakra is not particularly personal or intimate and it will sweep the individual with it as it moves along.

As we mentioned earlier, at the genital chakra our awareness of ourselves is not completely assured. The genital chakra's sense of itself is discontinuous. There are moments when our experiences overwhelm us and our personal self awareness seems to disappear. The genital chakra's awareness is similar to a young child whose ego state is not yet fully formed. Sometimes a young child thinks of themselves as separate from their experience, while at other times they don't. Sometimes a young child will refer to themselves in the singular as I, while sometimes they will refer to themselves in the plural as we. The attainment of a stable, continuous sense of personal identity happens at the next chakric level, which is the solar plexus.

Solar Plexus Chakra

The solar plexus is the middle chakra of our outer awareness. It is the focal center of our outer reality. It is where we first establish a substantial sense of our self. At the solar plexus we take all of our personal likes and dislikes and we put them into a pattern that we use to describe who we are. It is where our sense of personal identity becomes stable. This identity becomes our outer ego. At this chakra we are also finally fully aware of our own awareness. We are self-aware.

At the solar plexus our sense of time is more developed than at the genital chakra. The genital chakra sees life as a string of separate present moments. The solar plexus begins to see all these individual moments in a connected pattern. The past is real to the solar plexus. The present is also real to the solar plexus. Yet the future remains a theoretical possibility to the solar plexus. While the solar plexus has a much stronger sense of time's continuity than the genital chakra, the solar plexus is still unsure about the actuality of the future. It wants to believe in the existence of the future, but it isn't absolutely certain of it. Therefore the solar plexus trusts the past more than the future. It sees the past as a reliable anchor. The solar plexus has lived through the past. The future may not be so kind.

The solar plexus is much more sophisticated than the genital chakra. The solar plexus perceives more complex relationships than the genital chakra. This does not mean that the solar plexus is an intellectual giant. It is not. It simply doesn't have the same naive acceptance of surface reality that the genital chakra has. The solar plexus notices undercurrents, looks for hidden relationships and assumes that there's more going on than meets the eye. The solar plexus is capable of cunning. It can keep secrets. It can deceive. The genital chakra can only lie by choosing not to mention something, or by misdirecting attention. The solar plexus can lie by presenting something that is false as actually being true.

The creation of our identity and the protection of that identity is the main concern of the solar plexus. The solar plexus deals poorly with confusion. While the genital chakra shuts down when it is confused, the solar plexus will often attack what confuses it. The solar plexus is active and it aggressively protects itself. Sadly, it can actually deceive itself as a form of self protection.

The genital chakra naively accepts whatever facts are in front of it. It may have opinions about those facts, but the facts still remain what they are. But the solar plexus manipulates its reality. The solar plexus picks and chooses its facts, decides what is and isn't relevant and true. The solar plexus determines the nature and meaning of the facts that it chooses. The solar plexus writes its own history and continually rewrites that history to protect itself. (The genital chakra is unable to rewrite history, it can only selectively remember or forget.) The solar plexus uses its memory to shapes the meanings of its experiences. It then defines itself through those meanings. Because the solar plexus creates a definition of itself and of its world, it becomes invested in those definitions. The solar plexus deeply identifies itself with the world that it creates.

At the third chakra our possessions become part of our identity. We own something, either physically or experientially, that gives us a sense of personal definition. We belong to someone or something and someone or something belongs to us. The solar plexus is largely about possession. We contain and hold experiences, skills, memories, beliefs, objects, relationships, and so forth. All of these things create our sense of identity.

The solar plexus introduces us to social awareness. Our sense of personal identity is placed into a social context. We create a cultural sense of ourselves at the solar plexus. We relate to the world around us according to a set of cultural rules. We use social definitions to make sense of our world. We also use our society to identify our place within the larger cultural framework. This can be a sense of belonging to a social class, or to a social group such as a city or nation, or some other socially determined group. We may be leaders, followers, or we may see ourselves as outlaws - but in each instance we define ourselves in terms of the larger social group.

Simply put, the solar plexus chakra is the organization of individual parts into a whole. In social terms, it creates the ability of people to fill different societal roles, which allows them to function together as a whole. These roles are determined by concrete activities. A construction worker has a specific social niche, a banker another niche, and a politician yet another. All of these roles are needed by, and created by, their society.

How we are perceived socially is based on either the physical objects we possess or the physical actions we perform within the larger whole. We associate ourselves with those objects and actions that define our social position. Our sense of social place is based on material reality.

The solar plexus chakra is the seat of our purely concrete desires. Here, what we want is defined in tangible terms. Even our desires for social approval involves some kind of tangible form. We may desire to buy something because it is held in high esteem and we wish to be admired. Or we may wish to do something heroic, such as save a child from a burning house, so as to be honored. Our skills become the basis of how others view us.

This awareness of a physically defined identity also sorts people according to their tastes and possessions. Social groups emerge. We align ourselves with people who are similar to us. We conflict with those of dissimilar tastes and circumstances.

As this self definition places us in a larger social context, we find the solar plexus opens the door to many problems. Stomach aches and pains often reveal an underlying disruption of our sense of self. We may feel guilty for not living up to what we consider to be our social obligations. We may feel incapable of living up to our self definitions. We may feel that who we are is under attack by our social environment.

At the solar plexus we physically enact our sense of ourselves. Our actions both define us and are the result of who we think we are. We choose who we are and who we wish to be. This doesn't always mean that we always do good and moral things, either for ourselves or others. Our main goal is to defend and sustain our sense of who we think we are. If we do not like ourselves, then we may do things that hurt us. If we don't like others, then we may do things that hurt them.

The solar plexus is willing to fight for its definition of itself. It is unwilling to quietly accept conditions that it feels damages its sense of identity. At this chakric level we may prefer to die rather than accept an inaccurate or degrading social definition of ourselves. We are also willing to kill other people to sustain our social identity.

The solar plexus is not quite rational. It is cunning, but it isn't able to think in logically consistent, complex ways. It builds it's knowledge on the like or dislike, trial and error, awareness of the genital chakra. It also knows relative strength and weakness. It knows when it must be submissive and when it can command. But its thinking process is unsophisticated. The solar plexus is capable of understanding much more complex situations than the genital chakra, but that isn't saying a great deal. When the solar plexus runs into something, an idea or a situation, that is beyond its scope it becomes bewildered. Suddenly, the solar plexus's order is upset and it no longer trusts its world. This can make for a very upset stomach. And extreme defensiveness.

The strength of the solar plexus is that it is active. When it is sure of itself and what is going on around it, it interacts with its environment efficiently and comfortably. It can be generous and kind. It also is fairly creative. It manipulates relationships and creates new meanings and connections. A healthy solar plexus accepts the world around it and participates cleanly in that world. Self-doubt is minimal and the world is seen as basically manageable. The solar plexus feels safe and it comfortably allows autonomy to the people around it.

The weakness of the solar plexus is that it is nervous about its own safety and worth. It can become highly competitive. It can become jealous. It may feel that it is losing in the social competition. Other people own more and have better things. They are happier. They are more, while I am less. Because of all these comparative judgements, the solar plexus can feel that it is under attack. It may fight with what it feels is attacking it, or it may give up, withdraw and allow itself to be overrun. The solar plexus can become argumentative, quick to anger, hard to please and live behind a protective wall. It can become neurotic and live in a world filled with overwhelming problems and brutal enemies.

The solar plexus may also defend a very narrow definition of reality. It may feel overwhelmed by anything that makes the world larger than it can immediately comprehend. It can become narrowminded, petty, and cruel. The solar plexus can try to make everything around it smaller so that it can feel bigger. Wars are fought because of the solar plexus. The scale of these wars can be extremely small and personal, or they can involve nations.

This shows the importance of the solar plexus. The solar plexus is the focal point of our time and space reality. It is the pivot point of our awareness of outer physical existence. It is the home of our concrete, day to day, sense of self.

Many religions seek to transcend the solar plexus, not so much to eliminate it, but to make it part of a larger, more integrated reality. A healthy solar plexus understands that it is just one chakra among many others. It is willing to take its place in the larger context of our chakric awareness, just as it is willing to take its place in the larger context of our social reality.

The solar plexus does respond to the other chakras. It does not act in isolation. The main problem with the solar plexus is its need to have a reality that is familiar. It will deny facts that contradict its habitual reality. It will claim that the facts are wrong in some way. The solar plexus is moderately open to change, but generally it prefers a status quo.

The solar plexus can be aloof from its experience. This means that it is able to override what it feels. While it is capable of tremendous empathy with those around it, it is also capable of deciding to only pay attention to itself. This means that the solar plexus can be extremely detached. This ability to choose to feel or not to feel something can be a strength. The solar plexus can, by sheer force of will, decide to ignore all distractions and press on toward its goal. It can also be an extreme weakness when the solar plexus decides to ignore all the facts that prove it is definitely wrong.

As the focal center of our time space reality, the solar plexus is extremely important. It is the center of our personal complex conditioning. It tries to function through habits as much as possible. The solar plexus sizes up a present situation and tries to plug in a prior response. This prior response may be from either our personal experience or our culture's experience. Unfortunately, these plug ins are not always adequate to the problem at hand. Because it is not very agile, the solar plexus often finds itself beyond its depth. It may try to hold onto an inadequate sense of reality rather than go through the difficult process of changing and adapting to a new situation. It is troublesome for an old dog to learn new tricks.

For example, at the beginning of the European Renaissance astronomical observations showed that the earth was not the center of the universe. The earth, along with the other planets in our solar system, circled the Sun. These findings contradicted Church Doctrine and commonsense. The prevailing cultural belief was that the earth was surrounded by the heavens. The earth was still and the heavens moved around it. It was difficult for people to change their beliefs in light of the new facts. The old facts were tied into a comfortable sense of identity with humanity at the center of a smaller, less complex, universe. It was traumatic to question the reliability of the old ideas. The new facts implied possibilities that were uncomfortable to our familiar sense of who we were.

By creating our self definition the solar plexus shapes our world. This is why many religious systems seek to modify our solar plexus's habits. The more mystical Christian monastic orders will impose silence as a means of overcoming our habitual responses. In Tibetan Buddhism one of the first things they address is our conditioning, or the solar plexus. The solar plexus must be gently told that the world is a far bigger place than it may have imagined. At the same time the solar plexus must always trust its reality. If it does not, it will either withdraw into isolation, or attack what it feels is undermining its sense of reality. If we gently prod our outer ego it will feel some discomfort as it notices that its world is changing, but it will adjust.

Generally, it is a mistake to attack our own ego as a way of seeking spiritual growth. While the solar plexus chakra does have limitations, it is a part of our consciousness. As the center of our time space reality it is not really wise (or possible) to remove it from our awareness. We merely have to put our solar plexus's self awareness into its proper larger context.

Many "spiritual" people loathe themselves because they can't remove their solar plexus. It often becomes an extremely absorbing, wasteful game. It ends up going something like this: "I'm a good spiritual person and so I will remove my bad physical ego because it is so petty and defensive." Well, the bad physical ego cannot go, doesn't want to go, and so it fights back. The harder the fight, the more spiritual we feel. We congratulate ourselves for fighting so hard to be spiritual. Meanwhile, our solar plexus's belief system is largely left untouched and our world view is little changed.

The best way to transcend the solar plexus is to show it how it fits into a much larger world. The solar plexus is not an intellectual giant, but it knows when the world is beyond its grasp. It doesn't have to attack what it doesn't understand. Usually, when our solar plexus realizes that it is merely part of a larger whole - but still safe - it will let go of attitudes and ideas that do not fit the new larger reality.

With each rise in chakric level the scope of our awareness broadens. Each lower chakra cannot quite comprehend the reality of the chakras above it. They end up taking the higher chakra's reality on faith. This requires trust. For the solar plexus trust is built on reliability. This sense of security is what it seeks both from the outer world and ourselves. It's outer circumstances may change, but so long as it's sense of self remains intact it can usually handle it fairly well.

Heart Chakra

The heart is where the concrete perspective of the lower three chakras meets the abstract perspective of the upper three chakras. This makes the heart the nexus of our higher and lower realities. It is the central chakra of our inner awareness and it is our inner focal center.

Our emotions and our feelings are who we generally feel ourselves to be. When we ask someone how they are, what we are really curious about is their emotional state. If they reply that their intellectual concepts have taken a huge leap lately, we are surprised. Similarly, if they reply that their social status just keeps getting higher and higher, we would also be a bit surprised. Usually we live in our emotional state. The expected response to asking how someone is would be 'I feel fine.' referring to their emotional state.

The heart is not linearly rational. As the seat of our emotions, the heart is where our inner abstract reality meets our world of outer fact. At the heart, outer facts become symbols of inner reality. For the heart, everything can have symbolic content. The heart takes us into a dream like world of fantasy which reveals hidden meanings. Everything reflects our inner sensibility. For example, a star filled sky becomes the ballet of the heavens, the cosmic dance of creation. Or chancing upon our reflection in a broken mirror, we may see the shattered hopes and dreams of our soul.

The heart connects things in a loose, associative way. For example, a gun becomes a penis, which becomes a snake, which becomes linked to temptation and culturally linked to the knowledge of good and evil, the lost innocence of the Garden of Eden, God's anger, and on and on. If we string enough of these associations together, we eventually connect things that are rather dissimilar, even as we emotionally meld their meanings. It is easy to see where the heart can become very confusing and how its symbolism can be difficult to consciously trace and understand. If an event has an overwhelming emotional impact we will create such a swirl of associations that they may become a total blur.

The heart has a very powerful impact on our lives because it defines everything in extremely personal terms. We react to things according to how our heart feels. It tells us what something means to us. It fits the outer world into our inner personal desires. Most of the meanings that we carry in our hearts are assumed. Things feel a certain way because that is just way they are. This means that the heart's unquestioned associations define our internal world.

It is virtually impossible to know exactly what another person's inner symbols are. The associations involved are so rich and private that it takes a long time to begin to understand exactly what the various symbols mean and how they interconnect. This is why Jungian psychoanalysis takes years. It takes a long time to map out our inner symbolic landscape.

The emotional state that the heart taps into has a tremendous impact on our health. Our emotional state often uses physical disease to symbolically reflect how it feels. This emotional viewpoint sees illness as a creative expression of the individual. The heart integrates our inner feelings, needs and desires with our outer circumstances. Illness can result when we are unable to achieve a satisfactory balance.

Our bodies tend to follow the lead of our hearts. Many illnesses can be seen as symbolic expressions of our emotional state. This is not to say that a person deserves whatever illness they may have, rather that a particular illness or injury can be traced to a psychological source. This describes the process: a woman was finding herself exhausted and over committed because she was having trouble saying no to people's requests. At the exact moment that she was thinking about how much she needed some rest, she slipped and injured her ankle. This injury forced her to cut back her hectic schedule and get the rest she so badly needed.

The physical impact can also be our body's attempt to deal with what the heart and mind cannot: a gentleman becomes ill with pneumonia because he is unable to emotionally grasp a disturbing experience. He sleeps a great deal in order to allow his unconscious mind to process the meaning of what he experienced. If the meaning remains emotionally unresolvable, he may actually physically die.

To the heart, our reality is pure symbolism. The heart is not concerned with the static facts of life, but with the dynamic meanings of life. Meaning overshadows fact. This makes some of the decisions that the heart makes seem very strange and impractical. The heart is not rational in a mathematical sense. Its decisions are based on expressing symbolic meanings. Therefore the heart strives for goals that do not necessarily make sense on physical, social, or intellectual levels.

Another part of the reason that the heart is able to express itself through our body, even to the degree of our own death, is that the heart has a sense of personal continuity that extends, somewhat irrationally, beyond death.

The heart knows that the future is going to happen. The genital chakra believes only in the present moment. The solar plexus primarily believes in the past, even as it lives in the present and hopes that the future will happen. In contrast, the heart is absolutely certain that the future will happen, even beyond our physical death.

This sense of personal continuity is reflected in popular love songs that speak of lovers sharing a love that will last forever. With the heart we have risen above the limitations of time and space. Our emotions exist in a realm that 'neither rusts nor decays'. Our emotions create a psychic momentum of consciousness that endures beyond our physical death. There are many reports of people whose love in one lifetime reunites them in another. One such account is told in "The Search for Om Sety" which is about a woman who was born (or reborn as she saw it) in early twentieth century England. She remembered having a distant past life where an Egyptian Pharaoh was her beloved. She and he are reunited, after a fashion, in the twentieth century when she returns to the temple where she used to live in ancient Egypt. He visits her in dreams and as an astral presence they continue their relationship under most unusual circumstances.

There are many other similar stories. Because our emotions and desires rise above the physical facts of our existence, they can endure beyond our physical death.

Our consciousness is like a spinning top. The faster it spins the longer it stands. The less friction there is, the longer it spins and therefore the longer it stands. As we rise up the chakras there is less and less friction. The more abstract a chakra is, the longer it can maintain its momentum of awareness. The longer the momentum lasts, the broader the span of time a chakra's consciousness can remain cohesive.

The root has a time frame that is connected to the human race. It sees millennia as mere moments. But it is trans-personal and doesn't provide a beyond death foundation for an individual's consciousness. The genital chakra is extremely personal, but it is intimately connected with the physical body and has a very short time frame of awareness. The genital chakra's awareness ceases at the moment of our physical death. The solar plexus is still essentially physical in its perspective although it has a sense of there being a future because it knows there was a past. Our solar plexus's awareness lasts approximately seven weeks after death. (This is time frame found in the Tibetan Book of the Dead and its descriptions of the Bardo, or the place where our consciousness goes between lives.)

As we saw in the Om Sety story, the heart, or our astral body, when it is given enough investment, can persist for thousands of years after death. This is because the heart is both abstract and concrete. It joins the ideal and real in our experience. Romantic love is perfect for creating a personal ideal connection to an actual external object. The outer beloved is usually rather idealized. (The problem becomes disillusionment when the projected inner idealization runs into the more tawdry details of real life.) The heart lives in its own feelings, passions and desires. Normally, the heart doesn't live in a world entirely of its own creation. The facts still exist, it just adds its own inner resonance to it's outer reality. Sometimes these outer facts become a point of departure for the heart's inner ideals. As we noted earlier, the heart is not practical, it is symbolically expressive.

Still, the heart tries to maintain a balance between our inner feelings and our outer world. A weakness of the heart is that it can try to force the outer world's facts to fit how it feels. At its worst, the heart may become disconnected to the world around it. The heart may become so enmeshed in its own symbols that it distorts outer reality, sometimes beyond recognition . When Sigmund Freud ran into this problem, he decided that the reality principle was ultimately stronger than the fantasy principle. The problem is that we live in both inner and outer worlds and that both are equally important to us. If our heart's illusions are harshly revealed to us, the result can be a kind of emotional and psychological death. In its worst form, we may actually commit suicide or get sick and die. If our hearts are unable to idealize, to fantasize about what could be, to have hope, then we are emotionally crippled. The world feels flat and lifeless as we endure a life that has no connection to our souls. We feel like we are dying just a little bit each day.

At its best, the facts of our lives fit nicely with our ideals. We feel an inner connection to our outer reality. This means that our outer lives are charged with inner meaning. This does not mean that we are always happy. It means that our emotional responses give us accurate information on which to judge how we feel and what we want.

While the genetic and cultural heritage that we receive from our families is obvious, we also inherit an emotional perspective. Every family has an overall mood. This becomes the tinted emotional glasses of the family's group perception. By being born with our genetic heritage we acquire an emotional predisposition that is to a degree biochemically determined. We also, just by being within our family, acquire an emotional mood, or astral vortex that envelops each family member. This abstract emotional perspective is part of our family's lineage. In a sense, each family has an emotional cloud that surrounds each of its members. This emotional vortex can be supportive or destructive. While normally it serves as an emotional backdrop, this emotional cloud can become a presence in its own right. Sometimes this presence becomes dominating and disruptive. Then the family mood, what causes it, what it believes and why, will need to be directly dealt with.

By their nature, our emotions are not very fluid. It is hard for us to move about emotionally. It is like trying to run through a waist high pool of water. It is difficult to move through the water very quickly. (By contrast, our mind is much more fluid and we move through ideas as easily as our bodies move through the air. The solar plexus is sort of like walking through ankle deep muck. This is part of why social change takes so long.)

The strength of the heart is that its feelings anchor us. Our emotions are a fairly clear signal about what things mean to us. We usually trust how our heart feels.

A weakness of the heart is that we may see life through a particular emotion's perspective. We may become comfortable with a certain mood, ignoring those other moods, other emotions, that do not fit our familiar emotional space. Usually we will come to see one emotion as more truthful than the others. This is like saying a particular color of tinted eyeglasses is more truthful than the other tints.

Another weakness of the heart is that it sometimes cannot see the context of its feelings. It is difficult for the heart to see itself and to grasp how the situation it is in may be dictating its feelings. The heart can feel like it is the victim of what it feels, rather than the creator of what it feels.

Often when an event happens we merely replay how we already emotionally feel. This means that we aren't dealing with how we actually feel and what we actually want. The heart can also be unable to see how it is helping to create the situation that is causing it pain. There is a "which came first" problem, the emotion or the situation. "Who is causing who?" becomes the issue.

At their best our emotions give us information that enables us to choose what we want and create a world that more completely expresses who and what we are internally as well as externally. Our outer world is connected to us through emotional rapport. We feel that we personally have meaning and that the outer world has personal significance for us as well.

Finally, the heart is the seat of the soul. It is the inner core of our being. It is the chakra that binds all our worlds, our inner and outer, as well as our real and ideal worlds, together.

Throat Chakra

Like the solar plexus, the throat is extremely aware of relationships. The throat has a far more complex world view than the solar plexus. The throat can see multiple levels of relationship simultaneously. It can place the same thing into many different contexts at once. It can see how a woman is a mother, a wife, an employee, a poet, a daughter, religious, hungry, happy, dreamy, practical, foolish, and so on, all at once. The throat creates the concepts that provide the context of our lives. The throat determines, either by conscious choice or by unthinking assumption, the context of our understanding.

Each chakra has its own type of desire, its own wants and needs. The throat likes to passionately care about its own ideas. It desires to be smart. The throat wants to be respected and esteemed for the brilliance of its observations and thinking. In many ways it is very similar to the solar plexus chakra. Only here the social connections are through ideas rather than based on physical factors.

Our ideas shape our experiences. They determine what we will do. For example, a man meets a woman. He notices that she is very attractive. He also notices that she is married. But his ideas tell him that marriage doesn't really matter and so he makes a pass at her. Meanwhile, in her mind marriage does matter and so she rebuffs him. Another man meets the same woman and notices that she is very pretty. He decides that it would be nice to paint her portrait to further understand what makes her so beautiful. He respects her marriage as it is a part of who she is and part of why she is pretty. She, after telling him how much her marriage means to her, finds the idea of her portrait being painted quite flattering and she agrees. In this we can easily see how each person's ideas shapes how they choose to interact. Not surprisingly, our concepts shape the way that we feel at the lower chakras a great deal.

While it is fairly typical for people to use their minds to question their culture's assumptions, we rarely question our own throat's intellectual assumptions. We accept our core ideas and concepts quite unthinkingly.

Because ideas are very fluid, they tend to change, develop and evolve fairly quickly. Ideas grow in complexity as they are refined. They evolve into more detailed sets of relationships. Newton's Mechanics worked well as a theory of physics until it had to deal with relationships that were discovered through the properties of radiation. Einstein's Theory of Relativity solves the problems of Newtonian mechanics, but it doesn't deal adequately with the random order (or disorder) of subatomic particles. So, each new perspective both solves one mystifying set of relationships and eventually leads to a new set of unexplained facts.

This means that our intellectual understanding can never be complete. Each answer leads to more questions. At the same time, there is always another way of looking at the same set of facts. In the mind's eye, the world is a completely relative, totally fluid series of relationships. And all the relationships that we perceive depend completely on our point of view. Ultimately, what the throat chakra knows is always subject to reformulation and reinterpretation. There are few, if any, absolutes.

This can give the intellect an underlying sense of insecurity because Truth is so illusive. Sometimes the mind feels like it cannot rest. There is always some intriguing puzzle that calls for investigation and understanding.

Sometimes a new idea may completely change many of our prior notions of what was true. So long as the mind understands the new concept, it generally is able to handle the changes. The lower chakras often lack this flexibility. We may embrace something intellectually, but our cultural traditions or emotional needs may not as easily adjust to the new order.

The throat chakra works in much the same way as the solar plexus chakra. Both chakras are indirectly aware of their environment. Because of their slightly removed perspective, both chakras are more aware of the role that they play in their own awareness than the other chakras are. The throat chakra is the home of Descartes' famous statement "I think, therefore I am." Our awareness of our activity of being aware is particularly accented in both the solar plexus and throat chakras. As we mentioned earlier, the throat chakra is the abstract mirror image of the solar plexus chakra. It is the home of the little voice in our heads which we know as our inner sense of self. It is the voice of the thoughts that swirl within our mind.

The throat is our first fully abstract awareness. The heart was a blending of abstract and concrete awarenesses, whereas the throat is completely abstract. Because the throat has virtually no concrete awareness, it relies heavily on the lower concrete chakras for the information, or the data, that gives it the substance of its awareness.

The throat is similar to the solar plexus in its quest for power. The throat labels things in an attempt to understand and control them. In ritual magic to know the Name of an Entity gives you control over that Entity. You can summon or banish an Entity through its Name. Similarly, the throat uses symbols to identify, label and manipulate reality. This abstract reality uses symbols to represent things and to manipulate relationships. Some symbols are quite abstract, such as theoretical mathematics, while others are more connected to what they concretely represent, such as the blueprints of a house.

Language aptly describes the way the throat works. The sounds that a given language makes have no intrinsic meaning (at least not anymore). A verbal language's sounds are pure abstract symbol. It only has meaning through cultural agreement. A word denotes what it does because enough people agree it is what that verbally created sound 'means.' The sound of the word for home is different in English, French, or Chinese, and yet they all mean essentially the same thing. The mind uses conceptual symbols to represent actual reality. At the same time the word "home" has a different connotation than the word "house." The two words may refer to the same physical object, but their emotional meanings are very different. A house may or may not be a home. The mind recognizes and plays with these subtle differences.

If our mind's abstract symbols are accurate enough to represent a situation adequately, then our thinking will work. If our mind's abstract symbols do not adequately account for all the factors involved, then our thinking will not work very well. Our thinking will also be inaccurate if our logic is faulty, and we do not connect things in ways that are reasonable. For example, "Cats scratch themselves to get rid of fleas. If I scratch myself, then I must have fleas." is poor logic. It may be true, but it would only be by coincidence as the relationships are not well connected.

The throat chakra is where we develop rational mental constructs. It is where we develop logic and symbol systems. This enables the mind to quickly and easily visualize relationships between things. We can use a system of logic to see things in our mind and understand what will and will not work. This saves us the trouble of having to learn everything by trial and error. This is a huge leap over the sensate and solar plexus chakras whose awareness is based almost completely on trial and error.

This means that the throat can move beyond having to directly experience something to understand it. We can use our mind to create conceptual frameworks of relationship. We can take the facts that we experientially know and use a conceptual framework to fill in any gaps that exist in our experiential knowledge. We can use what we know to determine what must be in those gaps, even though we don't have any direct experience or data. We can reliably infer or deduce what must be true. What we know becomes a springboard for extending our understanding.

The throat organizes and shapes so much of our awareness that it is hard to overstate how important the throat chakra is. Our inner sense of identity is tied to what we think and what we believe is true. At the throat we determine, in fairly personal terms, if something is true or false. Because of it's ability to create logic structures, this chakra can shape everything around it according to what it believes to be the Truth. This lining up of the facts to support a premise can lead us to use some very shaky logic and data in order to maintain the appearance of a concept as being true.

For better or worse, any notion (regardless of its ultimate relationship to reality) only needs to be accepted as true for a person to use it to define their reality. A false notion can serve as the basis of our actions just as easily as a true notion. The closer an idea fits our experiences, or conforms to our inner feelings and desires, the more accurate that idea will seem to us.

Concepts are extremely social in their impact. At the throat we decide what we do and do not believe. Because it is fairly easy to hide behind our ideas, our throat can feel like it has much more freedom than the solar plexus chakra. At the same time, our ideas also become another kind of social identity. People group together according to their shared ideas. Our ideas become a form of social currency which we buy and sell to each other.

Despite the connection between the physical brain and our consciousness, esoterically our mental awareness is seen to be intangible. This means that the mind's consciousness exists beyond the confines of normal time and space reality. Because it is totally abstract the throat chakra's awareness has a momentum that lasts even longer than the heart's emotional awareness. In terms of our personal conscious continuity between incarnations, the mind is quite long lived. It is the abstract nature of the mind that gives it the ability to endure outside the realm of physical reality. As we move up into the more abstract chakras, our consciousness creates a personal momentum that endures far longer than our physical bodies. At the throat our awareness uses concepts to create ideals that can endure for an extremely long time.

Yet for all of its abstract qualities the mind is extremely real. The mind has substance even though it is extremely subtle. The mind can be seen as sending out and receiving the equivalent of radio waves. Telepathy uses such means to connect people. This can be seen when you call someone on the telephone and they say " I was just thinking about you." Like radio waves, people can be thousands of miles away from each other and still be in telepathic rapport. All this describes how important the mind is in creating and shaping our connection to the world around us.

The throat chakra defines our inner reality just as completely as our solar plexus chakra defines our outer reality. The throat and the solar plexus are intimately linked. If we are thinking and have a startling realization, then our solar plexus will be shaken up and have to adjust to the new idea. If something shakes up our solar plexus, then our throat has to grasp the new situation. Generally, the mind is nimbler and quicker to change than the lower chakras are.

The strength of the throat chakra is that it sees multiple contexts. It can place something into many different kinds of relationship simultaneously. This allows us to discover connections and influences that are not readily apparent.

A weakness of the throat is that it can try to make everything around it conform to its ideas. Another weakness is that because the mind is so fluid and quick it can make an erroneous idea seem to work. It can use slight of mind to delude itself.

Another weakness of the throat (which it shares with the solar plexus) is that it can become isolated. Others may be unwilling to accept a person's ideas. While unpopularity and general rejection doesn't mean a concept is wrong, it is still a difficult position to be in.

The throat can also try to force its ideas on others. Political and religious movements have destroyed many people who didn't agree with them. Sadly, the detachment of the throat allows it to be aloof and unemphatic as it brutally purifies the world according to its ideals. A great deal of suffering can be inflicted on others in the name of serving the Truth.

The throat may also find that it's knowledge is inadequate for a given situation. We may react by becoming withdrawn and aggressively deny that there is a problem. Or if we are unable to allow ourselves the luxury of being ignorant, we may seek greater understanding.

A healthy throat is able to play with its own ideas. It trusts that it will eventually acquire an adequate understanding. When its ideas don't work, it looks for new ideas that do work. At its best, the throat is creative and willing to modify its ideas as the situation requires.

The throat can be surprisingly passionate about its ideas. Although the mind can be coolly analytical, the nature of the throat tends more toward excited investigation. The throat can be very playful and curious. It enjoys a problem and likes to play with possible solutions. It can burn with the desire for understanding. It needs to know why. Sometimes the throat's passion can cross into obsession.

An unhealthy throat is unable to let go of ideas that do not work. It clings to its assumptions and will not adjust to circumstances. This can lead to a form of conceptual blindness.

The throat can find itself in situations far beyond its understanding. Then it needs to gather information. It may be impossible to get the data that is needed. Or we may be unable to think of an idea that accounts for all of the facts at hand. The result is that the throat may find itself out of balance, unable to adequately explain something.

When the throat is out of balance, there is a tendency to obscure things. The throat also tends toward melodrama.

The throat is a surprisingly good actor. The throat is capable of conning other people. It can present an illusory idea as being true quite effectively. This is because the throat dwells in a completely abstract reality, where the truth is an idea rather than an actual thing.

The throat can also use its ideas to nurture others and also to be nurtured as well. The mouth, nose and ears are physically and symbolically connected to the throat chakra. This implies that the throat chakra takes in food and breath, which are vital to our well-being. The throat reaches out through words and ideas, while it simultaneously uses words to take in abstract nurture. For example the words "I love you." can be extremely nourishing.

The throat is our most complex conscious awareness. As our highest dualized (fully conscious) chakric level, the throat is where we try to understand our brow and crown chakras. But, as we already know, with each rise in chakric level the field of our awareness becomes larger. This means that the throat cannot entirely grasp the awareness of either the brow or crown chakras. It can only understand aspects of their awareness. Both the brow and the crown chakras are aware of things that the throat cannot directly comprehend. But because the throat is able to use its systems of logic and knowhow to determine what must be true, it can get some idea of what the brow and crown chakras perceptions are.

Brow Chakra

The brow chakra directly intuitively 'sees' in much the same way that the genital chakra directly sensately feels. The brow is the abstract counterpart of the genital chakra. The genital chakra uses physical sensations to know something. The brow chakra uses intuition to know something. Both chakras use a form of direct experience. At the brow we abstractly perceive something's essence. This is where we visualize the potentials of situations and things. We intuit many interweaving levels of relationship and potential.

When we go above the throat, into the brow and crown chakras, we enter preconscious levels of awareness. We have no personal external expressive function at the two upper most chakras. In our awareness these two chakras function wholly internally. This means that we cannot directly externally dichotomize our awareness in these two chakras. Due to the lack of intrinsic inner and outer contrast, it is extremely difficult for us to be consciously aware of what we know at the two top chakras. The result is that our intuition often has an elusive, slippery, dream like quality. We know something, but exactly what we know and how we know it, is difficult to grasp. It is hard to put what we intuitively perceive into an adequate context.

For example, we go to a party. On walking into the crowded room we have a strong negative reaction to one person and a strong positive reaction to another person. On an intuitive level we have already visualized who these people are and how they could connect to us. Our reactions are a form of decision. The brow, like the genital chakra, uses an attraction and repulsion response. We are intuitively drawn to something or we are intuitively repulsed by something. Like our physical sensations, we do not necessarily understand the reasons behind our reactions.

This is why our intuition can be so annoying. We are sure that we know something, but we are not sure exactly what, or how to use it. Also we have to learn the difference between our imagination and our intuition. This is because our intuition often clothes itself with the same stuff that our dreams are made of. Unfortunately, this dream like quality also blurs the context of the brow's perceptions.

Then, when we add the fact that the brow tends to create in actuality what it visualizes in the abstract, the brow's awareness becomes even slipperier. The realm of the brow is somewhat magical. It straddles the line between perception and creation. It becomes a kind of chicken or the egg question: does it see a potential that already exists, or does it create the potential by visualizing it's existence? (This idea was the crux of the highly popular Dune trilogy.)

Our intuition connects our inner, or spiritual will to the potentials that are constantly swirling all around us. The brow chakra is where we visualize how we will ensoul our inner spiritual being in time and space. This intuition can be life shaping, such as when a person meets someone that they intuitively know will be their spouse, or it can be fairly simple such as intuitively knowing what the best time is to make a minor business call.

The brow chakra looks out at time and space and sees relationships and their possibilities. It visualizes what something is in its inner essence and what it could be. The brow imagines how things will interact and what, of their own nature, they would become. This is important because nothing can be a part of something that contradicts what it truly is.

For example, our inner being, or spirit, can attempt to deny its own nature, or even it's own right to existence. When this happens, you will find people acting in contradiction of their own intrinsic being. When we try to act against our own nature, we become disconnected from our own being. Since our spirit is eternal, it cannot die, so it cannot truly commit suicide. On a spiritual, or psychological level, we can only attempt to hide from ourselves.

Suppose that we do something that we morally disapprove of. We may come to dislike ourselves. This can lead us to try various ways of escaping from ourselves. We may use drugs, or drink too much, or to we may try to hide from ourselves through risky activities. These behaviors cover up our feelings and their self damaging results serve to dramatize our remorse. Eventually we should realize that our life is still what it is no matter how hard we try to escape from it and we just have to deal with it. Often, after a person has hidden from themselves for a long time, the inner person will suddenly awaken and radical changes occur in their lives.

At the third eye, or brow chakra, our spiritual inner will chooses our lives. By choosing which doors to open and close, we create who and what we are. There are many romanticized stories of the powers of the third eye. The third eye is depicted as seeing the future. It is depicted as seeing deep into the heart of someone or something. The third eye is credited with being able to act as a literal magnifying lens. It is enough to say that the brow chakra sees abstract realities that are both actual and possible. Different people see different things through their brow. Some people are detail oriented, while other people are big picture oriented.

Because conscious awareness is based on dichotomies, we have to look outside of ourselves to find the outer context of our brow's inner intuitive awareness. Without an external context for our inner intuitions, we cannot be sure that we are not just letting our imagination run wild. The brow will also attempt to use the crown chakra to check its perceptions. We will try to use the crown's very broad sense of pattern to give our intuitions a context. Also, we will use our throat's intellect to analyze what our intuitions seem to know. Unfortunately, our intuitive awareness sees relationships in wholes which are often beyond the scope of the mind to fully comprehend. To gain a conscious awareness we must try to break the whole down into intellectually understandable parts.

The brow's awareness has tremendous resonance. Because of the large scope of its awareness, it sees many layers of relationship simultaneously. This is both confusing and exhilarating. One of the biggest problems we have with our awareness at the brow is trusting what we know. It is difficult to step outside of the boundaries of our mind and trust that something will work just because we intuitively 'see' that it will. And our brow, because it sees things differently than our lower chakras, may have different goals than what a lower chakra may desire.

In contrast, the brow can easily see the desires of all the lower chakras. For example, a woman is dating two men. One of them is wealthy, owns a big luxurious home, and has a prestigious job. The other is economically barely getting by, and has a house that is small and in need of repair. The woman's solar plexus, or social identity, prefers the wealthy man. The woman's heart feels more comfortable with the poorer man. When she tries to think about how she feels about each of them she gets confused. The wealthier man makes more sense. Her life would be easier with him and he is a nice guy. A bit self-absorbed, but nice. But the poorer man makes her heart feel lighter and when he looks at her, he seems to see right through her to her very soul.

It is a classic head and heart conflict. She is stuck. The solar plexus doesn't quite understand the heart's emotional concerns, while the heart does understand solar plexus's social concerns. She goes into her brow to tap into her intuition to help her make a choice. On a solar plexus level she is surprised to intuit that she really doesn't care that much about her heart. 'Romantic love is for fools.' her solar plexus says. She intuits that he will be gone a lot traveling on business. Her intuition visualizes herself having a series of brief affairs within the context of her wealthy lifestyle. When she moves to her heart, she is surprised to find how little her social status matters to her. Looking at her heart, she intuitively visualizes a deep connection and emotional bond slowly being built with her poor but emotionally connected spouse. At the same time, she intuits losing most of her friends because she cannot afford to go out and play with them anymore and she will become socially isolated.

In the midst of all this, she has the intuition that she should do nothing. There is a third option. She feels that if she waits another gentleman will show up in her life that is better suited than either of these two current gentlemen. This vague sense of something better down the road is strong and so she trusts it. Her brow's intuitive awareness looks out beyond the awareness of the lower chakras and sees possibilities that are unknown to them.

So, when we step into intuitive realms we may be surprised to discover exactly what it is that will probably happen on a particular chakric level. The larger time frame and broader context of the brow's awareness is outside our normal day to day reality. The brow may see things in terms of a step by step process, rather than as taking a certain amount of calender time.

Just as the heart is allegorically expressive, the brow is spiritually ensouling. The goals of our brow's inner spirit may differ from the goals of our solar plexus or heart. Ideally, at the brow the desires of all of our lower chakras are taken into account. But this is not always the case. The brow tends toward the magical and mystical. This perspective is not always satisfying to our lower chakras. Where the brow sees mystical layers of tightly bound connection, the solar plexus may see impractical ideas that will not bring any profit.

The brow's ability to be highly imaginative can also be a problem. It may see a tremendous number of possibilities and be unable to judge how probable any of them are. It may naively believe that just because something can happen, it will happen. This can lead to an overly optimistic (or fearful) outlook. We are so optimistic that we keep making foolish decisions based on an improbable set of circumstances falling into place. Or we may expect so many bad things to happen that we may become frozen in fear.

Ideally, the brow helps us accurately see a set of circumstances and know what is both possible and probable. This helps guide our choices so that we create a world that tangibly works and a life that spiritually fulfills us. Normally, the brow is preconscious and it acts in the background of our awareness.

At its worst, the information we receive at the brow is either overwhelming, or simply inaccurate. We may project our own prior experiences and personal desires onto our intuitions and so inaccurately perceive things. Using our prior example, the woman may think she intuitively visualizes the wealthier man as becoming a doting spouse, or she may see the poor man's moderately productive business as suddenly becoming extremely successful. The brow can be a teasing form of perception because we truly see what we wish to have happen as becoming real. This can render the use of divinatory tools such as astrology or the tarot useless. They end up simply echoing our own desires back to us. Our divinations mirror our wishes, rather than give us accurate information about a situation.

Complicating things even more is the magical push the brow can give to what it sees. This makes the prophecy of the brow self fulfilling. Once again we have to realize that we are always creating reality to fit our self image. This is as true at the higher chakras as it is at the lower ones. Normally the decisions that we make at the brow go unnoticed as we unconsciously accept the life we unknowingly create.

At its best, the brow accurately perceives possibilities and easily integrates our own desires with the desires of those around us. Life flows smoothly as our will enacts who we are on a deep level. Our world is a richly textured weaving of many levels of reality. The brow pushes its creative conceptual perceptions into existence fluidly and respectfully.

Crown Chakra

The top chakra is our most abstract perspective. It is the chakra with the largest scope of awareness. Because the crown, like the brow, also lacks an outer experience function, the crown is also a preconscious awareness. Unlike the brow, it is doubtful that our awareness of the crown can ever be more than only partially conscious. As the crown is the abstract equivalent of the root chakra, it has the same transpersonal qualities that the root chakra has. At both of these bracketing transpersonal chakras, the crown and the root, we are connected to something greater than just ourselves.

At the crown chakra we see abstract patterns that are beyond our personal creation. The crown is aware of multiple levels of integrated simultaneous creation. What appears to be a contradiction at a lower chakra is turned into a unified harmony at the crown. This is mostly due to the large scale of the crown chakra's perspective. It sees night and day as different aspects of the same thing, while a lower chakra may see night and day as two contradictory states.

The crown chakra has a unique perspective on the nature of our concrete reality. At the crown we look up and perceive the pure energy that underlies all being. This energy seems to flow out of nothingness or out of a shimmering void. This pure energy is felt to move down into increasingly tangible form. To the crown chakra, the tangible world is the motion of pure energy in repetitious patterns. This means that the tangible world can be affected by the abstract realm of the crown. Spirit can impact matter because matter is spirit. The distinctions of abstract and concrete blur.

Because of the large scope of what the crown perceives, it has tremendous resonance. The crown touches a realm that feels infinite.

The crown is the mystic's paradise. It is where we tap into the mind of God.

The crown also connects us to various forms of collective human consciousness. For example, through the crown we connect with the conceptual pattern behind a group's awareness. This group mind is apparent when we use the crown deal with collective assumptions of relationship and order. Each groups uses their own set of abstract assumptions to guide their actions. This can be as simple as a social group's rules of conduct. When we play a game such as chess, we are entering into an abstract set of rules that govern the rules of the game of chess. These rules are the creation of the collective minds of the people who have played chess. While inflexible at a given moment, these rules are subject to change. If enough people agree, a new set of rules will be adopted. Even at the crown, the relationships involved aren't absolute. What guides these changes at the crown is it's purpose.

Through the crown chakra we connect to the collective mind of a group of chess players. We can personally engage the group assumptions. How competitive they are, how concerned about winning they are overall, how much their sense of the game's elegance and beauty matters to them, how serious they are about playing well, how much it's an excuse for a social gathering; all these things become factors within a given group's mind set.

The crown chakra connects the us to the group mind corresponding to what we are doing. If we are in a church, then that particular church's group mind's beliefs are dominant. If the church is affiliated with a larger body then that group mind becomes a backdrop for the assumptions of the local church. While driving on a highway the rules of the road of the local community as well as the nation acts as the abstract pattern that we participate in. This makes it so that we all know which side of the street to drive on throughout the country. An obvious, yet important rule that we must all agree on. If we suddenly had to change sides of the street when we went from one town to another the accident rate would be enormous. This is a very non-mystical way of looking at the crown. In this perspective the crown chakra merely provides the abstract pattern that organizes our lower chakra's interactions.

At the same time the crown can be extremely mystical. We have a very idealized sense of reality at the crown. There is a vibrant dynamic quality to all of life at the crown, just as there is at the root. There is a sense of an underlying cosmic order, or divine plan, at the crown. This sense of order appears to go far beyond our human constructs.

This means when someone enacts their crown chakra they often have a highly idealized sense of mission. Under the inspiration of the crown chakra people have done things that change cultural assumptions. This can lead to the founding of major religions. At the same time the inspiration of the crown chakra may result in acts that are not entirely reasonable. Adolph Hitler had a profound sense of being on a divine mission. He also did unspeakable acts in the name of his ideals. He was delusional and rationalized his own atrocious acts as being the result of the faults of other people. Because his ideals were pure he wrongly assumed that his actions were as well.

This is the problem of the crown chakra: it can be self betrayed. A person can become so mesmerized by their divine commission that they lose all sense of proportion. To make matters even more confusing, the normal social rules do not necessarily apply to the crown chakra. The crown chakra has such a large perspective that it sometimes actually does transcends our normal moral structures. This makes it quite difficult to maintain personal equilibrium in the vast perspective of crown chakra. It also makes it difficult to judge the actions of people taken while they are under the sway of the crown chakra. As Buddhists have noticed, a person who has suddenly attained Enlightment may or may not act in accord with standard social rules.

Like the root chakra, the crown is not really a conscious awareness. The root is unconscious, while the crown is preconscious. Just as the individual can become lost in the vastness of the root chakra, we can also become lost in the vastness of the crown. Another mistake we may make is thinking that we actually personally contain the vast perspective of the crown chakra. This can lead to feelings of tremendous power. We see ourselves as floating above normal mundane existence. The extraordinary fluidity and vast scope of the crown chakra feels like it is at our command. But just because reality is very fluid and magical in the domain of the crown, it does not mean that our personal will is omnipotent.

The interaction of personal and collective realities needs to be kept in balance at the crown just as it has to be kept in balance at the root. It is one thing to sense the dynamic creativity of the universe and quite another to feel that one is the creator of that universe.

At its best, at the crown everything is in equilibrium. There is virtually no sense of conflict, only fulfillment. The crown sees everything as so integrated that everything moves together in a flowing dance of mutual accommodation. This becomes an occult axiom of all interaction. Everything interacts with everything else in some form of mutual, reciprocal balance. The crown chakra is where we abstractly connect ourselves to the potentials of the world around us. Prayer is a perfect example of an individual will seeking to integrate with the world around it. At its best, we have a fluid give-and-take in prayer. We respect our personal wants and needs, just as we respect the wants and needs of the world around us. We look to the larger creative force (God) to fulfill all these various needs.

The brow and the crown are where the magical activity of our consciousness takes place. Most of the magical acts that we do run on autopilot. Normally we are not consciously aware of the impact that our abstract will has on the world around us. It is a bit tricky to try to consciously establish something at these levels. Because we are acting from deep within our preconscious core of being, trying to enact anything shallower than our true self is usually ineffective.

At the crown chakra we enter into the divine and we participate in the core fluidity of creation. At the crown we take the pure formlessness of pure potential reality that resides above the crown and mold it into a form that is real to us. Our consciousness normally creates our reality by riding on a lot of prior assumptions about what 'reality' is. This can become our fulfillment or our prison. In either case, it is in sync with our own larger pattern's sense of reality.

The power of positive thinking can work so long as our core believes in the reality of what we are creating. A house cannot be divided against itself or it will collapse. We will build by day and tear down by night. Our conscious sense of will must be integrated with our deeper preconscious core reality.

At its worst, the crown can use a sense of having Divine Permission to justify our own desires. Or it can box us into a world of ideal perfection that is hollow and lifeless. The essential creativity and wonder of the crown is lost in long list of 'shoulds'.

At its best, we live in a universe that is rich and which cares about everything in it. The world is a place of fulfillment, not of confinement. The impossible becomes possible if the larger Cosmic Will wishes it to happen. In other words, nothing is seen as being impossible before God. The entire fabric of the universe is alive and radiant with the inner presence of that which is above and beyond our understanding. It is through the crown chakra that we see the dynamically fluid creativity which is possible in our universe. We participate in this fluid creativity without fully understanding how or why it happens.

This concludes our look at the individual chakras. These brief chakric descriptions are only rough guidelines. As you explore the chakras in your own life you will create your own understanding of them that will be far richer and deeper than what is presented here.

A Chess Game Seen Through the Chakras

We play chess on a board that has eight squares per row and eight squares per column, giving it sixty-four squares total. The squares alternate in two different colors. We move sixteen pieces on this board which symbolize various parts of our army. The object of the game is to capture your opponent's king. Without going into too much detail, each of the pieces has its own distinctive way of moving on the chess board. Through the use of various strategies we can coordinate the movement of our pieces on the symbolic checker board field of battle as we seek to gain an advantage and eventually capture our opponent's king.

In purely physical terms the chess board and the pieces that move on it describe the root chakra level which provides the physical actuality of chess. Then the genital chakra level would provide our ability to see and actually reach out and move the chess pieces. This is our sensate experience of chess. Playing chess is not a very sensually stimulating experience, although some chess boards and chess pieces are very elegant and ornate. Often they are designed to appeal to the eye as art objects. But because the idea behind the game is a symbolic battle, the game pieces are essentially abstract representations of battle forces as these are created by the mind at the throat chakra. In terms of the genital chakra the main sensate events are visually scanning the board, touching the pieces, and moving them. Chess is more of a meeting of minds in symbolic battle than it is the gritty sensate reality of the bodies of men bleeding and being destroyed as they fight in a life and death struggle. In the experiential terms of the genital chakra, chess is a extremely tidy form of warfare.

Socially, chess is a competition between two sides, usually two people. One side wins and the other side loses. Occasionally they tie. This competition is, for many players, the prime motivation for playing chess. It is an aspect of the solar plexus chakra. How everyone fits into their social group's hierarchy completes the solar plexus level of chess. There are chess tournaments and ranking systems for many levels of skill and competition. A player can find any caliber of competition that they desire.

For one player chess can be a means of rising into social prominence. For another player it may be a form of social comradery. Some people love the competition and the emotional charge they get from winning. Others love the excitement of the social swirl of a chess tournament. Some people enjoy sharing their interest in chess with other players.

Some people enjoy the feeling of adrenalin when playing a tournament match. Other people consider chess to be elegant and beautiful. Others romanticize the prestige and glory they will gain through becoming a great chess player. This describes how the heart chakra may relate to chess.

The game requires a great deal of strategy. In order to get better, some people read books and study games played by recognized champions. They think about the board itself and how to move the pieces in order to best control the board. They study opening moves and gambits, read books written by master chess players and try to learn from them. In short, they bring their entire intellect, or throat chakra, into the game.

In the middle of a game an intuition as to what move a player should make can occur. Although they don't have a complete intellectual grasp of why they think a particular move is good, they do it anyway because it just feels right. Their intuition has come into play. The brow chakra is involved.

It is our social agreement on the structure of the rules that enables us to play chess together. A transpersonal order which patterns the rules and goals involved in the game of chess is required. This brings the crown chakra into the game. We see the game and its place within the overall structure of our human experience. The present day's rules have evolved over many generations of players. The traditional foundations of the game have been sufficient, at least until now. At the present time, there is a concern that a supercomputer and a good chess program will eventually make it so that the outcome of a game of chess will become a foregone conclusion. A game will have already been won simply by having the first move. This would render the game of chess academic. So the question has been raised as to how to change the game's structure to make the outcome more uncertain. Perhaps by making the chess board into a twelve by twelve square, rather than the current eight by eight square. Or perhaps randomly placing the more powerful eight pieces on the back row, rather than in the same predetermined order they are now placed in, which will increase the game's mathematical possibilities. There will have to be some kind of social consensus (solar plexus) about any changes in the overall pattern and structure of the game (crown chakra). The players will have to agree upon the rules in order to be able to play the same game together.

This example shows how the chakras work together and how a single situation can bring all of them into play. No chakra is an island. They each have a unique perspective that works with the other chakras to create our highly nuanced and complex awareness.

The Higher and Lower Chakras Contrasted

The main distinction between the higher and lower chakras is their relationship to cause and effect. The lower chakras are very mechanistic - a cause enacts an effect. Ultimately, these cause-and-effect mechanisms are based on the physical interactions found at the root chakra. The world is seen as a predictable set of interactions of physical forces. There are physical relationships that are constant and reliable. A stronger force will dominate a weaker force. The speed of light is constant. The world is based on causes and their effects.

In the higher chakras relationships are based upon affinity rather than causality. The higher chakras are best described as a dance between mutual partners who have an affinity for each other. This creates a world that is not linearly causal. There is still an abstract kind of cause and effect relationship being enacted, but the mechanism involves mutuality of interests. On the abstract levels, the force that is capable of the greatest amount of attraction will cause things to happen in accord with its will. Things come together due to their mutual affinity with the desires of the strongest will. The closer a person is to their spiritual core the deeper and stronger their will becomes. The closer we get to our spiritual core the more completely we live a world of interconnection. In a totally abstract sense, God is the Pure Will at the Center of all Being. The difference between the lower chakra's physical mechanistic relationships and the higher chakra's enactment of seemingly magical coincidental affinities is quite striking. The higher chakras live in a world that is physically much more fluid but requires the application of Will to achieve its results.

The Chakras and Astrology

The Difference Between the Astrological Signs and the Planets

When we look up at the night sky we see the starry heavens. According to our eyes the stars do not move. From ancient times we have connected the stars together to form images. The twelve constellations are images from antiquity that circle the world in the heavens. These are the twelve astrological signs.

In contrast to the unmoving astrological signs (each of which is associated with a particular chakra)€ are the astrological planets which do move through the sky. We see the planets move from one constellation to another. Each of the planets moves a different speed through the twelve signs. Their rate of speed depends on the length of their orbit around the sun. Astrologically, there are ten planets. (Pluto remains an astrological planet despite the astronomer's downgrading of it). In chakric astrology we are concerned mainly with the seven inner planets. The outer three planets were unknown to ancient astrologers and they play a secondary role in chakric astrology.

The Astrological Signs and the Chakras

There are twelve astrological signs and seven chakras. As seven does not go into twelve evenly, we will have to distribute the signs among the chakras in a way that is uneven. Each chakra has an inner and outer function. This helps us arrange the astrological signs in a way that describes how our chakra's awareness works.

The left, or outer experiential side, of the chakras only has five astrological signs. The top two chakras are empty. In contrast, the right or inner side, has an astrological sign on every level.   This imbalance describes the way our consciousness works. It reflects how our internal awareness is more developed than our external awareness.

Our awareness needs to contain a dichotomy in order to consciously understand what it knows. This dichotomy enables us to see the context of our awareness. (The root chakra, as we have already seen, is a special case.) From the genital to the throat our chakras contain an inner and outer dichotomy. At the top two chakras, we only function on the inner right side. This means that the top two chakras are preconscious , or an awareness that we are not quite fully conscious of. Therefore we have trouble placing our crown and brow chakra's awareness into an accurate outer context.

When we distribute the twelve astrological signs to the seven chakras what we get looks like this:

Outer Sign	Glyph	Chakric Level	Inner Sign	Glyph
		Crown	Cancer	♋
		Brow	Leo	♌
Gemini	•	Throat	Virgo	♍
Taurus	♉	Heart	Libra	♎
Aries	♈	Solar Plexus	Scorpio	♏
Pisces	♓	Sensate	Sagittarius	♐
Aquarius	♒	Root	Capricorn	♑

The chakric diagram presented here enables us to take a person's birth time and locate each planet's place according to their astrological sign. We then use the planet's astrological sign to find the planet's chakric location. For example, if the Moon is in the astrological sign of Virgo at the time of a person's birth, then their Moon is placed at the inner throat chakra. We use the same method with the rest of the planets, using each planet's astrological sign location to find their chakric location. This is how we use astrology to create a person's chakric diagram which reveals their chakric accents and chakric interactions.

Meaning of the Chakric Structure

The imbalance of the five external functions and the seven internal functions has tremendous implications. We have already mentioned that the top two chakras are preconscious in our awareness. This is reflected in the chakric diagram by the two empty areas on the outer side. The lack of an outer function means that our two upper chakras do not have an intrinsic internal dichotomy of awareness. We are unable to easily place their inner awareness into an outer context. This is why our brow's intuition is so difficult to understand. We are usually unable to place what we know within ourselves confidently into an accurate external context. The same thing is true of the crown's abstract sense of order, it is difficult for us to accurately see where it comes from or what it really means.

Assuming that our human consciousness is growing and evolving, eventually we will have active functions on the outer left side at both the brow and crown chakras. Until then our awareness will remain slightly out of balance, with our being more fully internally aware than we are externally aware.

Let's look at what this imbalance means.

Depending on which side of the chakras we emphasize, inner or outer, we end up with two very different perspectives. If we emphasize the outer world and the world of objective experience, we have a five tiered consciousness with a focal center at the solar plexus chakra. If we accentuate our inner subjective awareness then we have a seven tiered consciousness whose focal center is the heart. The outer perspective focuses on tangible objects and events and their social significance. The world is a bunch of tangible facts and statistics. The inner perspective focuses on how we emotionally feel inside, on how we and the world around us emotionally feels. The world is a bunch of emotional fulfillments or disappointments.

The differences in perspective really becomes noticeable when we contrast how each side deals with the top two chakras. In the outer awareness, the functions of the brow and the crown chakra are felt to be beyond the scope of our own being and are enacted by something external to us. We usually assign this external higher, "magical" consciousness to "God." On the inner side the brow and crown chakras are contained within our own awareness. We feel that the "magical" aspects of the higher chakras are a part of our own being. Magical acts do not have to rely upon an external agency. "God" may or may not exist, but we can personally enact the "magical" awareness of the top two chakras without the need of Divine assistance.

Two major religions describe the differences between the outer and inner perspectives rather well. Christianity describes a primarily left side, outer awareness focus; while Buddhism describes a primarily right side, inner awareness focus. The differences in their world view reflect the fundamental differences of their primary chakric side orientations.

In Christianity humanity is the creation of a God (who resides above us in Heaven) that is above and beyond our scope of awareness. There's a gulf between man and God that is humanly unbridgeable. Humanity is quite limited in its awareness and is blind to the Big Picture which is known only to God. God guides and prods His creation from high above, in Heaven. We strive to join God in Heaven, both here and now as we live on earth and especially after our death, when we hope to ascend to God in Heaven. Humanity has to reach up to God and attempt to discover God's Will. Only then will an individual have a chance to knowingly live in the larger pattern. Our goal is to align ourselves with God and to attentively discern God's Will, which is shown to us through magical coincidences, sudden intuitive flashes of insight and other forms of spiritual guidance.

In the Christian world view, God sent Himself, in the form of Jesus, to die for the sins of humanity (the cause of the gulf between man and God). God's power is seen through a variety of miracles and Jesus' Resurrection from the dead. God is seen as a personal deity who is active in the lives of those that accept His salvation and miraculous guidance.

Salvation is given to us through the benevolence of a greater spiritual power: God. It is our purpose in life to personally realize this gift of Salvation and then try to live in accordance with God's Divine Will. The goal is to walk with God while we are alive on earth and after our death to ascend to God in heaven. All real power in both heaven and on earth resides with God. Even when people pray for divine power to help them, the power always remains God's.

Christianity's world view fits the five tiered outer chakric perspective very well. An external superior God supplies us with the information to act within a pattern that is larger than we can personally know. This information is received through intuitions, voices and visions that are given to us by either spiritual agents such as angels, or God Himself. Because of our human limitations, there are many things that we must resign ourselves to being unable to understand.

Without God our highest human awareness is our intellect. This fits the Renaissance's Rational Humanist response to Christianity in Europe. The European Renaissance paradigm was dominated by the underlying assumptions of Christianity. The intellectual humanists eventually found themselves in a world where they only trusted what they could empirically measure and rationally understand. This world view is also completely dominated by a five-tiered, external objective perspective. This is the perspective of the objectively focused, outer chakric mind set of the west. In purely scientific terms, we can only know what we can observe and measure. We are limited to the mundane physical world of mechanical cause and effect. The existence of God is possible but scientifically unknowable. In essence, Western Rational Humanism shrugs and says it is impossible to say God does or doesn't exist. The awareness of the upper two chakras is empirically untestable, untrustworthy and therefore to be ignored.

In Buddhism, our own consciousness is considered to be what we primarily experience. Our awareness is felt to be both self sustaining and self contained. The primary concern of our conscious awareness is to perpetuate itself. Unfortunately, this self perpetuation happens at the expense of a clear and undeluded sense of the larger Self. For the Buddhist, salvation is attaining a state called Enlightenment. In order to do this we need to escape from the limitations and delusions of our lower levels of awareness. We need to disengage from a personal world view whose delusions buttress our sense of possessing a 'separate' personal existence and we need to return to the vastness and inclusive freedom of the higher Self. The existence of God is somewhat irrelevant in the Buddhist world view. Our real problem is our own self limited awareness. Because our awareness is our own creation it is something which only we can change. There is no external source of salvation. Each person must work their own way through their own inner self-deception to the clarity of Enlightenment. Others can only tell you about Enlightenment, you must achieve it yourself. It cannot be given to you.

Gautama, the Buddha, was the first person to become Enlightened. He told other people about his experience and his understanding of the way the mind worked. He assured other people that they could also become Enlightened. Becoming Enlightened entails an experiential awareness of the higher state of interconnectedness that we see at the crown chakra. In order to consciously live in the awareness of the crown chakra you have to still the demands of the lower chakras. This is done through meditation which quiets the mind and body. For the Buddhist, salvation is achieved by changing our chakric awareness from an emphasis on the lower chakras to an emphasis on the highest chakras. Because it is your own perspective that needs to change, no one else can enlighten you. The Buddha could not make anyone else Enlightened. He could only help them in the process of opening themselves up to their own inner enlightened state of awareness.

In the Buddhist world view we already contain the higher enlightened awareness. Everyone is already intrinsically enlightened. We have merely allowed ourselves to get wrapped up in our mundane desires and existence which obscures this underlying illumined state of awareness.

To the Buddhist spiritual power lives within each of us as individuals, for magic and the miraculous are intrinsic to the nature of the universe. This means that our human consciousness is capable of many magical acts. Indeed, we are continuously using the magical realms to create and sustain our deluded state of awareness. Our intrinsic nature includes the magical/mystical awareness of the top two chakras. But, again our magical capacities, while fun and perhaps even of benefit, are still ultimately just another set of entanglements that enable us to maintain our personal delusions.

The Buddhist world view fits the inner seven-tiered side quite well. Everything is essentially contained within our awareness. Our goal is to uncover an awareness that is already within us and make it consciously known. Even the Buddhist idea of reincarnation fits the seven tiered side's personal sense of completeness. Physical incarnation, or our rebirth, forces our awareness within the smaller scope of the lower chakras. Enlightenment integrates our awareness with the crown chakra so completely that we no longer feel drawn to rebirth. For the Buddhist, salvation is getting our awareness into the realms that exist beyond the cycles of birth, death, and rebirth. It is getting us to live out of the crown chakra rather than the middle five chakras.

As you can see, merely shifting our focus on the inner or the outer chakric functions has a huge impact on our world view. Both the inner and the outer perspectives are accurate, only each perspective focuses on part of the whole truth. Most people gravitate to either the inner or the outer world view as their primary perspective.

To finish up on our investigation of the impact of the structure of our chakras let's take a quick look at how our chakras interact with other people. Our chakras do not act in isolation. Our chakras are designed to interact with our environment and to help us to interact with each other. This next diagram will show how two people interact on a chakric level. Imagine that the two people are facing each other so that their subjective inner activity is on the outside and their objective outer activity is on the inside, between them. Their purely personal reactions happen on the far left and far right edges as they interact. The middle is where they mutually interact and experience what each person considers to be the objective outer experience of the other person. The two upper chakras are only personally active on the inner levels. Between the two individuals on the upper two chakra levels is a set of shared concepts and goals which they both use to structure their interaction.

Using chess as an example, both players know that they need to take turns moving the pieces. They both also agree on how the pieces move and what the goal of the game is. Our two chess players are acting under a set of shared assumptions which enables them to actually play the game of chess together. Between the two people, as an unspoken and assumed presence, is the set of rules and purposes that they've brought into their interaction.

The following diagram shows two people's chakric diagrams as they are facing each other during an interaction. In the middle we see that they both share a mutual purpose and pattern. Their shared abstract assumptions are the rules (shared pattern) and goals (shared purpose) which enables them to interact effectively. Their interaction will be thwarted if they don't share the same assumptions of rules and goals at the two mutually enacted upper chakras.

Person A	Shared Activity		Person B
Cancer	(Shared Pattern)		Cancer
Leo	(Shared Purpose)		Leo
Virgo	Gemini	Gemini	Virgo
Libra	Taurus	Taurus	Libra
Scorpio	Aries	Aries	Scorpio
Sagittarius	Pisces	Pisces	Sagittarius
Capricorn	Aquarius	Aquarius	Capricorn

The Planets and the Chakras

The planetary assignments (also called rulership's) of the chakras are assigned like so:

Chakra	Planet	Glyph
Crown	Moon	☽
Brow	Sun	☉
Throat	Mercury	☿
Heart	Venus	♀
Solar Plexus	Mars	♂
Sensate	Jupiter	♃
Root	Saturn	♄

These chakric rulership's are permanent. A planet's connection with a chakra doesn't change. For example, the Sun always rules the brow chakra. No matter what astrological sign the Sun may be found in, it still rules the brow chakra. As the Sun moves from astrological sign to astrological sign it takes the brow chakra along with it. This is how we connect the brow chakra to another chakra. It is the placement of the chakra's ruling planet that connects one chakra to another chakra. A planet takes the chakra that it rules and places it into the chakra where it's astrological sign position at birth is found.

The Sun rules the brow chakra and if the Sun is located in the astrological sign of Scorpio when you were born, then the Sun places your brow chakra into the chakric placement that Scorpio is assigned to, which is the inner solar plexus chakra. Therefore, the Sun takes the brow chakra's awareness and places it into the awareness of the inner solar plexus because that is the chakric position where Scorpio is located. This simple method of using the astrological sign location of a planet to reveal the flow of one chakra's awareness into another chakra is the core of chakric astrology.

As the planets are always in motion, their locations are continuously changing. In chakric astrology, to get a glimpse of a person's manner of chakric interaction we look at the planetary locations at the moment of their birth. The birth time is used to locate the astrological sign of each of the planets which gives us their placement in the chakric diagram. We use the locations of the planets to see how a person connects their chakras.

The signs, as we have seen, are associated with the chakras in a basic universal structure. Everyone has the same twelve signs in the same chakric locations. All of us have the same planetary rulers for the same chakras. It is the astrological sign locations of the planets that varies between different people and which enables chakric astrology to reveal the distinctiveness of individual personalities.

This is how we use astrology to see how an individual links their chakras together: the sign locations of the planets show us which chakras a person links together. It reveals their personal style of chakric awareness.

In the traditional house-based astrology, each of the planets has a unique character. They each symbolize a distinctive kind of activity. In chakric astrology the planets unique qualities are unimportant as the planets are basically just chakric location markers. Yet the nature of the chakra that each planet is assigned to fits the classic astrological symbolism of the planets quite well. In fact, they fit so well that you may find yourself wondering if the chakras are the ultimate source of astrology's classic planetary symbolism. Therefore, if you are already familiar with the classic astrological planetary characteristics it may help you to understand the chakras.

Still, be aware that in chakric astrology the planets do not act the same way as they do in house wheel astrology. For example, in a house-based astrology the nature of the relationship between two planets is defined by how many degrees of arc they are away from each other in the heavens. These spatial relationships (called aspects) use the distance separating two planets to define the quality and nature of their mutual interaction.

In chakric astrology the planets do not form such spatial aspect relationships with each other. There are no degrees of arc available to measure such a spatial relationship between the two planets. In chakric astrology the planets are only used to reveal relationships between the chakras.

The planets also have no symbolic significance. The planets don't represent any kind of activity. In chakric astrology the chakras themselves are the active factor. It is the perspective of the various chakras that are active. We are only using the planets to see how the seven chakric perspectives interact. This reduces the planet's role in chakric astrology to being mere markers. They only serve to show a connection between one chakra and another chakra.

In assigning the planets to the chakras, we started at the top with the fastest moving planet and moved downward to the slowest moving planet. The Moon is at the very top, then the Sun is next, moving on down the chakras in the same order as their orbit. The slowest moving planet known to the ancients was Saturn. It is assigned to the root chakra. The fastest moving planet is the Moon, which is assigned to the crown chakra. The planetary assignments move down from the throat chakra in this order: Mercury, Venus, Mars and Jupiter.

This planetary sequence also brings us to the distinction between the heliocentric, or sun centered, appearance of planetary motion and the geocentric, or earth centered, appearance of the same motion. From a heliocentric point of view, the Sun is still and the planets move around it. From a geocentric perspective, the Earth is still and everything else is seen to move. From a geocentric perspective, the Sun takes on the motion of the Earth and serves as an allegory for the Earth. This symbolically implies that we view the Earth as the realm of our intentions, or as the field of our potential being, rather than merely as the place of our factual existence.

The geocentric perspective also creates an optical effect where a planet is sometimes seen to move backward in their orbit. This is called retrogradation. When a planet is retrograde in classic astrology, its function is turned inward. It is seen to be subjectively focused and withdrawn from the outside world. Chakric astrology is already extremely subjective. There is no direct reference to any outer event in chakric analysis. This means that a planet's being retrograde in classic astrological symbolism doesn't add very much to chakra astrology. Therefore retrogradation is ignored in chakric astrology.

Again, in chakric astrology our interest in the planets isn't in the classic astrological symbolism of the planets. The planets aren't symbols, instead the planets help us to see and understand one chakra's relationship with the other chakras.

For example, the location of Mars, the solar plexus's ruling plant, tells us which chakra provides the context of the solar plexus's awareness. The awareness of the solar plexus is sublimated to the chakra where Mars is found by astrological sign. If Mars is located in the sign of Capricorn then we see that Mars places the awareness of the solar plexus into the root chakra. This tells us that their solar plexus's social identity is placed into the context of their inner awareness of concrete transpersonal pattern. Their social identity serves their root's transpersonal momentums. This person's social identity must include their sense of personal place within their subjective sense of the larger context of humanity's destiny.

Continuing with our example of Mars in the root chakra, this means that within the root chakra's awareness, the solar plexus chakra's concerns become emphasized. The root chakra is aware of, and deals with, the solar plexus chakra's issues. Their personal social concerns are placed into the root chakra's big picture perspective. Their solar plexus activity is also brought into the service of the root chakra's awareness. Perhaps their place in society must measure up to their subjective sense of human evolution. Or perhaps their sense of social identity takes on a fated quality, for better or worse. It also moves a conscious awareness (the solar plexus) into an unconscious realm (the root).

If say, Venus, is found on the throat level, then the heart chakra's emotional awareness is seen through the lens of our intellect. We would use our mind to understand our emotions. Our throat would both express and analyze our emotions. We may verbally say how our emotions feel, perhaps through song, poetry, or prose. Our mind is also used to help us understand our emotions. "Why do I feel this way?" becomes a concern of the mind and then it uses its logical rational perspective to place our emotions into a context.

If Venus is found on the heart level, then our emotions would provide their own context. This self contained awareness would both strengthen the heart chakra's overall impact in our awareness and tend to isolate our emotions. The heart's perspective would become more pronounced if only because it is self contained. It will be easy for us to feel our emotions and difficult for us to place them into a context for understanding.

The important thing to remember is that a planet carries the awareness of the chakra it rules with it wherever it goes. Later, we will go into greater detail on how the full sweep of planetary locations can be used to understand exactly how someone's chakric activity is integrated. But first we need to get a general overview of how the chakras interact.

The way that any two chakras interact with each other depends on their relative positions. A higher chakra will organize and generalize a lower chakra's awareness. It will see the lower chakras awareness as specific instances which it seeks to classify by type. Meanwhile, a lower chakra will express and make specific a higher chakra's principles and types. The higher chakra gives the organizing idea while the lower chakra gives the specific facts. In other words, the awareness of the lower chakra provides the details while the higher chakra provides the general pattern.

For example, if Mars is found on the throat level in a chakric diagram, then social reality becomes an important aspect of their mental landscape. The solar plexus's specific experiences are noticed by the throat chakra. The throat chakra then lends its abstract understanding to the solar plexus's specific beliefs and experiences. This means that they will intellectually refine their solar plexus chakra's awareness. The raw data of the solar plexus's specific experiences becomes the foundation of the throat chakra's theories. Ultimately though, it is their throat's perspective that dominates their understanding of the solar plexus. They will intellectually define their social position and cultural beliefs.

The raising of one chakra's awareness to another chakra is called an evolutionary process. The lower chakra's awareness expands in scope when it is put into the context of a higher chakra. At the same time, the higher chakra has to adequately account for whatever facts that the lower chakra presents to it.

The opposite process occurs when we move down the chakras. The general idea of the higher chakra's awareness is expressed through the lower chakra. The higher chakra's premises shape the more specific awareness of the lower chakra. If Mars is found at the genital chakra, the cultural definitions of what an experience means and how it feels may dominate our actual sensate experiences. The notions of the solar plexus become expressed through the specific details of our genital chakra's experiences of reality. Cultural assumptions may have a huge impact on what we believe we feel, as well as what experiences we choose to reject or to allow ourselves to have.

The involutionary process can become a problem when the higher chakra's assumptions contradict the lower chakra's actual reality. The involutionary process has a bad reputation. The involutionary process is a bit trickier than the evolutionary process. In our rush to enact our assumptions, we may lose sight of the relevant facts. We usually presume that the higher chakra's perspective is superior - up until it becomes impossible to force the lower chakra's reality to conform to the higher chakra's notions.

The involuntary process has a certainty to it. We believe that we know what we are doing due to our prior experiences. In contrast, during the evolutionary process we start off more tentatively. We are looking for an accurate way to understand the facts. While we may have various initial assumptions and we may become confused when our assumptions don't work, in the evolutionary process we rarely lose sight of the facts.

For example, let's put Jupiter in the solar plexus chakra. Here our genital chakra's sensate awareness is placed into the context of our cultural identity. We will interpret our sensations through our solar plexus's awareness. This means that if we experience something that is outside of our culture's awareness we will have trouble knowing what it means. Suppose we lived five thousand years ago in small isolated village. Suddenly we hear a loud sound and we look up into the sky and see an object fall and hit the ground with a bang. There is a small hole where the object hit the ground. When we look in the hole we find a small chunk of gleaming metal. We suspect that this is an important omen, but we don't know what it means. When we try to tell our friends about the thing that we saw fall out of the sky, they remark that we tell really funny stories. God does not send anything down from the sky except rain and lightening. We go to the elders and tell them our story. We show them our piece of metal. They have never heard of such a thing ever happening before. They are polite but dismissive. We begin to wonder if we are cursed. Or crazy. We clutch the small piece of metal as if holding on to our sanity. Our culture's knowledge apparently doesn't include meteorites. Our individual understanding of our experiences is usually aided by our culture, but not always. This experience falls between the cultural cracks. We are on our own in creating a solar plexus understanding of the event. Are we blessed or cursed by the heavens? Hopefully time will tell.

Or perhaps our culture tells us that pleasure is a sign of frivolity and weakness. We will seek to avoid feeling pleasure. No matter how wonderful something might actually feel, we will try not to enjoy it. If we somehow actually do feel pleasure, we will lament our moral weakness. In a culture where pleasure is allowed, or even encouraged, we would not suppress our appetite for pleasure at all. We certainly wouldn't reproach ourselves whenever we felt it.

Let's look at some of the differences between the evolutionary and involutionary processes. For example, suppose we find someone physically attractive. When the raw data of our physical sensation is placed into our social context, it could go something like this:

"I find them very attractive. Is it going to be possible to act on my attraction? I wonder if they are available? Perhaps they are married?" Our sense of the meaning of what we find physically attractive is shaped by our solar plexus reality. The motion is from the experience of the genital chakra (the attraction) and to the social pattern of the solar plexus chakra (wondering if are they married). This is an evolutionary process.

Reverse the motion and we see an involutionary effect. The solar plexus chakra seeks to create or shape the experience of the genital chakra. Then when we see someone that we think is attractive. It might go like this: "Everyone thinks they're really hot... so they are extremely attractive... I wonder if I'm good enough to go out with them... if they go out with me that'd mean I'm hot... so I want them, just like everyone else." Our sense of solar plexus reality defines what is attractive and shapes what we think and how we feel.

A quick description of the evolutionary and involutionary processes which gives us a rough outline of how to interpret chakric interactions is that in the involutionary process a rule or a principle is expressed through the facts of a lower chakra's awareness. (But remember, a principle is only good if it actually works.)

Involutionary	**Evolutionary**
(higher moves lower)	(lower moves higher)
A Higher Chakra's	A Lower Chakra's
Understanding is . . .	Specific Experiences . . .
. . . made Specific	. . . are shaped
and Experienced	and Understood
At a Lower Chakra	At a Higher Chakra

In the evolutionary process the raw data of a lower chakra's awareness is placed into a higher chakra's understanding. The facts have no meaning until they are placed into an adequate context and comprehended.

The exception to this involutionary rule is the root chakra which is transpersonal. When a personal chakra (the middle five chakras) moves down into the root, it may attempt to impose itself on the root chakra. The problem is that the root has a larger perspective than any of our personal chakras. While the motion makes our general understanding specific, the root is largely unconscious and obscures the conscious awareness of the higher chakra. The root's perspective envelopes the higher chakra.

In the evolutionary motion the awareness of a lower chakra is seen through the eyes of a higher chakra. The higher chakra defines the meaning of the awareness of the lower chakra. For example, if the genital chakra goes up to the solar plexus then the cultural awareness of the solar plexus understands and judges our sensations. The higher chakra will interpret the lower according to its perspective, but may even try to dictate the experience of the lower chakra. It may try to ignore or explain away whatever disagrees with its current framework of understanding. While the facts ultimately remain what they are, their interpretation can vary greatly.

In the involutionary motion if the solar plexus moves down into the genital chakra, it may attempt to shape the experience of the genital chakra according to its dictates. This can be something like telling yourself that you're a serious person and therefore you will not enjoy that frivolous hedonistic music and you definitely will not dance to it. (Despite the fact that you are extremely sensually stimulated by it and are already unconsciously tapping your foot in rhythm.) The influence of a higher chakra on the meaning of a lower chakra's experiences can sometimes ignore the actual awareness of the lower chakra. You may attempt to reshape the reality of the lower awareness to fit the higher's vision. Using the prior example, you might stifle yourself and become detached from your desire to dance and flow with the music. The involutionary motion has many 'shoulds'. The evolutionary motion doesn't have many 'shoulds'. It is a little bit more open ended and it asks more questions. In the involutionary motion our understanding is assumed to be adequate. The involutionary motion often acts in the background, it's assumptions shaping the lower chakra's perceptions. In the evolutionary motion an adequate understanding is usually still being sought and so our lower chakra is seen as a valuable source of information.

If the "I am too serious for frivolous behavior" presumption gets carried too far, we may actually deaden ourselves to our genital perceptions and reactions.   Or perhaps the lower chakra may completely rebel against the input of the higher chakra and act with reckless hedonistic abandon trying to make the point that we are being too serious.

The point is that both of the chakras need to work together in order to create an adequate understanding. Ultimately, it is useless to say that either the involutionary or the evolutionary process is of greater moral worth. They both have their uses.

The Outer Planets in the Chakras

In chakric astrology the three outer planets symbolize humanity's collective chakric awareness. The three planets beyond Saturn represent a generation's shared collective chakric perspective. This collective perspective serves as an underlying set of assumptions which each generation has about who they are, or their group social identity; their reaction to their physical world, or their collective sensate experience; and the underlying set of structures that create the environment that they live in, or the physical structure of their collective circumstances (which would include their technology). Each generation lives in their own particular mix of collective assumptions which generally are taken for granted, in much the same way that we assume the presence of air.

Just as our individual consciousness evolves from the lower to the higher, so does our collective chakric awareness. Astrologically humanity didn't have a true global collective awareness until fairly recently. Our concepts were always confined to our region of the globe and there wasn't a single culture that grasped the entirety of the world. The discovery of Uranus in 1781 symbolized humanity's first step into a global collective consciousness. With sailing vessels and their regular circumnavigation of the globe on the seas, humanity finally developed a group mind that was truly aware of the world as a whole.

As the first of the trans-saturnian planets to be discovered, Uranus (glyph ♅) coincided with the awakening of a collective root chakra, which coincided with the struggles to replace authoritarian monarchies with democratic governments. The next planet to be discovered was Neptune (glyph ♆). It reveals the creation of a collective genital chakra, or shared sensate reality. The inventions of the late nineteenth and early twentieth century, such as the telegraph, telephone, and recording devices such as the phonograph, photograph and motion pictures enabled people to share experiences. We could see someone from the other side of the planet or talk to people on the other side of the globe. The last of the presently used trans-saturnian planets is Pluto (glyph ♀) which denotes the appearance of a collective solar plexus. The creation of nuclear weapons enabled us to unleash destruction in an extremely effective, large-scale and impersonal way. Nuclear weapons enable us to destroy ourselves quite quickly and effectively.

Remember that in chakric astrology the placement of the three trans-saturnian planets (Uranus, Neptune and Pluto) describe the over all perspective of a generation. These planets do not describe an individual's awareness, but rather their peer culture's attitudes. These three outer planets represent their generation's shared assumptions which becomes the underlying context of our individual perspectives.

Cultural Planet	Outer Sign	Chakra	Inner Sign	Personal Planet
		Crown	Cancer	Moon
		Brow	Leo	Sun
	Gemini	Throat	Virgo	Mercury
	Taurus	Heart	Libra	Venus
Pluto ♀	Aries	Solar Plexus	Scorpio	Mars
Neptune ♆	Pisces	Sensate	Sagittarius	Jupiter
Uranus ♅	Aquarius	Root	Capricorn	Saturn

Theoretically, the heart will be next collective chakric level of our awareness to become active. Hopefully the heart's capacity for love, connectedness and generosity will become more prevalent and dominate our collective actions on the world stage. Perhaps we will even actually care for each other rather than primarily exploit each other. This is not to say that we are on the verge of a utopian era, as the heart has it's own imperfections and problematic attitudes. But when the heart is finally a part of our collective awareness it will be another step in humanity's evolving consciousness.

The cultural planets are connected to the outer function of awareness, which assigns Pluto to Aries, Neptune is assigned to Pisces and Uranus is assigned to Aquarius. The personal planets become a individual counterpoint to the collective perspective.

Prior to the discovery of Uranus the world was purely personal in scale. The awareness of a single individual could encompass the consciousness of the entire human race. In the era ushered in by the trans-saturnian planets our collective awareness became greater than any individual could encompass. At that point the knowledge possessed by the human race became too complex and too vast for any one person to contain. Individuals had to become specialized in what they knew. The scale of human knowledge had became transpersonal and with only the collective awareness of humanity capable of dealing with all of it's parts. No individual can keep up with the diversity and wealth of information that human knowledge now possesses.

The trans-saturnian planets are placed on the left or outer side because it is in the outer external world that we ultimately share reality with other people. The collective, or transpersonal, reality is a realm which we experience as external from ourselves. The trans-saturnian planets rule this collective objective realm.

Uranus is the first of the collective planets to be discovered and it is connected with the outer functions of the root chakra. The sign of Aquarius, at the outer root chakra, is also connected to Uranus. The next collective planet to be discovered was Neptune and it is associated with the outer functions of the genital chakra. Neptune is associated with the astrological sign of Pisces. The last of the outer planets to be discovered was Pluto. Pluto is associated with our collective solar plexus chakra and with the astrological sign Aries.

The next planet that we discover in our solar system will be assigned to the heart chakra and the astrological sign of Taurus. It will signify the emergence of a collective awareness of the heart chakra. It is the next step in humanity's collective consciousness. Obviously, this implies that at this point in time humanity does not have a collective awareness at the heart chakra. The second planet that we discover beyond Pluto will be assigned to the throat chakra. Again, at this point the human race does not have a functioning collective throat chakra. Any additional planets that are discovered would be assigned in ascending order up the chakras according to the time of their discoveries.

The recent demotion of Pluto from planetary status by astronomers is symbolically interesting. So far astrologer's seem to be keeping Pluto in their system of thought. It'll be interesting to see what happens. Would the renunciation of Pluto symbolize a reversion back to the genital chakra as our highest collective awareness, if only for the moment? Or will astrologer's decide that they are engaged in a symbolic correlation of the heaven's and ignore the astronomer's concerns with the details of exactly what makes a planet a planet?

The Evolution of Consciousness

The rising of the cultural planets in our chakras in their order of discovery implies that our collective consciousness is evolving. Eventually, assuming that our evolution continues, humanity will have a collective heart chakra awareness. After that a collective throat chakra should evolve as a part of our collective consciousness. This same evolutionary process happened, and is still happening, on the level of individual consciousness. Each of us inherits our individual chakric structure in the same way that each of us inherits our individual human body. At this point in our progress in order for an individual to evolve in chakric awareness the whole of humanity has to evolve as well.

The spread of the astrological signs in the chakras implies some things about our awareness. That all seven chakras on the inside has an astrological sign associated with it, contrasts starkly with the five signs on the outside. Knowing that our consciousness rises in its evolution upward through the chakras, we can see that we do not have a fully evolved chakric awareness. We also can see that our consciousness functions internally before it functions externally. In other words, initially we are aware of ourselves before we relate that inner awareness to our outer circumstances.

The distribution of the astrological planets has different implications. Our personal chakric consciousness is fully evolved internally, therefore as individuals we have a planet for all seven chakric levels. Our individual awareness can also be seen to function both objectively and subjectively up to the throat chakra. In contrast, our collective awareness only functions through the lower three chakras. We have a personal awareness at the heart and throat chakras, but we don't have a collective awareness on those levels. The highest collective perspective we have at this point stops at the solar plexus. This is part of why humanity presently has various cultural and national conflicts over power and control. The solar plexus is the highest form of collective action that we presently can fully comprehend.   Another implication of the contrast between our personal and collective planets is that our collective awareness does not have an internal awareness. This implies that the collective mind is not directly capable of self reflection.   Apparently, our collective consciousness is not very self-aware. It is up to us as individuals to supply the internal counterpoint which creates the dichotomy needed to establish a collective self-awareness.

Or another possibility is that our collective consciousness operates on both sides of our chakric awareness and looks something like this:

Outer Sign	Chakra	Personal Planet	Cultural Planet	Inner Sign
	Crown	Moon		Cancer
	Brow	Sun		Leo
Gemini	Throat	Mercury		Virgo
Taurus	Heart	Venus		Libra
Aries	Solar Plexus	Mars	Pluto	Scorpio
Pisces	Genital	Jupiter	Neptune	Sagittarius
Aquarius	Root	Saturn	Uranus	Capricorn

Pluto would be assigned to both Aries and Scorpio, Neptune to both Pisces and Sagittarius and Uranus would be connected with the root and the signs of Aquarius and Capricorn. This arrangement makes our collective awareness (as symbolized by the trans-saturnian planets) both subjective and objective. There is a tendency to think of our collective awareness as something external and objective. At the same time we contain it within ourselves. There is a good argument for either cultural planet correlation arrangement. The question becomes the relationship between our personal and collective levels of awareness. Is the collective awareness of humanity the creation of a joining together of individuals, or is the individual a particularized offshoot of the collective whole? Once again the problem becomes very much a matter of which came first: the chicken or the egg?

The question becomes how much does the individual affect the whole, and how much does the whole affect the individual. Ultimately our consciousness will probably evolve so that it will eventually look astrologically like the following diagram, despite the fact the gods that would be assigned to the outer heart and throat are associated with planets that have not been discovered yet, like so:

Cultural Planet	Outer Sign	Chakra	Inner Sign	Personal Planet
		Crown	Cancer	Moon
		Brow	Leo	Sun
Coeus	Gemini	Throat	Virgo	Mercury
Eleus	Taurus	Heart	Libra	Venus
Pluto	Aries	Solar Plexus	Scorpio	Mars
Neptune	Pisces	Genital	Sagittarius	Jupiter
Uranus	Aquarius	Root	Capricorn	Saturn

This gives the addition on the outer cultural planetary side of two Titans: Eleus, god of compassion; and Coeus, god of intelligence and deep pondering. Eleus is assigned to Taurus and Coeus is connected to Gemini. Beyond that one hesitates to even guess. It is possible that someday we may personally and collectively enact the outer functions of the top two chakras. This would mean that the psychism of the brow chakra will become much more reliable. The crown chakra's awareness will probably always remain slippery despite any internal dichotomy due its transpersonal nature.

To get a better grasp on our own awareness let's look at what an amoeba's chakric diagram could look like. An amoeba is a simple single celled organism. It reproduces itself through cellular division. It has no nervous system and probably is only vaguely aware of sensation. It uses a simple attraction repulsion mechanism for its movements toward food and away from danger. It has no social organization, amoebas don't gather together and hunt for food. It has no heart and it is not emotionally aware. It doesn't possess a mind either. Is it intuitively aware? Doubtful, but possible. Does it believe it has a role in a larger cosmic purpose? Again it is doubtful, but impossible to know for sure. We surmise that our amoeba's chakric structure looks something like this:

Outer	Chakra	Inner
	Crown	
	Brow	
	Throat	
	Heart	
	Solar Plexus	
	Genital	Active
	Root	Active

There are no chakric functions on the outside. Because there are only two active functioning chakric areas, an amoeba probably would see the world as a vertical dichotomy: instinct and individual response to sensation. There would be only two astrological signs. One sign would represent the genital chakra, while the other sign would represent the root chakra. The genital chakra would be functioning in those moments when the amoeba had an individual experience. The root chakra, which is probably the amoeba's dominant chakra, would be active at those moments when the amoeba is functioning either instinctively or on purely biochemical levels. In this analysis, an amoeba would not have any internally dichotomized chakric awareness, and so it wouldn't be what we would consider at all self aware.

Or perhaps an amoeba's chakric awareness looks like the following diagram in which case the root chakra is sort of self aware. It is still pretty much limited to an instinctive response system.

Outer	Chakra	Inner
	Crown	
	Brow	
	Throat	
	Heart	
	Solar Plexus	
	Genital	Active
Active	Root	Active

Or perhaps it's chakras function like this:

Outer	Chakra	Inner
	Crown	
	Brow	
	Throat	
	Heart	
	Solar Plexus	
Active	Genital	Active
Active	Root	Active

In which case it would actually be consciously aware of it's environment and actually be making choices about how it feels and how to react.

The assumption in all of these diagrams is that there is probably no active awareness above the genital level, or more accurately, the sensation level. It is hard to tell exactly how much of an outer awareness an amoeba has. It may have no outer functions on the left side. Or may be active externally only at the root. Or perhaps it is externally active at both the root and the genital chakras.

On the right inner side, it definitely has a root chakra as seen in its genetic heritage and physical existence. It is also sensately aware, for it uses sensation to move, to go toward food to feed itself, or to flee from danger. Does it have an internal preconscious awareness of the solar plexus? Is it aware of itself within a larger context? Is it aware of itself within a social hierarchy? Probably not. Do amoebas have a cultural heritage? No. Within an amoeba's consciousness everything above the genital chakra is probably far hazier than our human preconscious awareness of the brow and crown chakras are. Still, an amoeba may be highly intuitive. It may use intuition to choose which direction to go in. All of the internal functions of the seven chakras may be active in an amoeba's awareness. In which case the inner awareness is fully formed from the moment of it's creation and it is the outer functions that are undeveloped. Then the amoeba's awareness would be seen as evolving in outer awareness upward through the chakras in an ascending grasp of greater and greater external awareness.

The issue becomes a matter of volition. Does our conscious awareness evolve by choice, by chance, or a combination of both? Does life choose its own form, or is the form imposed upon it from without? Is there a preexistent abstract dimension of awareness, such as God, that designs the concrete levels of awareness? Or are the abstract dimensions of awareness (the higher chakras) the accumulated result of aeons of concrete experiences? Is the abstract awareness of the upper chakric levels the result of concrete actuality? Or is the concrete actuality of the lower chakras the result of a higher abstract awareness's design?

Put another way: is God the abstract creation of a concrete universe? Or is the universe the concrete creation of an abstract God? Which came first, the Creation or the Creator? Or are they constantly simultaneously co-creating each other?

Which brings us back to our amoeba. How much volition does an amoeba have? What is the scope of its will? Does it have an intrinsic awareness that includes the higher abstract levels? That would mean that it has all seven chakras as a latent preconscious awareness on the right side. Or does such an abstract awareness reside somewhere outside of the amoeba, in, say, the mind of God? That would mean that an amoeba would not contain any abstract or outer awareness. Then its chakric structure could look somewhat like this:

Outer	**Chakra**	**Inner**
	Solar Plexus	
	Genital	Active
	Root	Active

All this raises questions whose answers are impossible to know for sure. But geologic evidence shows that single celled organisms were the only form of life on earth for a very, very long time. Once the single cell barrier was broken many kinds of multi-celled organisms rapidly evolved. The multiple celled organisms developed specialized cells to fulfill particular needs. The functions that once were carried out completely within a single cell: sensation, ingestion, digestion, reproduction, and so on, become functions of specialized groups of cells. A new multi-celled unit of consciousness emerged. The identity of a single cell was transmuted into a similarly unique identity based on an individual multi-celled organism. The new life forms quickly diversified into many different species. The evolution of organisms with increasingly complex levels of awareness followed soon after.

Divine/Avataric
Angelic/Buddhic
Human
Animal
Plant
Single Celled Organism
Mineral

Classically the evolution of awareness in eastern thought is seen to run from the bottom to the top as shown above.

The mineral level is the basis of the physical universe. It is a realm of pure cause and effect. Molecular interactions are based on chemical attractions and repulsions. Chemistry shows us how mechanical the mineral realm is. Apply enough heat to water and the molecular bond holding the oxygen and hydrogen atoms together will be broken. The mineral level is extremely mechanistic. Mineral compounds do not have feelings. Their world does not require sensation, nor do chemical compounds like or dislike what happens to them.

The single celled organisms are sensately aware (although not necessarily self aware). They experience their environment. They interact with their environment in ways that use the mineral level's chemical interactions, but they are more complex. They are alive. If they do not acquire certain resources, they die. Minerals do not live and die.

The multiple celled structure of plants reveals a form of social awareness, but plants do not have an emotional awareness. The relatively static quality of social hierarchies is reflected in the immobility of plant life.

The heart level, with its emotional awareness, is assigned to the animal kingdom. Here we find an emotional relationship to the environment. Animals have been seen to dream. With the plant world physical mobility was extremely limited. At the animal level life becomes very mobile. Animals can move about. Also an individual animal can rise up to become the leader of its social group, while the bark of a tree must always hold the same place in the tree's 'social' structure.

With the mental level we reach humanity. Here we find the capacity to think and reason. This level is completely abstract. The components of the mental vehicle are wholly symbolic. Through them we can articulate ourselves through symbols and share our ideas, experiences and feelings with others. Interpersonal cohesion can be based on shared concepts and ideas, whereas before they were based on shared familial, ethnic and emotional bonds. At the throat chakra we can write books or paint paintings that talk to multiple generations.

It is impossible to date exactly when we first developed an outer awareness at the various chakras. When did the solar plexus chakra first acquire a full dichotomous inner and outer awareness? When did our heart chakras develop a left side awareness? Was it when we first developed the capacity for monogamous romantic relationships? When we first cared about our children more than ourselves? It is also impossible to say how long the development process behind each rise in chakric level took. All that can be said for certain is that the consciousness of person has a much greater degree of complexity than a single celled organism's awareness.

Yet, humanity's full acquisition of the mental level is in all likelihood a fairly recent achievement (evolutionarily speaking). The throat chakra was probably first evident when we began to use tools and language. It probably wasn't fully established until we began to use the logic structures of mathematics, a cognitive skill which we probably initially developed in order to make large scale buildings, such as temples and palaces.

The next step in the evolution of our individual, personal awareness is dichotomizing the brow chakra. Then after that a dichotomized crown chakra awareness is next. It is impossible to know how long this process will take, or even if it will happen at all. It could be that our personal individualized consciousness is fully evolved.

Perhaps the next step in our evolution is the development of a collective awareness above the solar plexus chakra.

Metaphysical Implications

Because the upper three chakras are totally abstract, they do not require a physical focus to exist. In one school of thought, in order for us to transcend physical death, we only need to create enough self awareness to generate enough momentum to maintain our consciousness at these higher levels so that can they continue after our physical death. We have already discussed how romantic love can endure beyond death. It is also possible to use the mind and its ideas to create an awareness whose momentum continues after death. Simultaneously, it is possible to use the brow and crown chakras to create spiritual momentums that will endure beyond death. The goal of many spiritual schools is to make the abstract realms of our higher chakric awareness more real to us. Some groups use astral projection to make the heart level more real. Some groups teach mental discipline and seek to hone the mind to make the mental realm an enduring home for our individual conscious continuity beyond death. Other groups use prayer, with it's seeking after miracles, to connect us with the enduring awareness of the brow and crown.

These ideas beg the question: Is a person's present chakric consciousness something they created in a prior lifetime? Or does our present consciousness emerge from a blank state? Is it the product of random factors present at our birth, which we spiritually inherit, much as we inherit our physical body? Is it God's doing? Why does a person get one chakric diagram rather than another one? Again, the questions are impossible to definitively answer. Although they imply some intriguing ideas.

Chakra Experience Exercises

Solitary Observation

Now that we have some sense of the chakras, here is a simple exercise that we can do to help us understand the chakras. First, be alone in a quiet room. What we're going to do is take one of our chakras, visualize it and try to feel it. Then we're going to take another chakra and visualize it and try to feel it. Some chakras will be more accessible to us than others. One chakra may feel tight and slightly nervous, while another may feel light and breezy. The key is to get into the chakra and feel its awareness. Also, how a chakra feels at any given moment changes a great deal depending on our circumstances, our mood and what we're thinking about. Initially, in this exercise all we're trying to do is gather information.

If one of the chakras feels stressed, pay attention to how it feels. Where do these feelings lead? Observe any thoughts, images, or associations that arise. Our chakras do not feel things in a vacuum. There are reasons for the way they feel.

Assuming we are alone in a quiet room, the only thing a chakra is experiencing is itself. These may be the chakra's reaction to our passing thoughts, feelings or memories. Each of the chakras contain prior experiences and memories. That is their purpose. Our chakras become predisposed to feeling (and thinking, in their own fashion) in a habitual way very quickly. Accumulated experiences condition chakric expectations. So, what are we feeling and in which chakra? Think about the perspective that each chakra has. Is our solar plexus tight? Is our social identity under stress? Is our spouse upsetting us? Or do we feel unloved? Unable to understand things? Or perhaps we are overwhelmed by our possibilities?

At the same time, realize that each chakra has its own particular set of needs and desires. Are those needs being fulfilled? Does a particular chakra feel hungry? If so, for what?

Once we feel comfortable with each of the chakras individually, we can start to connect one chakra with another chakra. How does one chakra react to another chakra? If we place our throat chakra into our brow chakra how does our throat chakra feel? Does our throat go "this place is vast and amazing" or "this place is vast and scary"? Can we feel why a chakra reacts the way it does? How does the brow chakra react to the throat chakra's presence? If the throat has a pleasant reaction to the brow chakra, is the brow comfortable with the throat? If the throat finds the brow chakra scary, does the brow find the throat irritating? There is no correct way for our chakras interact. Just observe.

Understanding how one chakra reacts to another chakra is the key to understanding chakric astrology. Obviously, it is also helpful in our learning to understand ourselves. When we find areas of tension try to notice which chakra is stressed. Try to notice if the same chakra is calm when connecting to a different chakra. What we are trying to do is see how well, or poorly, our chakras interact. Later we can think about why one chakra would or would not get along well with another chakra. Does our solar plexus try to force its will upon our sensate chakra, making us believe that we like things that we don't really like, or dislike things that we actually like? Is our throat ignoring our feelings at the heart? Do we have a bad memory residing in a chakra? Was there a moment when we felt like we let someone down and we don't really like to remember that? Did something happen in the past that completely confused us? These are the kinds of questions that we can ask ourselves as we to try to uncover what might be the source of the stress in our chakras.

Public Place Observation

This exercise involves a public place because the chakras not only store memories, they also interact with our environment. In order to do this exercise we are looking for a quiet place that has some social activity. A park or coffeehouse could be suitable. Look briefly at a person, get a sense of who they are and then look away. Then feel your own body and try to sense what chakra was involved in the observation. You might actually find that you may still be chakrically interacting with that person even after you've looked away. The chakras reach out and touch the world around us. They know things through contact. What we're trying to do is notice the living organic nature of the chakras in a real time, present moment experience. We are trying to notice which chakras reach out and interact with which people.

Look at another person. Feel who they are with your chakras and note which chakras are active, and which are withdrawn. Again, there is no right or wrong here. We're just looking for information. Sometimes the memories within a chakra will superimpose themselves onto the experience of the present moment. If so, is the projection accurate and helpful? Or is it just using the present moment to replay the past? Realize that our chakras store our prior experiences and those experiences may impact our interaction with the present. The person we looked at may remind us of someone from our past and our chakric reactions to them may be based on our memories rather than our present experience.

It may take a while to get comfortable with noticing your chakra's interactions with other people. But remember that this process is constantly taking place below the threshold of your normal conscious awareness. It is natural and normal. While becoming consciously aware of the activity is a bit strange at first, just observe. Eventually you will become relaxed and your chakras will simply become yet another source of information about how you feel about the people around you.

The chakras react differently to different people and places. Notice these reactions and eventually you will begin to notice some patterns. The goal is to understand yourself and the way you interact with your environment more fully. After a while you may see reflexive reactions to people or places that you don't find helpful. It is difficult to get out a rut (there is a reason that the etheric vehicle, or the chakras, is called the habit body), but if you try you can undo your inappropriate habits.

Use a mix of both the public and private place observations to create a well balanced awareness. Remember that the chakras are both storage containers of prior events and they interact with the present moment. What you're trying to achieve is an awareness of both yourself and your environment.

Creating an Astrological Chakric Diagram

To create a person's chakric diagram we need to know the locations of the planets at the time of their birth. Computer programs that calculate these planetary locations are readily available. With chakric astrology the planetary locations don't need to be very exact. All we need to know is the astrological sign of each of the planets when a person was born.

As we saw before, we use the planet's astrological sign to see where to put each planet in the chakric diagram. We place the planets next to the sign that they are in. For example, if the moon is in Pisces then we put in on the genital chakra level on the left, outer side. This is because that is where the sign Pisces is found in the chakric diagram. (Small example diagram below. See the Appendix for a Chakric Astrology Worksheet designed to be to be photocopied for your own use.)

Once we get all the planets placed in the chakric diagram we quickly glance at the diagram to get a rough grasp of how their chakras work. First, we look at how the planets are distributed in the diagram. Are they evenly scattered? Are the planets clustered on either side? Does one planet stand out somehow, perhaps by being separate from the rest? Are most of the planets in the higher chakras? In the lower chakras? Does one chakra have the majority of the planets? Is only one chakra empty? Does only one chakra have planets on both sides?

What we want to do is notice whatever stands out. These basic planetary patterns can give us a quick idea of who they are. It is a way of swiftly grasping the overall balance of a person's diagram.

The next thing we do is look at how the chakra's relate to one another. To do this we draw lines connecting each the chakras. Each planet takes the chakra that it rules with it to the chakra where it's ruling planet is located. This gives us seven lines of chakric motion, as each chakra's ruling planet is placed into their chakric location by the astrological sign where the planet is found.

After we have all the connecting lines placed on our chakric diagram, we draw out how the chakras interact. Once again we will start with the general pattern. We look at how integrated the chakras are. Are all the chakras connected to each other? Do they flow in a straight line or do they form loops? How many lines or loops are there? Do these loops and lines interconnect, or are they separate? Are some chakras isolated? If a chakra contains its own ruling planet then the awareness of that chakra doesn't move on to another chakra. Often this stopping point becomes a focal point of their chakric awareness.

What all these connections tell us is how integrated or fragmented their chakric awareness is. If there are a lot of small units that are not connected to any other units, then this person's awareness is not very integrated. Some areas of their chakric awareness are isolated from other areas of their awareness. When the chakras act in isolation there is a tendency to move from one separate unit of

Chakric Astrology Worksheet For_____

Born ____/____/____   Time____:____ Am/Pm   Time Zone _____   Location_____

Outer Sign	Chakra & Planet	Inner Sign		
	Crown			**Chakric Motion**
	☽	♋		
				Up (Evolutionary)
				Down (Involutionary)
	Brow			**None** (Stopper)
	☉	♌		
	Throat			**Cultural Motion**
♊	☿	♍		
				♀ (Solar Plexus) up/down to
	Heart			♆ (Sensate) up/down to
				♅ (Root) up/down to
♉	♀	♎		
				Chakric Integration
	Solar Plexus			
♈	♂	♏		
	Sensate			
♓	♃	♐		
	Root			
♒	♄	♑		

awareness to another separate unit. The person flits between different, competing areas of focus. For them, life is compartmentalized. Usually their problem is bringing the various separate parts of their awareness together into a more coordinated whole.

If all of the chakras are interconnected, then their awareness is unified and all facets of their awareness work together. There is usually an easily identifiable focal point in their awareness. This becomes their problem area. For them, the issue is how the focal chakra deals with the built up psychic tension. A single chakra, or a two chakra loop, sometimes carries the weight of their entire awareness. It has to satisfy the needs of all their chakras. Their problem becomes either releasing the built up pressure, or else realizing that the other chakras also matter, even if they aren't at the forefront of their awareness.

We should also check the overall motion of the chakras. Is the motion mostly upward? In which case they learn from experience. Is the motion mostly downward? Then they try to impose their beliefs and prior experiences on their present situation. Are the higher chakras connected to the lower chakras? Do their abstract and their concrete levels of awareness interact with each other? Is the person primarily on the left experiencing side? Or are they most concerned with how they feel inside at the right side? Then lastly, what is the pattern of their chakric integration? Is it simple? Complex? Does one hand know what the other hand is doing? Does their awareness end up in a context that is not fully conscious? (The brow or crown chakras.) Does their awareness go into a context that is unconscious? (The root chakra.)

Now let's put what we have just discussed to work. We will look at some chakric diagrams and analyze them, to bring the ideas we have just looked at to life.

First Example Chakric Diagram

All that we need to get a full understanding of how their chakras interact are the planetary locations, by astrological sign, at the moment of their birth.

For this person they are:

Moon in Gemini	Jupiter in Taurus
Sun in Scorpio	Saturn in Libra
Mercury in Sagittarius	Uranus in Cancer
Venus in Sagittarius	Neptune in Libra
Mars in Capricorn	Pluto in Leo

When we put the planets into their chakric diagram (see the following chakric diagram), we find that they have no empty chakric levels. In quick overview we see no dynamic stress point. There are two planets on the left expressive side. If there was only one planet, that chakra would have been a strong focal point. A single planet on a side makes both that side and that particular chakric level very important in a person's awareness.

Two things do stand out: the throat is the only chakra that is empty on the right side and the heart is the only chakra that is active on both sides.

The throat's lack of an inner function implies that when they talk they are noticing what they internally think by communicating it to another person. For them, talking is not just a means of contact with another person, it is also how they come to know and process their own thoughts.   Because the throat is the only empty chakra on the right side it becomes emphasized in their internal awareness. We would guess that inwardly they don't feel they are very smart. The empty right side makes them feel that they lack inner intellectual substance. This may create a sense of an inner lacking that they seek to overcome. This may motivate them to study and learn so that their sense of weakness may actually be turned into a strength.

The Moon in Gemini brings the perspective of the crown down to the throat. Their throat knows that the world is highly integrated and abstractly structured. They express to others that the world is very magical and orderly. Their mind assumes there is an underlying cosmic structure and purpose and it becomes a part of how and why they touch the outer world. They enjoy sharing through verbal communication and it makes them aware of the bigger pattern in which they live.

The ruler of the throat, Mercury, goes down to the genital chakra on the remembering right side. What they

For __FIRST EXAMPLE_____ BORN____/__/___ At
___:_____ Am/pm

Chakra &
Outer Sign - Planet - Inner Sign

Crown
☽   ♋   ♅

Brow
☉   ♌   ⚢

Throat
☽   ♊   ☿   ♍

Heart
♃   ♉   ♀   ♎   ♄   ♆

Solar Plexus
♈   ♂   ♏   ☉

Genital
♓   ♃   ♐   ☿   ♀

Root
♒   ♄   ♑   ♂

sensately feel is impacted by what they think they will feel. In other words, they use the outer throat chakra to shape their genital chakra's sensate experiences. Their mind, in a behind the scene's manner, helps define the scope and meaning of their tangible experiences. Since they are externally focused at the throat, they may allow how others think to influence how they feel. The genital chakra also becomes how they know and understand what they think. They seek to sensately experience their mind's ideas.

The heart is the only chakra that is active on both sides. This heightens their awareness of how they emotionally feel. Their heart is where they are most self aware. It is where they link their inner and outer worlds most completely.

The heart contains Jupiter (the ruler of the genital chakra) in Taurus on the left expressive side. Neptune, the cultural ruler of the genital chakra, is also found at the heart level on the inside. The tangible world's richness of sensation feeds their sense of emotional connection to their external world. Interestingly, at the heart they internalize their culture's genital awareness (Neptune in Libra on the right side) while they externalize their personal genital awareness (Jupiter in Taurus on the left side). Experiences become imbued with rich personal significance. Their experiences become emotionally charged personal symbols which add depth to their actual physical experiences.

Next we draw the lines of planetary rulership. To do this we take the chakra that a planet rules and draw a line from that chakra to the chakra where the planet is found. In this diagram the root's ruler, Saturn, is found in the heart on the right side. We draw a line from the root to the heart, using an arrow to point the direction of the motion. We repeat this procedure with each of the chakras.

We find that the example diagram's chakras move like so:

Crown	to	Throat
Brow	to	Solar Plexus
Throat	to	Sensate
Heart	to	Sensate
Solar Plexus	to	Root
Sensate	to	Heart
Root	to	Heart

Now we can begin to look at how the chakras work together as a whole. This means that we are looking for lines of connection, circular loops, isolated chakras, chakras that don't move to another chakra (stoppers) and how integrated their chakras are as a whole. To keep it simple we will start at the crown and follow it through to whatever chakras it ultimately connects with. We will follow the crown chakra's line of connection until we have: accounted for all the chakras; returned to a prior chakra; or come to a chakra that does not move on.

If we return to a prior chakra, we will have uncovered a self-contained loop. If we reach a chakra that doesn't move on to another chakra we have uncovered a stopper. We mark off each chakra that we run into. After we are done tracing out the crown chakra's connections we will take the next chakra from the top that hasn't already been traced out and see its lines of connection. If it is the brow then we will trace the brow's connections. Then we will move down to the throat and so on, until every chakra's connections are diagramed. Their chakras go:

Crown to Throat; Throat to Genital; Genital to Heart;
    Heart to Genital

We have found a loop. It is a simple loop, containing only two steps: the heart to the genital chakra and then the genital back to the heart chakra. The crown and the throat chakras both feed into the genital. We view the two feeding chakras like tributaries of a river. The genital chakra's awareness becomes emphasized because of the two chakras adding their awareness it. We mark off the four chakras that we found tracing out the crown line. This leaves three chakras to account for: the brow, solar plexus and root. So we go to the brow (the next one down from the top) and trace the line of motion:

Brow to Solar Plexus; Solar Plexus to Root; Root to Heart

We stop at the heart because we've seen it before. When we draw out the chakras in this second line, we have accounted for all of the chakras. (We are done with the chakric diagram in purely personal terms. We will look at the impact of their culture - Uranus, Neptune and Pluto - on their awareness later.)

This second line of motion feeds into their heart, which then feeds into the heart-to-genital loop. All their chakras connect into a single mechanism. The ultimate focus of their awareness is the heart and genital loop. All of their chakras feed into this two-step loop. A simple dichotomy that plays their sensate experiences off their emotions is the crux of their awareness.

Their chakras are somewhat balanced. Two chakras flow into the genital, while three chakras flow into the heart. The heart ends up carrying a bit more weight, but not a great deal more. Each side of the genital/heart loop has a transpersonal chakra which also helps to even out their relative strength.

Their brow flows into their solar plexus, which in turn flows into their root, which then flows into their heart. Meanwhile, their crown flows into their throat, which then flows into their genital, which then moves into their heart. Both of these motions are entirely one-way. Both of these tributary lines do not have any direct interaction with each other.

Looking more closely at each of the tributary lines we find:

Brow to Solar Plexus to Root to Heart

The brow places its preconscious intuitive decision-making process into their solar plexus's social identity. They use their intuition to augment their concrete social identity. Their intuition has a practical tenor. Social reality becomes the focus of their intuition. Their solar plexus is then placed into the context of the root. Their personal identity is compelled to deal with the larger matrix of humanity. They are aware of the impact that underlying physical structures have on who we are. The physical form of being human matters to them. Their social identity is concerned with those structures.

Then the root moves to the heart, adding its depth into their emotional awareness at the heart. They connect the root's larger picture to their personal emotional awareness. They are aware of the interaction of the root and their own emotional state. They probably need to emotionally approve of how well they fulfill their sense of personal destiny which they find at the root. This is not necessarily self aggrandizement, but rather a need to feel that they are doing their part in what they see as the larger picture.

Each of these chakric steps happens on the inner, remembering side. This line of chakric integration is rather subjective and largely hidden from outer view. The motion is downward until the last step which rises to the heart. Up until the last step they move from principle to fact. This downward movement carries the risk that they will try to impose their assumptions on the actuality of their experiences.

Their awareness then moves from the heart back to the genital. This moves their emotional awareness into the context of their sensate awareness. Their tangible experiences tend to confirm their emotional premises. They seek to use the actuality of their experiences to help prove what they already emotionally believe.

But because of the genital and heart chakra loop, the genital chakra also feeds actual data to their heart for analysis. This adds a wrinkle to their heart's awareness. It is attempting to symbolically shape the emotional meaning of their experiences while it is simultaneously using their emotional awareness to understand what their actual experiences mean.

Now we are beginning to see how their chakras work. The other line of connection goes:

Crown to Throat to Genital to Heart

The crown moves its abstract sense of order into the context of their intellectual awareness. They seek to express their sense of higher order through ideas, through verbal communication. They probably talk to other people to help them understand their crown chakra's set of assumptions and sense of order. For them the crown's higher pattern is readily seen through intellectual social gatherings, such as classes, seminars and workshops.

Then the throat is placed into the context of their tangible sensate experience. They seek to tangibly feel and touch what their mind believes. They try to place the abstract ideas they believe in into a form that can be concretely experienced. This means that their throat also tries to shape their actual experiential awareness. Their genital chakra is being pressed to conform to both their emotional and intellectual judgments about their sensate reality.

First they talk with other people and give their intuitively perceived situation intellectual form. Then they try to make their ideas actually work. Ultimately, for them (in a two step process) the physical becomes the embodiment of the spiritual. They have a strong sense of an underlying intangible presence within their tangible day to day world. Their physical world isn't seen as being automatic or mundane, it is spirit made flesh.

A possible problem is that they may use the higher chakra's perspectives to project things onto their actual physical awareness that do not conform to the reality of what they may actually experience. Their ideals and emotional symbols may be out of step with their sensate reality. This may create tension. On the plus side, they probably get a great deal out of tangible reality. On the minus side, they are trying to make tangible reality conform to a lot of emotional and intellectual assumptions.

Then they take this second line of awareness and move it up to the heart. As we mentioned earlier, their heart orders and interprets the meaning of their experiences at the genital chakra. They use their heart to understand their sensate reality. By extension, their heart also ends up ordering their intellectual and spiritual perspectives as these are filtered through the genital chakra's experiential awareness.

Once again, their genital chakra is brought back up to the heart for further refinement. Then their heart's awareness returns to the genital chakra to be physically realized once again. Left on its own, this loop could theoretically refine an single experience-emotion indefinitely. In reality, this process continues to refine a particular focus of awareness until a new experience or emotion pushes it out of the loop. Then the new focus of awareness becomes refined until it is displaced by another more recent experience.

Because they're dealing with a simple dichotomy, they have a tendency to flip back and forth from using the heart as the basis of their actions, to using the genital chakra as the basis. Their awareness will jump from the heart to the genital fairly rapidly, as they use one chakra to try to understand the other.

When they are in their heart chakra, they will tend to be a bit idealistic and slightly impractical despite the tangible here and now input of the genital chakra. When they are in their genital chakra, they will be more pragmatic and yet feel restricted by circumstances because of the idealism coming from the heart.

Both the brow and the crown chakras act as underlying starting points in their awareness. They perceive things at these two levels without any other chakras impact directly modifying their awareness. Because they are a few steps back from the focal loop, the brow and the crown chakras operate in the background and provide a backdrop in their overall awareness. They think of themselves as being spiritually grounded because these two chakras are the starting point of each line of their awareness.

Now let's look at the three peer cultural planets. We see they are all evolutionary in motion. Their culture's sense of social identity moves to their brow chakra. (Pluto in Leo.) The culture's impact on their ability to ensoul themselves (Leo and the brow chakra) is intuitively processed. They use the larger culture's sense of collective identity as a context for their own personal possibilities.

When we compare the placement of Mars to Pluto we get a glimpse of how their personal view of the solar plexus differs from their peer culture's. The contrast is between the inner root (Mars in Capricorn) and the brow (Pluto in Leo). Their culture see's the solar plexus through the lens of a will to be, whereas they personally see their solar plexus in an unconscious internal structural context. Their culture envision's possibilities, while they personally see the limitations of the demands of their fate.

Their peer culture's root chakra flows into the crown. (Uranus in Cancer.) Their culture sees the root in terms of the crown's large scale abstract pattern. Their culture's tangible structure is seen in the context of abstract ideals. There's a collective desire to change the way their culture actually is, into what they idealistically feel their culture could be (rather than should be). The crown is the foundation of their peer culture's collective awareness.

Their personal context for the root chakra is the heart. (Saturn in Libra.) They see the root in the context of their own personal emotional pattern which they create and sustain at the heart. For them the heart becomes the bedrock, or foundation, of their personality. They see their feelings and emotions as being the core of who they are.

Perhaps most significant to them is that their collective peer culture's genital chakra moves to the heart. (Neptune in Libra.) Their peer's treatment of physical experience is similar to their own. (Jupiter in Taurus.) Both they and their culture use the heart to explain tangible events. This gives a cultural echo to their own personal process. It also emphasizes the genital-to-heart leg of their own chakric loop. An underlying sense of social affirmation is added to their using the heart chakra to process the sensate awareness of their genital chakra.

This first example introduces us to analyzing a chakric diagram. Hopefully the ideas are clear to you. Basically it is a matter of learning how the awareness of one chakra is seen through of the awareness of another chakra. Let's look at another example.

Second Example Chakric Diagram

Moon in Gemini	Jupiter in Capricorn
Sun in Leo	Saturn in Scorpio
Mercury in Virgo	Uranus in Sagittarius
Venus in Virgo	Neptune in Sagittarius
Mars in Sagittarius	Pluto in Libra

On first glance at this chakric diagram we notice two things: the only empty chakra is the crown and the only chakra that has a planet on the on the left side is the throat. The single planet on the left side implies that their outer environment at the throat is the focal point of their awareness. They experience the world through ideas and they express themselves through ideas. Their throat chakra is their primary way of interacting with the world around them.

By overall balance, The crown also is important in their chakric awareness because it is their only empty chakra. This creates a heightened sense of lacking at the crown. It becomes a kind of psychological hunger. They are a bit haunted by a sense of missing the active presence of the crown chakras's bigger picture . They probably have a nagging feeling that something just beyond their grasp is going on. It is as if they believe that some of the rules behind life are always hidden from their view. Because the crown moves to the throat, they look to their culture's abstract intellectual awareness to help them understand the hidden larger picture.

Next we notice that there are only two chakras that have more than one planet: the throat and the genital chakras. This means that by planetary weight their throat and genital chakras are the most important. They are their busiest chakras. Internally, the genital chakra carries the heaviest load. But more significantly, their throat chakra is the only chakra that has planets on both sides. This means that the throat chakra is their only fully dichotomized chakric perspective. Therefore it is their most fully conscious chakric awareness. They understand their own mind's thinking process and how it works fairly well. They are aware of how various ideas affect how they think. They can also see how their ideas impact their interactions with their outer environment. So, as well as being the focal chakra due to it's having their only outer planet, it is also their only chakra with planets on both sides. This means that their mind matters a lot to them. And they know it.

For SECOND EXAMPLE _____ Born ___ / ___ / ___ At ___
  ___ : ___ Am/pm

Chakra &
Outer Sign - Planet - Inner Sign

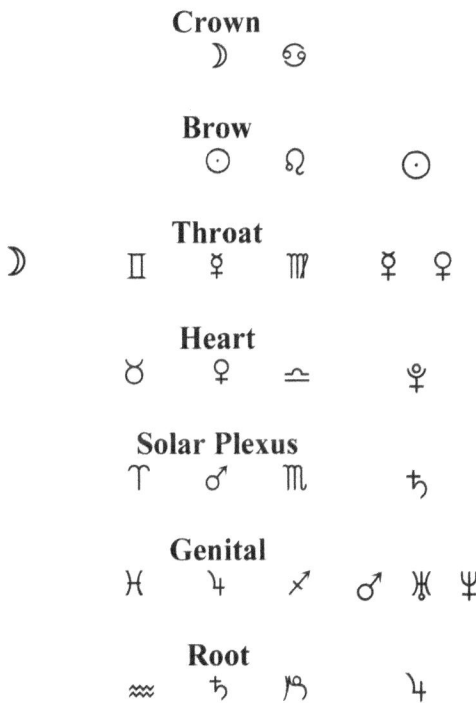

Crown
☽   ♋

Brow
☉   ♌   ☉

Throat
☽   ♊   ☿   ♍   ☿   ♀

Heart
♉   ♀   ♎   ♀

Solar Plexus
♈   ♂   ♏   ♄

Genital
♓   ♃   ♐   ♂   ♅   ♆

Root
♒   ♄   ♑   ♃

Next we look at the motion of the planets. We find that in this diagram two planets move evolutionarily upward. Three planets move involutionarily downward. And two planets act as stopper's, or are on their own level. The motion is fairly balanced. They tend to impose their views on the facts a bit more than they let the facts tell them what is going on. They are not so easily pushed around by circumstances, as would be the case if there was lots of upward motion. Nor are they constantly trying to impose themselves on everything, which would be true with lots of downward motion.

Crown	to	Throat
Brow	to	Brow
Throat	to	Throat
Heart	to	Throat
Solar Plexus	to	Genital
Genital	to	Root
Root	to	Solar Plexus

When we delineate how the chakras interact - draw out the lines of rulership that connect the chakras to each other - we notice that they have three separate subdivisions within their chakric awareness. This implies that their overall chakric awareness is not very integrated. They are apt to have a tendency to compartmentalize their life. Each of these separate parts of their awareness remains distinct from the other parts of their awareness. The first problem is trying to determine which of these components of their awareness is dominant. Then we need to see how the other two parts fit into their awareness. From our quick glance at the overall balance of their chakric diagram we assumed that their throat is most important. So, let's take a deeper look at their chakras.

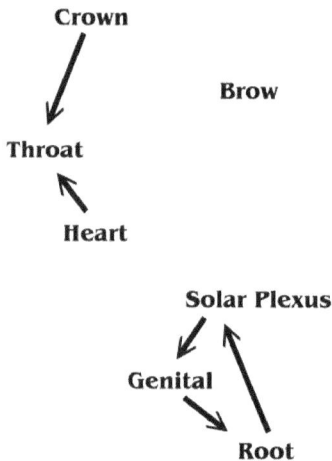

The brow is a "stopper" and stands alone. None of the other chakras feed into the awareness of the brow, nor does the brow connect its awareness to any other chakra. In both of the other components of their awareness three chakras are involved. One component is a three-step loop, where all three chakras create a circular motion. The other component has two chakras feeding into a third chakra, which is a stopper.

When we look at these three components more closely, we see that the brow stands by itself and so their intuitive sense of possibility doesn't directly connect to the rest of their awareness. This gives their intuitions greater freedom but it also makes it harder for them to connect their inner wishes and dreams to what they consider to be the 'real' world.   This means that their abstract sense of personal preference is isolated and alone. They probably have some difficulty taking who they feel they are on an inner spiritual level and connecting it to their daily life. They probably feel that who they really are is somewhat remote from the world around them.

At the same time, in their second component of chakric awareness, their crown and the heart chakras both feed directly into the throat chakra, which then acts as a stopper. This placement gives them the ability to rationally understand their own emotional feelings. They understand the context of their emotions fairly well. They are probably able to place their emotional state into a larger context. They conceptually grasp the abstract patterns that shape their world and investigate them in an analytical way. They use their mind to try to grasp the big picture, stuff such as 'why were we born?' and so on. The lines of connection shows us what their throat is most directly concerned about. This doesn't mean that they don't think about the rest of their chakric awareness, only that concerns of the crown and heart are at the forefront of their thinking. Their throat's being a stopper adds to it's focal position in their awareness.

In their third and final chakric component, the solar plexus flows down into the genital, which then flows down into the root chakra, which then flows back up to the solar plexus, creating a continuous circle. The motion is primarily downward, with the only upward flow being from the root. These chakras are the only ones that are purely concrete and totally time and space oriented. This person seeks to make their concrete world conform to their wishes, even as they are being pressed to fulfill the demands of the root's transpersonal structure which upholds their tangible world. They have definite ideas about the way things should be. At the same time they understand that there are rigid physical structures that make things the way things are.

The root chakra impacts their solar plexus chakra, leading them to believe that their social reality and social identity are ultimately the result of humanity's biological roots.   Physical reality sets the underlying tone for social reality. When the solar plexus moves down into the genital chakra, they interpret their sensate reality through the lens of their culture. They are quite aware of the social rules. They know how they are supposed to feel, act, and look upon the genital level's tangible experiential reality. Then their genital chakra's actual experiences are placed into the context of the human race's physical awareness at the root. Their personal tangible experiences are used to create their own pattern of the root chakra's awareness. They believe that they how they personally feel is simply an aspect of the overall human condition. They experience the same things that everyone else does. They feel the same way that everyone else feels. Then their root chakra's awareness moves back up to the solar plexus where it helps to reshape their social awareness. They see how the demands of physical reality create the structures behind our social systems. How our social culture is the result of geographic and hereditary factors beyond the individual's control. And then they see how these factors shape our experiences at the genital chakra level.

The three lower chakras run round and round, with each successive pass refining their perspective a bit more each time. This nonstop loop enables these three chakras to digest an experience extremely thoroughly. The weakness of a loop is that our awareness can keep reworking the same thing over and over, becoming increasingly concerned with minor details and pointless nuances. A further problem in this particular case is that the loop is isolated from the other chakras.

This person lacks an intrinsic cohesiveness in their chakric awareness. This fragmentation is heightened even further by the complete separation of the higher and lower chakras from each other. Their world is compartmentalized into separate abstract and concrete realms and they feel a greater personal affinity to the abstract realms.

We have seen that on the plus side a loop can help us to rethink and refine our awareness, while on the minus side a loop can lead to an obsessive overworking of detail. Usually, life is busy enough that the focus of the loop, the initial event that entered our awareness in the first place, will be displaced by a new, more recent event that will take over our attention.

It should be obvious how a stopper also serves to focalize our awareness, except that rather than shift an incident continuously through a set of chakras in order to get a different perspective, the stopper holds the event in itself until it has a realization that dissipates the tension. When no such realization is already on hand, the stopper tries to reach a critical point of tension that enables it to have a breakthrough realization. The new interpretation then dissolves the psychic tension. The problem is that there can be a lot of stress involved. Plus the breakthrough may not happen.

Occasionally we may find ourselves stuck on a major event and find it difficult to move on. The problem then becomes getting a fresh perspective. Both the loop's continuous reworking and the stopper's extreme focus seeks to uncover a missing detail that will suddenly make everything clear. The problem is that usually we lack an adequate context and that is why we don't understand something. More details added to an inadequate idea doesn't help. We need to step back and find a fresh idea and this is not part of either the loop's or the stopper's natural process. This means that when we find ourselves in a looping pattern, repeating the same thoughts and feeling again and again, we have to consciously step out of the repetitive loop. And the stopper's style of digging deeper and deeper, using sheer intensity of focus to force a breakthrough can sometimes merely lead to overwhelming tension. Again we have to make the effort to consciously step out of the stopper's awareness to acquire a fresh perspective.

We already saw that this person's upper chakras are separate from the lower three chakras. This implies that this person sees the concrete physical world as very distinct from the upper chakra's abstract world. For them, spirit is very distinct from matter. Like oil and water, the two don't readily mix.

The circular motion of the lower three chakras means that this person continually refines their concrete awareness. The root chakra feeds into the solar plexus and brings its underlying sense of structure to it. This gives their social reality depth and resonance. The solar plexus then moves down into the genital chakra. This implies that they have a tendency to force themselves to physically feel and want things that conform to their sense of cultural reality. They are probably extremely aware of how their culture believes they should feel. They are probably capable of pushing themselves into experiencing what they their culture dictates they should be experiencing. They also probably think that they actually like the things that society has decided that they ought to like.

Then the genital chakra flows down into the root and how they actually feel is unconsciously noted. Their reactions to their genital chakra's experiences is placed into the context of the impersonal root's structures. This can become righteous indignation at the inequities of social structures limitations to their experiences or a feeling of helpless despair in the face of transpersonal structures indifference to how they personally feel. There personal reactions get filtered by the root and then gets fed back up to the solar plexus. And a new cycle in the refinement of their awareness takes place. Because the genital chakra moves through the root it is unlikely that it has much influence on the solar plexus. How they feel personally is obscured by the root's collective awareness. Given their overall separation of abstract and concrete realities, they probably feel that the physical world is a vast structure that is indifferent to their personal wants and needs.

The other three part component of their awareness operates a bit differently. The crown feeds its awareness to the throat. This gives their intellect an intuitive resonance and depth. Their thinking is probably a bit idealistic. Their thinking also probably picks up a bit of a magical quality as well. They probably often feel that things should be a certain way, even though they cannot logically explain why. At the same time, their heart feeds into their throat. This causes them to think about their emotions and think in emotionalized terms. It also causes their heart to focus more on the abstract than the concrete aspect of its awareness. Their thinking acquires a bit of the heart's fancifulness. Because their throat acts as a stopper, their mind provides the point of resolution and is the final context for both their crown and heart chakras. Their thinking is actually probably quite convincing and their mind moves rather fluidly. Their mind has some romanticized and magical aspects, but they should be able to logically think their way through them. Their mind is agile, partially because it is not tied down to a world of solid, intractable facts.

Their least complex awareness is at the brow chakra, which is a stopper and stands alone. Their inner will is unencumbered by any other direct considerations. They probably have a fairly strong intuitive sense of themselves and what they want. They are also probably fairly decisive. The main problem they run into is that who they feel they really are is outside the realm of their tangible circumstances. Their tangible reality isn't seen as reflecting their inner soul. This means their inner sense of who they are and what they want may remain largely unaffected by their outer environment. They may feel somewhat aloof from their outer environment and act a bit opportunistically, due to feeling slightly disconnected from the world around them. They may feel that a pane of glass separates who they really are from the world around them. Or they might feel like a puppeteer, standing above their world, pulling strings and making things happen that aren't quite personally real.

As the final overall detail, when we look at their chart we see that the Moon is the only planet on the left, or outer side. It is in the throat chakra. The Moon is also the ruler of the crown chakra which is the only chakra which is empty on the right side. Both these facts emphasize the importance of the Moon and its placement.

This person seeks to express their ideals through the throat. They are aware of the abstract patterns underlying their ideas and seek to use these idea-patterns to express themselves. They seek to bridge what they see as the gap between themselves and the world around them through the throat. They bring the world into themselves through their throat chakra and they also use the throat chakra to reach out from themselves.

Their throat is active on both sides and so they are fully aware of their own thinking and its expressive impact, both on themselves and on the world around them. They use their throat and the world of communication and ideas to try to see and how the world is 'meant to be'. They also use their throat chakra to know the presence of the divine or the transcendent.

Now we will look at the three trans-saturnian planets which describe their peer culture's awareness. Uranus and Neptune are both found at the genital chakra on the inside. Pluto is found at the inner heart chakra. Uranus places their culture's collective root awareness into the genital chakra's experiential context. Their peer group uses the genital chakra to experience and understand the root chakra. Their peer group probably believes that how we experience reality is mostly due to the physical design of the human body. We feel the things the way that we do, because of the way our body is made. Our sensate experiences are hardwired, making it so that we have to feel the way we feel. Their peer culture believes that the echoing resonance of the root's structures is apparent in our sensate awareness at the genital chakra.

Neptune, which is associated with the collective genital chakra on the outside, is found at the genital chakra on the inside. Their peer culture feels that a deep connection to the outer world is found through physical sensations. Physical experiences are felt to have a lot of depth and reverberation. In their peer culture's view, the outer world is experienced so deeply and richly that it becomes a part of the inner person. (In personal terms, Neptune symbolizes an extreme sensitivity to physical nuance and undercurrent.)

In contrast to their peers, this person takes their own genital chakra's awareness and sees it through their root chakra. (Jupiter in Capricorn.) This is an interesting personal movement in the opposite direction of their peer culture's perspective. For them, the way that they physically experience the world is both shaped and obscured by the unconscious nature of the root. Their genital perspective may even try to dictate the meaning of the root's awareness. This isn't really going to work, for it is kind of like trying to have a drinking glass hold all the water in a lake. Yet they do see how their personal like/dislike responses at the genital chakra are connected to the more instinctual trust/mistrust responses of the root chakra.

The last peer culture planet is Pluto which is found at the inner heart chakra. Their peer culture's social identity impacts their heart. Because Pluto is the only planet they have in the heart chakra, their culture's social identity becomes the most active component of their heart chakra's awareness. They personally emotionally identify with their peer culture's somewhat idealized sense of it's own collective social identity. They use their peer culture's collective sense of identity for emotional reassurance. They empathize with the identity struggles of their peer group. They see these struggles as symbols of their own attempt to create a personally meaningful life.

The overall chakric motion of the three cultural planets is upward. Their peer culture sees the three lower collective chakras awareness as data to be analyzed. Their culture does not seek to impose a set of assumptions on things. It does not seek to shape the meaning of what it experiences. Their peer culture lets their awareness lead them to their conclusions, rather than uses their conclusions to define their awareness.

Importantly, this person uses their culture's collective awareness to connect their lower chakric loop to their higher chakric awareness. They use the collective social awareness symbolized by Pluto to bring a solar plexus awareness up to their heart. Then they personally connect their heart to their throat. Their peer group's solar plexus perspective gives them a means of connecting the concrete and the abstract aspects of their personal awareness. Their peer culture's social perspective enables them to create a connection between the abstract and the concrete aspects of life which if left on their own they would not personally be able to make.

Now that we have a general idea of their internal process, let's try to see how it might work in real life. How would this person go about romantic love? Suppose they meet somebody at a party. They find them attractive (genital chakra). Part of why they find them sensately attractive is because they fit their inner social sense of what is desirable. (Mars in the genital chakra, inner.) But the interaction is about romance and so we look to the heart. There we find that their personal feelings are initially dominated by their culture's social reality. This person uses their culture's concept of romantic desirability (Pluto in the heart chakra, inner) as initial point of selection. Then their heart moves up to the throat, where they rationally analyze their romantic attraction. (Venus in the throat chakra, inner.) Here they take their peer culture's ideas of desirability and make them much more personal. Their heart's feelings, which were initially stirred by their culture's values, are re-examined in more personal terms. They actually use their heart's cultural awareness (solar plexus, Pluto) in a two step process to connect the awareness of their lower chakric loop to their abstract awareness at the throat.

When they look at a potential romantic partner it probably goes something like this: "My, they really look sexy. Plus their style of dress fits a social group that I'm comfortable with. Let me think about this for a moment. Yes, they're really cute and the way they act is charming. Assertive without being arrogant, relaxed and yet self-aware. Judging from the way they talk, they are smart. I am pretty sure that if I play slightly hard to get, aloof, slightly interested and beguiling, I'll have them eating out of my hand by the end of the evening. Is this what I really want?"

What do they do to establish an emotional connection? How do they feel romantically connected to someone else? With Venus in the throat on the inside and the Moon as the only outer planet, they would probably talk. In order to feel connected they would need to be able to share ideas. They would need to communicate who they are and how they feel in words to a romantic partner. If they can't establish an intellectual rapport they will disengage from the potential partner no matter how socially perfect they are. For them the social context merely allows the door to open. It is at the throat that their heart becomes fully engaged. For this person, the physical experience of romantic love is almost totally defined by their culture. They accept their culture's preferences and manners fairly comfortably. Meanwhile, they are actually personally more romantically engaged through their mind then they are through their body. When it comes to physical attraction they are willing to accept their peer culture's values. They know their culture's values and are willing to play by it's rules to get what they want. At the same time, their own sense of attraction, what really matters to them personally, is found at their throat.

Now let's look at how this person deals with their solar plexus. How do they establish their social identity? How do they deal with their culture?

When we look at their solar plexus, there is only planet, Saturn in Scorpio on the inner side. In a sense, their solar plexus carries the weight of their root chakra's awareness. They probably feel a fairly strong sense of obligation to their family and their cultural heritage. At the same time, Mars is found in the genital chakra in Sagittarius on the inner side. This implies that who they feel they are at the solar plexus impacts what and how they sensately feel. Their sense of social identity determines the kind of sensate experiences that they will choose to have. It also helps shape how they feel about those experiences. They will also strive to connect themselves to other people through their sensate experiences and their personal reactions. They will use their genital chakra's experiences to share social reality.

Pluto, the cultural planet ruling the outer solar plexus, is found in the heart chakra on the inside. Their prevailing peer culture emotionally internalizes their cultural beliefs. Collective cultural perspectives becomes translated into personal symbols. For example, a diamond is seen as a social sign of a special romantic bond. The social reality of romantic love becomes idealized by their peer culture in the transition to the heart.

This person desires to believe in their peer culture's perspective. They understand their peer culture's symbolic emotional style of creating a social identity and they also personally use their culture's emotional symbols. Yet, how they personally establish their own sense of social identity is much more physically experiential then it is abstractly symbolic. They need to experience something which their solar plexus makes happen in order to make their social identity real to themselves.

Again, we must remember that the chakric diagram is only a mirror which merely reflects someone's life, it doesn't make anything happen. Until the facts of a person's life are added to the diagram, everything we see in the chakric diagram remains mere theory.

Third Example Chakric Diagram

Moon in Sagittarius	Jupiter in Leo
Sun in Libra	Saturn in Virgo
Mercury in Libra	Uranus in Scorpio
Venus in Scorpio	Neptune in Sagittarius
Mars in Scorpio	Pluto in Libra

At first glance, we notice that all the planets are on the right, inner side. This person probably feels things deeply and at the same feels disconnected from the outer world. Most of their planets are also found at the solar plexus and heart. These two levels are where our personal awareness is naturally centered. Taken together, all this implies that this person lives in a very personal, intimate world. Their extreme inner focus overshadows their direct experience of the outer world. They are busy dealing with their own inner reactions and psychological process. This person lives entirely within themselves. Because they have no planets at the root or the crown chakras, they also have no direct focus of attention on either transpersonal level.

They are only indirectly aware of the transpersonal levels. This extreme inward focus is unusual.

They have five involutionary and two evolutionary placements. Their overall inclination is to impose a set of assumptions on things. They feel things 'should' be a certain way. This generates tension as they try to impose their internal 'shoulds' on the actualities of their life. The only two chakras that respond to a lower chakra's awareness are the throat and brow. These two chakras are the only places where they let the facts speak for themselves.

When we follow their lines of chakric connection, we find all their chakras join together into a single unit. There are two distinct chakric lines that the feed into the heart. Then the heart feeds directly into their solar plexus. Their solar plexus acts as a stopper, making all of this person's awareness ultimately focus on their solar plexus chakra. As everything is on the inner remembering side, one would guess that they are extremely self-conscious, as well as very self aware. They probably feel inundated by various chakric awarenesses that their solar plexus notices but doesn't really understand.

One chakric line contains four steps. These are: the crown flows into the genital, which then flows into the brow, which then flows into the heart, which then flows into the solar plexus. The second line contains three steps: the root chakra flows into the throat, which then flows into the heart, which then flows into the solar plexus. The heart chakra places all of their chakric awareness into the solar plexus.

Despite their solar plexus being the final reaction point, first they have to understand what everything means to them emotionally and symbolically at the heart. Then they take their emotional reality and place it into their solar plexus. The lack of outer activity in the chakric diagram doesn't mean that they have no external experiences. What it means is that they view their objective experiences in a highly subjective way. They internalize their outer awareness, move it through their chakras in a kind of inner psychological digestive process, and then eventually they move it through their inner heart down to their inner solar plexus thereby completing their chakric process.

Their heart chakra is the key filter of their awareness. Before anything gets to the solar plexus it must first go through the heart. Although the solar plexus is where their awareness ultimately stops, the importance of the heart is magnified by both chakric lines meeting at the heart.

For __THIRD EXAMPLE_____ Born____/__/____ At ___:_____Am/pm

Chakra &
Outer Sign - Planet - Inner Sign

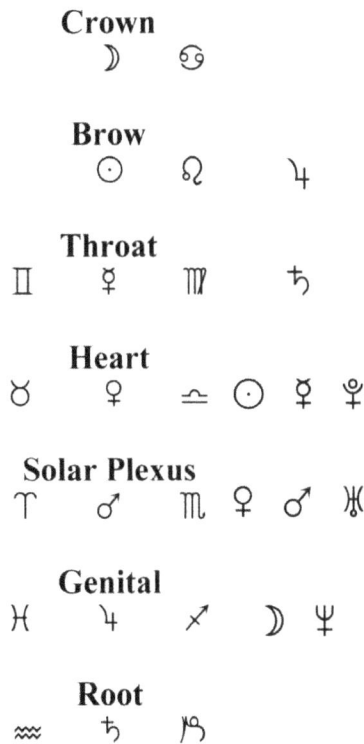

Crown
☽   ♋

Brow
☉   ♌   ♃

Throat
♊   ☿   ♍   ♄

Heart
♉   ♀   ♎   ☉   ☿   ♀

Solar Plexus
♈   ♂   ♏   ♀   ♂   ♅

Genital
♓   ♃   ♐   ☽   ♆

Root
♒   ♄   ♑

They live in their heart and express their heart's awareness through their solar plexus. They live in a world that is full of private, personally meaningful symbolic details. We would expect that they would have minor physical problems that symbolically express how they feel psychologically.

This inner focus on the heart implies that they have a strong sense of emotional connection to the world around them. They probably romanticize the world around them. Most likely they are a bit harsh with themselves due to their idealized sense of their own social identity (heart moving down into the solar plexus). Yet, it is at the solar plexus that everything must ultimately prove itself to them.

Along with demanding a strong pragmatism, this adds pressure for their own emotional attitudes and symbols to be socially viable. On one level everything must fit within their social reality. On another level their social reality must be able to express their inner emotional state. This puts them in a sort of internal social limbo. They probably argue with the inadequacy of prevailing social opinion even as they try to satisfy it. Yet, due to everything being on the inner side they have an inner reserve, where they feel who they truly are is protected from the immediate impact of external reality. Hopefully, they do not feel boxed in by a sense of inner isolation. But most of the boxed in feeling would be due to how they internally process how they feel, more than due to their outer circumstances.

Now let's look at their cultural backdrop. Uranus places their peer culture's root perspective into the inner solar plexus. With Neptune in Sagittarius we find their peer culture's genital perspective moves inward within its own chakric level and acts as a stopper. Pluto places their peer culture's solar plexus awareness into their inner heart.

Their peer culture's perspective toward experiential reality, symbolized by Neptune, takes an actual objective experience, feels it deeply, and internally tries to "know" what it means, what it really implies about the world. This gives physical sensations considerable resonance and leads to a somewhat mystical attitude toward the physical world.

This person takes their peer culture's genital perspective and uses it to add depth to their own genital chakra's awareness. Then they carry both genital chakra perspectives to their own brow chakra, which adds a personal intuitive dimension to their genital chakra's sensate awareness. The implications of their physical experience are carried into the realm of potential events. Their brow chakra's awareness is then brought down to the heart. The possibilities perceived at the brow simultaneously evoke and shape their emotional response. Their heart experiences what they intuitively perceive, adding its own emotional symbolism along the way.

At the same time, their peer culture's solar plexus perspective, symbolized by Pluto, is placed into their heart's awareness. Their peer culture adds a romanticized sense of self to their collective social identity. This can help give them social ideals to strive for, or it may assist them in glossing over the self serving reasons behind their social actions. In any case, their peer culture uses the heart as the context of their collective social identity while they personally use the heart as the pivotal filter of their awareness.

Meanwhile, their culture's root chakra is seen in the context of the solar plexus (Uranus in Scorpio). As a group, this person's peers feel they have a collective destiny that will impact and reshape their collective social structure and thereby shape their group cultural identity.

Simultaneously this individual feels affected by the larger cultural climate. Their sense of personal identity perceives shifts in their collective culture's social structures. Because this person's identity is the final focal point of their personal awareness, they easily notice the cultural tensions surrounding such changes swirling about them. They are aware of the changing cultural moods and climate on a fairly deep level.

Two things are striking about this person's chakric diagram. One, is that all of their chakric activity is on the inner remembering side. The other is that it is extremely integrated and focused. There are no diffusing chakric loops and there are no isolated chakras. Everything feeds through the heart chakra to a single focal point at the solar plexus chakra. This places a great deal of psychic energy in the last chakra in their flow of awareness. Their personal identity at the solar plexus becomes the point at which they must resolve all their psychic tension. This is similar to having water flow through a series of pipes until it all concentrates at one single narrow point. The water pressure is the highest at this final point.

The release of this psychic tension is a major issue for them. Because their awareness flows through their heart on its way to the solar plexus, they are probably inclined to deal with this pressure by having some physical ailments. (Remember the heart sees the physical body as a purely expressive symbol. This symbolic perspective enables the heart to use our body to manifest how it feels, whatever that may be.) Their body probably has lots of minor aches and pains, symbolic expressions that help them discharge some of their psychological tension.

How do they personally see their destiny, in contrast to their peer culture's perspective? Their root chakra goes to the throat, which implies that they think about their place in the flow of human progress. Then they move to the heart and see how they emotionally feel about their ideas about humanity's collective destiny and their own personal place in it. Lastly they move from the heart to the solar plexus and see, through the filters of the throat and the heart, how the root chakra affects their personal sense of social identity. This is where the collective and personal root chakras meet. They probably personally feel some of their peer culture's shared sense of destiny. Yet for them personally, this destiny probably feels like something that is fated to happen to them. Fate is a large, slow moving train that is running unstoppably down the tracks to a destination that they feel they cannot avoid. They need to realize that their fate is something that they can help to create, not just be stuck suffering.

Now let's take a look at their chakric flow and what is immediate and remote in their awareness. We can take each of the chakras and see how many steps it makes before it reaches the solar plexus. The farther away it is from the solar plexus, the less immediate it's awareness becomes to them. The more steps involved, the more a chakra's awareness becomes filtered by the awareness of the chakras that it moves through.

The crown chakra takes four steps to reach the solar plexus. This is the most steps that any of their chakras makes in their awareness. The awareness of the crown chakra is filtered through their genital, brow, heart, and solar plexus chakras. This multitude of steps weakens the immediate impact of the crown chakra. Other concerns overlay and obscure the crown. The crown becomes a background awareness that sets an underlying tone for the two primary players, the heart and solar plexus. It helps set the stage, but the drama centers on other chakras as the main players.

Their crown chakra flows down to their genital chakra. This takes the crown's preconscious awareness and uses it to shape their senate experiences. They probably have a mystical aura added to their sensate reality. They probably have the notion that through the physical world they see and touch the presence of the divine. Their genital chakra feeds into their brow. As we already know, the brow chakra is the abstract parallel of the genital chakra's physical sensate awareness. This means that they take their physical experiences and place them into the brow's intuitive perspective. This adds a much larger context to their genital chakra's reaction. Their sensate experiences acquire a spiritual overlay. The brow then moves down into the heart where the heart absorbs some of the brow's extremely fluid sense of possibility. The brow's perceptions mingles with the heart's imagination. Reality becomes very fluid in it's possibilities. The heart adds it symbolisms to the perceptions of the brow's possibilities as the brow imagines what it would like to have happen. So we can see why when their awareness does finally reach the solar plexus, their crown chakra's initial awareness has been obscured.

At this point in our analysis we would look at the section in the back on the planets in each of the chakras and see if the ideas presented in the final section of this text help us to more fully grasp who the person is. The section on Venus (the heart) in the solar plexus would be the first brief study we would look at. Then we would move on to the Venus in Scorpio description to make it specific to a side of our chakric awareness.

Tracing our way back up the chakra's flow chart we might also want to look at the throat's impact on the heart (Mercury in the heart chakra) and see if any of the ideas presented there help us. Because the brow chakra also flows into the heart so we might also look at the section on the Sun in the heart chakra. We look up each planetary section only as we feel a need to. Hopefully at some point we will acquire an intuitive 'Ah ha!' moment where we suddenly understand the person far beyond the ideas we found in planetary section.

Or we may continue to look up the sections on the planets in the chakras until we have looked at all of the seven chakric planets and still have only a swirl of disconnected ideas dancing in our mind. The problem with the planets in the chakras section is that the ideas presented in it are somewhat static and limited. A person's awareness is not just an accumulation of static parts, it is an active dynamic organic whole whose parts mutually interact and define each other. The purpose of the ideas presented in the planets in chakras section is to give us a starting point for our understanding, not to limit us to a few concepts that may not sufficiently fit the person in front of us.

These three examples offer a few ways of making a person's chakric diagram come alive. We can recognize what makes one chakra more important than another chakra within a person's awareness. Now we can tell if a person lives mostly within themselves or out in the world of outer experience. We went over most of the chakric diagram patterns that we'll see and learned what to look for in interpreting a diagram. We've plotted out the lines that reveal a person's chakric integration. We now have the tools to answer such questions as: Do they make their circumstances fit their assumptions, or do they gather information and then analyze it? How integrated is their awareness? What chakra is the focal point of the their awareness? How connected or fragmented is their overall chakric awareness?

How someone integrates their chakric awareness is always present within the diagram. But keep in mind that the interpretation of a chakric diagram is more art than science. Hopefully everything we've just seen will help us grasp someone's personality and so when we analyze a person's chakric diagram we will understand what it is telling us. This doesn't mean that we will understand the person perfectly. But we hopefully we'll have a good idea of the underlying mechanisms of their chakric awareness, of how they internally process their awareness. We will have a sense of which aspects of their awareness they are most involved in and most concerned with.

Connecting the Chakras to the House Wheel

Lets's look at one last chakric diagram in which we will investigate a specific problem that a young woman has come to us with: she is concerned about her current romantic partnership, which has always been rocky. She is asking us why.

We are going to use both a chakric diagram and a house wheel chart to together in order to get more information about her situation. First we will look at her chakric diagram and analyze it just as we have been doing. Then we will connect her external circumstances as these are seen through the astrological wheel of houses to her internal awareness as it is seen through the chakras.

For those of you that are already familiar with the classic meanings of the astrological houses the following interpretation of a classic astrological chart should be easy to follow. The most important thing is to try to keep the lines of relationship clear and simple. We are using the astrological wheel of houses to fill in the blanks about what kind of things their chakras are focusing on. As we already know, the perspective of chakric astrology is extremely subjective. By connecting the chakric diagram to the astrological house wheel chart we should be able to see some of the objective factors being dealt with by their chakra's internal process. In this way we hope to understand what it is that their chakras are actually dealing with.

But first we need to understand how her chakras interact. We look at the overall pattern of how her planets are distributed in the chakric diagram. There are five planets on the left and five planets on the right. Now, three of the planets on the right are cultural planets. Also, none of the planets on the right hand side is above the solar plexus. This means that her inner awareness is rather concrete and probably rather pragmatic. Overall, her inner awareness emphasizes her experience of the external world. It is important to her to interact with the world around her. It helps her connect the abstract and concrete levels of her chakric awareness.

By planetary distribution both the solar plexus and the genital chakras are the most important to her. Both of these chakras have three planets. The solar plexus has two on the outside and one on the inside, whereas the genital chakra has one on the outside and two on the inside. So far, neither chakra is decidedly more important than the other.

Knowing how the chakras work, we assume there is probably an emphasis on the solar plexus when she is actually interacting with the external world. When she's feeling more self expressive, she looks to the genital chakra and seeks either a situation or an experience that embodies her mood. We see from her lines of chakric integration that all of her higher chakras are ultimately focused on her solar plexus. She is probably always looking for the larger reason behind her social interactions and she feels all of her ideas and ideals should come alive through her solar plexus's social interactions.

Returning our attention to her chakric flow and how they integrate, we notice all of her chakras act together as a single unit and that they all ultimately focus on the genital chakra. Considering that she is asking about her love life we look at her heart chakra and notice that it is somewhat remote in the overall flow of her awareness. The heart moves to the throat and then to the solar plexus. And it's awareness then eventually moves, along with the rest of her chakras, to the genital chakra. It is at the genital chakra that all of her internal psychic tension seeks resolution. Ultimately she uses direct outer sensate experiences to relieve all of her pent up psychic energy. She tries to sensately experience the whole of her internal awareness at the genital chakra. This probably leads to situations that are a bit intense. Relieving her pent up psychic energy probably requires an occasional big intense experience, or a bunch of little, moderately intense experiences. Her problem is the release of her internal tension. Further complicating things is the fact that the whole of her awareness is filtered by the root chakra on its way to her sensate awareness at the genital chakra.

Looking more closely at her internal process as revealed by how her chakras interact, we see that on first meeting a potential romantic partner she uses her intuition to size him up. Then she uses her heart to see how he fits into her romantic ideals. Next, she thinks through how she feels and tries to intellectually grasp what is behind her emotional state. She is not a person that initially allows herself to get carried away by her emotions. She moves to the solar plexus and her romantic ideals and concepts about love are then attired in purely social terms. She judges her potential romantic partner by his social position and cultural attitude. Where he fits into the larger social matrix matters a great deal to her. It is her most consciously chosen basis of relationship.

During this process she probably doesn't make any movement towards actually entering into a relationship with her potential romantic partner. She is busy processing the situation. Then, without realizing it, she probably finds that her internal psychic tension reaches a tipping point and she spontaneously does something, probably of a sexual nature, which quickly precipitates a romantic relationship.

Once she is actually involved in a secure romantic relationship, their partnership probably acquires a competitive

Chakric Astrology Worksheet For_____

Born _May_ / _5_ / _1986_ Time_____ Am Time Zone _____ Location_____

Outer Sign	Chakra & Planet	Inner Sign
	Crown	
	☽	♋
	Brow	
	☉	♌
♀	**Throat**	
	♊ ☿ ♍	
☉	**Heart**	
	♉ ♀ ♎	
☽ ☿	**Solar Plexus**	
	♈ ♂ ♏	
♃	**Genital**	
	♓ ♃ ♐	
	Root	
	♒ ♄ ♑	

Inner symbols (right side): ♇ (Solar Plexus), ♄ ♅ (Genital), ♂ ♆ (Root)

Chakric Motion
Up 2   Down 4   None 1

Cultural Motion
♀ (Solar Plexus) to Itself
♅ (Genital) to Root
♇ (Root) to Genital

Chakric Integration

Crown → Solar Plexus
Throat → Solar Plexus
Brow → Heart → Throat
Solar Plexus → Root → Genital

quality, both between each other and with the world around them. She continually presses for an improved social position, both in her partnership and in the world around her. She feels that a successful partnership creates a place in society that fulfills her crown chakra's ideals, as well as satisfies her intellectual and emotional needs. For her the relationship is seen and judged through a social lens.

Then her social reality sort of tumbles down out of her conscious understanding into her root chakra and she finds herself having a nagging feeling that her partnership should matter in some basic fundamental way. This could be a need to have children, or for their partnership to have an impact on their social surroundings.

But she probably wont quite be able to articulate this need. Indeed, she'll probably notice it as a nagging sense that she and her partner have to fit into a meaningful structure. She will want something more than having a causal romantic affair from a partner. She is looking for someone to help her build a social springboard through which she can enact her ideals.

Then, moving to her genital chakra, she'll feel that she should be able sensately experience the impact that they have as a couple. She will want to see it, touch it and feel it in order to know that it is real. This could be going to social events such as seminars, honorary banquets, parties and the like. It could be working in an orphanage or something that fulfills her ideals. It could be having physical objects, such as a house, that display wealth and social prestige. Ultimately she is looking to use her romantic partnership to enable her to enter situations through which she can experience her social worth.

From all this we infer that for her romantic love isn't about poetry and swooning from overwhelming emotions. It's about the partnership's helping her to fulfill her need to be somebody socially. A romantic involvement has to help her tangibly experience a larger context. She looks at a romantic partnership as being as much a business enterprise as it is an emotional event. She probably is a bit unknowingly manipulative as she weaves her spiritual and social ideals into the fabric of her personal romantic relationship.

Well, this gives us a pretty good place to start. We ask her what she thinks the problem is. She tells us that he can't hold his own socially. He doesn't make enough money - which wouldn't be so bad except he doesn't seem to have any ambition to make something of himself. He has a low level job in an advertising firm. He is really very funny but he doesn't realize he should be out there performing stand up comedy - which he doesn't have the nerve to try - so that's a big disappointment. Plus he doesn't seem to understand her ambitions. He smiles, nods and looks at her like she's so cute when she talks about going overseas and doing some kind of social service with a non-governmental organization. She wistfully tells us he's really cute, but he no longer satisfies her in the bedroom either.

She asks us point blank what should she do.

We ask her what first attracted her to him. She replies that they meet at a party and his dimples were so cute when he laughed. And that he had a clever sarcastic wit that had an edgy bite. He had an assertive quality about him. He mentioned how it'd be fun to be a comedian. He looked like he'd be good in bed, which he was, at least at first, but now it's getting more and more routine. She's finding herself growing increasingly distant.

We tell her that it sounds like she isn't getting what she needs out of this relationship. We tell her that she is an intense woman who needs to be with someone who is as strong and passionate as she is. She laughs and tells us that she is way too intense for him. That she thought he was a tiger, but actually he's a kitten.

Because the chakras are purely subjective and make no direct reference to any actual external event, we now turn to the astrological wheel of houses which places a person into a neat framework of tangible circumstances. Since chakric astrology only gives us a picture of her inner being, when we combine her natal chakric diagram with her natal astrological house chart we should get a better idea how her inner being connects to her outer circumstances.

The wheel of houses breaks down our outer world into twelve basic interconnected external circumstances. (See the Brief House Rulerships in the Appendix for what each house is concerned with.)

The idea is simple, we use the astrological signs to find the relationship between a chakra and a house. In other words, we will connect a chakra's internal perspective with a house's external area of concern.

But first let's get a basic understanding of the houses.

In classic house based astrology the first house reveals a person's outer personality and their physical being as the means by which they enter into their world of tangible experience. Any of the twelve signs may be found at the ascendent. Which sign is at the first house cusp is very flexible and depends on what time of day a person is born at. This contrasts sharply with chakric astrology's more inflexible connection of the signs of Pisces and Sagittarius with the genital chakra and it's sensate awareness as our primary means of connecting to our world of tangible experience.

In the wheel of houses what a particular houses rules, or is concerned with, is inflexible. The first house is always the place of the self. The seventh house is always the place of partnership. The second house always rules the resources which a person possesses. How the planets and signs are spread out through the houses describes an individual's reaction to their circumstances in much the same way that how the planets are distributed through a chakric diagram describes an individual's chakric integration.

As we have seen, our chakric awareness uses dichotomies to create our consciousness. The same is true for the wheel of houses.

We use the contrast of inner and outer, along with the contrast of concrete and abstract as the basis of our conscious awareness in the chakras. Similarly, the wheel of houses uses two basic dichotomies to define our outer circumstances: self and not self as the foundation of our experience; and personal and collective perspectives as the foundation of our understanding. The ascendant and descendent axis (the horizontal line at the beginning edge of the first and seventh houses) is the focal point of our awareness of our own existence through our direct experiences. At the first house we find our physical body which is the experiential focal point of our conscious awareness. The first house is pure self. At the seventh house we find the not self with which we are in direct partnership. At the first house we find our self as the experiencer, which is then in direct polar contrast (and relationship) to the not self as what is being experienced. The second dichotomy is between the awareness of our personal subjective perspective and a collective transpersonal objective perspective. This axis of perspective contrasts our purely personal, inner spiritual perspective, or the privacy of our inner self which is found at the line at the beginning edge of the fourth house, with our purely objective social perspective, or our place in society, which is found at the midheaven, or the line at the beginning edge of the tenth house.

These two axial lines, one running from dawn to dusk and the other running from midnight to high noon, are the two foundational divisions from which the rest of the houses ultimately derive their meaning.

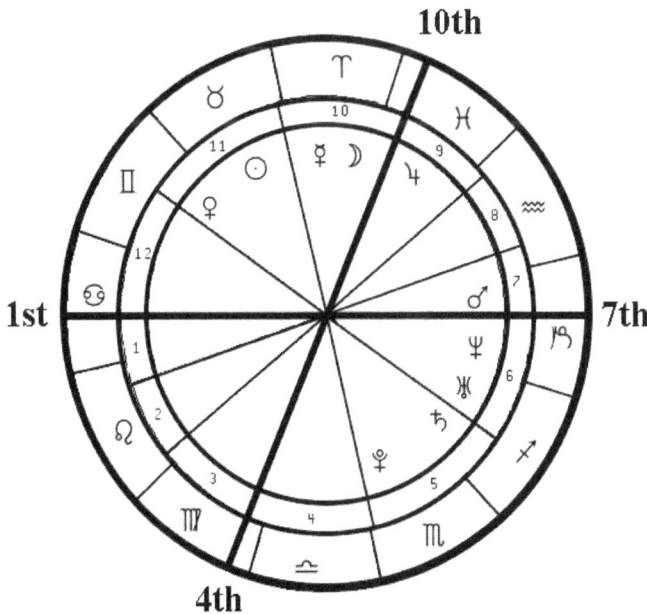

Our goal with chakric astrology is use the houses to see how a person's chakras connect to their outer circumstances. What we are seeking is which aspect of outer reality a particular chakra's awareness most naturally deals with.

In this example, in her house wheel the astrological sign Cancer is found at the starting edge of the first house. This means that she has a Cancer Ascendant. We would expect that her crown chakra's abstract ideals play a role in how she physically presents herself and the type of character that her personality tries to project. As the crown chakra is a pre-conscious awareness, she is probably normally unaware of the ideals that she uses to shape her personality.

Then she has Capricorn at the descendent (or the seventh house cusp) and so we infer that she uses her partnerships, particularly marriage, as an inner foundation in her world of day to day experience. As the root chakra is largely unconscious, she is probably hazy on exactly what kind of support she actually expects from a relationship. But she knows that her partnership has to provide a strong foundation.

When we look at her astrological house wheel we see that Pisces is at the midheaven, or the beginning edge of the tenth house. The midheaven, or tenth house, is the place of our sense of social position and honor. It is how others see us in terms of our place in society. Pisces rules the genital chakra on the outer experiential side. This means that her social position is based on her outer sensate experiences. Collectively, people see her as a person who experiences and reacts to things and they judge her according to sensate awareness. What she seeks to experience and her reactions to those experiences, forms the basis of her social position and prestige.

Interestingly, the sign of Aries is wholly contained within the tenth house and doesn't touch any house cusp. This implies that her outer solar plexus chakra acts in a hidden, indirect manner in terms of her outer social position and honor. How she feels at the genital chakric level is what most people see about her. Meanwhile, this has an impact on her outer sense of social identity which in turn affects how she presents herself at the tenth house.

The two systems, the chakric diagram and the house wheel so far seem to be mutually reenforcing each other.

When we looked at her chakric diagram we saw that the genital chakra is the ultimate focal point of her chakric awareness. Because Jupiter and the genital chakra it rules are so important in her chakric diagram we shall cut straight to the house position of Jupiter. It is in the ninth house. This means that circumstantially her internal chakric process leads her to the ninth house. The ninth house is associated with the higher mind, thinking and our philosophical foundations. This gives us further information on how she reacts to her sensate awareness. She thinks about her sensate experiences. She uses an intellectual framework to understand and interpret the circumstances behind her sensate experiences. In the outer world she is probably most comfortable in the observer role. Circumstantially she analyzes and philosophizes as she tries to use the genital chakra's sensate experiences to resolve her inner psychic tensions.

This brief study explains the basics of how she connects herself to her world. But because the question is about a romantic partnership we will now look at the house wheel's descendent and the seventh house, because the seventh house rules partnerships.

Earlier we noticed that Capricorn and root chakra are at the seventh house cusp. Now we also see that the planet Mars, the ruler of the solar plexus, is in Capricorn on the seventh house cusp. From her house wheel we see that circumstantially her solar plexus uses her partnerships, especially romantic relationships, as a personal foundation. She believes that her romantic partner provides, or should provide anyway, a foundation from which she can experience her social identity. So who she is with will greatly impact her sense of self. This added stress is largely unconscious (Capricorn and the root chakra) and she probably is unable to see why she is so distressed with her present relationship.

All she really seems to need from us is permission to exit the relationship. Which, from all indications, is what she wanted to do anyway. We tell her that unfortunately he doesn't seem to be quite right for her. Perhaps it is time to move on. We tell her that she seems to need a man as driven and passionate as she is. We say that she should probably look for a partner who already exhibits the kind of drive she requires. That, unfortunately, only a few men will fulfill her deeper needs. We suggest that she should pay more attention to how the gentleman fits into the bigger picture before she impulsively plunges into a relationship. While it seems doubtful that she'll change her initially deliberate and then suddenly impetuous romantic process very much, we are trying to get her to think in terms of a larger root chakra type context (Capricorn rules the seventh house).

Relieved to hear what see wanted to hear, she quickly agrees. She thanks us and then she leaves. As she leaves we imagine that the breakup itself will be fairly dramatic. She'll orchestrate the event and enact her feelings with great intensity. And then she'll suffer a mildly broken heart. But hopefully she'll refine her standards and her brow chakra's intuition may be more exacting as she selects her next partner.

Still, since her partnership needs are indirect and rather demanding, it may be difficult for her to get the kind of experiences she seems to need to reassure herself socially. Her need to sensately experience her reality will always be with her, no matter if she is single or involved in a romantic relationship, yet with Mars on the descendent we think that she will feel a strong need to be in a partnership. We hope that all of the various demands that she places on her romantic relationships will not make her unable to sustain a long term relationship as she would probably find such a stable foundation satisfying.

Now, if money had been her main concern (when most people consult an astrologer it usually concerns either romance or money) we would have looked to the second house cusp, which is concerned with money and possessions, to see which sign rules it. In her chart it is the sign of Leo, which is connected to the brow chakra. This implies that, for her, money is something that she doesn't really think about in an analytically pragmatic way, but rather she intuitively chooses her economic way. She probably expects money to just somehow appear if she really needs it. But for her money is most consciously connected to her heart chakra's outer perspective. She probably spends far more time envisioning the things that her money could do for her, rather than how much money she has. (The Sun is in the eleventh house which rules wishes, hopes and dreams, so she could also be spending her money on some lofty goal. The eleventh house also rules friendships, so it wouldn't be a surprise if she spends a good bit of her money on some sort of social activity with her friends.)

This only gives a brief glimpse of how we can combine the house wheel chart and the chakric diagram. But hopefully the potential of the method is apparent. The goal is to take the purely internal awareness of the chakras and use the departments of life assigned to the astrological houses see how a person connects their chakras to their tangible circumstances.

The Seven Chakric Planets
An overview with each chakric placement briefly examined

In this next section we will look at the seven planets that rule the chakras. We will look at their classic astrological symbolism first. Then we'll run through a brief interpretation of the planet in each chakra, including both sides of the lower five chakras. Keep in mind that these interpretations are designed to aid your understanding, not to provide a set of definitive meanings.

The classic astrological symbolism of the planets reveals a core affinity between a planet and the chakra that it rules. This means that we can use the classic astrological meanings of the planets to help us understand the chakras. This will help those who are already familiar with the astrological meaning of the planets to understand chakras. At the same time, understanding the chakras will also help us to grasp the astrological meaning of the planets.

We will start at the bottom with the root chakra and its ruling planet Saturn. Then we will move up through the rest of the chakras and their planetary rulers. The planet's are arranged by speed of motion, with the slowest planet at the bottom chakra and the fastest planet at the top chakra, which fits the character of chakras quite well. The lowest chakra is the most concrete and inflexible of them all, while the chakras become increasingly abstract and flexible as we move upward.

As you already know, in chakric astrology the planets merely show the flow of one chakra's awareness to another chakra. When a ruling planet moves one chakra into another chakra, the first chakra is seen up through the lens of the awareness of the second chakra. Each chakra has its own distinct color, and when it moves its awareness to another chakra, the two colors blend. The green of the heart blends with the yellow of the solar plexus. In the resulting blended color the green of the heart remains strongly green but it does acquire a yellowish tint. (The seven chakra's colors are arranged in the same way that light is refracted through a prism, going from red at the bottom up through orange, yellow, green, blue, indigo and finally violet at the top.)

Saturn: Root, point of self foundation; glyph - ♄

In classic astrology Saturn is the ruler of time. This fits the root chakra quite well. The root contains the underlying patterns, or cycles, on which our lives are built. Saturn is also the ruling planet of physical structure and tangible patterns of relationship. Saturn deals with the underlying biochemical processes that sustain our existence. Saturn is the basis of our physical existence. It is the underlying reality that sustains us and makes us who we are both personally and as examples of the human race.

Saturn provides all the tangible relationships that enable us to physically exist. It contains no intrinsic contradictions, because if it did, it's reality couldn't exist. This makes Saturn and the root chakra a good core reality check point. Although it is possible to hold two completely contradictory things in the heart or mind, the root chakra cannot indulge such a thing. If the reality of one of the higher personal chakras contradicts the root chakra, we know that it is the personal chakra that's doing something wrong. Whatever it is doing, it is something that reality ultimately will not sustain. In a conflict between our personal levels of awareness and the transpersonal concrete foundation of our reality, the transpersonal will win every time. This means that despite our fervent wishes (barring divine intervention) tangible reality will always win out. In classic astrological symbolism this is seen as making the planet Saturn seem mean and oppressive .

Because of its depth, Saturn makes the chakric level it is found on more serious. Saturn is not superficial and it is not charmingly witty. It is not lightly entertaining at cocktail parties. It is sensitive, realistic, and has a deep understanding of structure. This can make it feel heavy and ponderous. But it is totally reliable. Saturn's presence deepens the awareness of the chakric level it is on. The weight of the root chakra's foundations, which Saturn carries with it, initially slows down the receiving chakra's awareness. Before Saturn is willing to move, many things have to be taken care of first. But Saturn (the root) has a very strong momentum once it gets moving. Even if that momentum does start out at a snail's pace.

This isn't to say that the structures of the root chakra do not evolve. The root does change, only slowly. The reality represented by Saturn actually is fluid, but only as permutations that grow out of a pre-existing structure.

The chakra where Saturn is found becomes stronger and more foundational. The placement of Saturn lets us know which chakra serves as the bedrock of a person's awareness. It reveals the core perspective on which they build their awareness.

Saturn in the Root Chakra

Here the underlying presence of the human race as a part of our personal awareness is assumed. We have no personal disagreement with the basic structures that underlie our existence. We accept who we are and understand how it results from what we are physically. Because we accept the structures we inherit, we feel no pressure to consciously understand the underlying momentums of humanity that we are personally riding.

By placing the root into its own context of awareness, the root essentially stays unconscious. This means that when Saturn is at the root chakra level, the root operates automatically, without our realizing it. The root is emphasized, but our awareness of it's activity is also obscured.

With this Saturn placement, any chakra that goes down into the root also becomes obscured. The unconscious nature of the root clouds our awareness of the incoming chakra. Both the large-scale perspective of the root and its mechanical qualities tend to overwhelm any incoming chakra's awareness and it's attempts to guide the root.

The depth of the root makes it move slowly as it has a strong sense of how many interconnections underlie it's structure. There is a strong awareness of physical limitations. Attention is paid to the ability of a foundation to sustain what is built on them. This sense of structure creates a practical, pragmatic focus. If the underlying structure is considered inadequate then a project would have to either be modified or abandoned.

Saturn in Capricorn; on the right remembering side

Here the root chakra is placed into the context of its own personal understanding. This means that the root chakra remains largely unconscious in its activity. There is an underlying sense of an inner anchorage that helps to secure us individually. The larger social and physical structure is felt to sustain the us personally. It is felt to be a integral part of us and the larger structure is seen as intimate and personal. There is no deep-rooted quarrel with the way things are organized. There is no need to radically revise social structures. Although improvements can always be made, it is felt to be a matter of refining personal details, not overhauling the whole outer structure. Essentially, things are felt to function well enough. This means that good enough is left alone and we can generally ignore the root chakra and focus on more immediate concerns.

Saturn in Aquarius; on the left experiencing side

With the root chakra placed into the context of its own understanding on the interactive side, our sense of the underlying structure of the world and society is felt to be largely external from the individual. The root chakra is mainly seen in the context of social structures, which we experience as being external to us. With this placement, while the activity of the root chakra remains largely unconscious, there is an awareness of it's impact on our personal reality. While the root chakra's activities normally happen without our noticing it, when it is noticed it is usually because we feel that something needs to be changed. This produces a dynamic tension between us as an individual and the underlying structures of the world around us. There is a desire to understand and modify the underlying external structures that are part of our lives. There is an awareness of the impact external structures have on us and we seek to find what we can do to change these outer structures in accord with both our personal wants and needs and the needs of the larger world that surrounds us. Ultimately, this becomes the seeds of social movements seeking to modify social and physical injustice. They may also become the seeds of innovations which change how our society operates.

Saturn in the Genital Chakra

Saturn places the awareness of the root into the genital chakra. The root chakra's awareness feeds into our genital chakra's awareness. This is seen as the impact our genetically inherited body has on our own actual sensate experiences. We are aware that how we experience our own personal sensations is because of our body's biological structure. We feel that our personal sensations, although uniquely our own, are similar to the rest of humanity's sensations due to the shared design of the human body.

The shape and functions of our body tangibly reminds us of the root chakra's impact on what and how we sensately feel and know things. The body becomes a narrow window whose field of vision is determined by factors beyond our personal control. This can make us feel that all we can reliably know is limited to our physical sensations.

Our genital chakra's awareness is considered more reliable because of it's direct connection to the root. This gives our genital chakra greater stability. The large time frame of the root helps us to anchor the fleeting time frame of the genital chakra's awareness. The root is felt to be a repository of knowledge for dealing practically with our own personal experiences, even though the root's reactions are largely instinctual. This can be a reflex act, such as blinking, or an unconsciously anchored "sense" of whether or not a situation is safe.

Saturn sees our sensations as something more than fleeting or trivial. This can deepen the impact of our sensations. We may seek to find the underlying causes for why we react to an experience the way that we do. We may disdain purely personal reactions to experiences as being superficial, or not rooted in 'reality'. We may feel that our fleeting personal experiences are not carrying the significance that the root's depth demands of us.

Saturn in Sagittarius; on the right remembering side

Our inner genital chakra serves as the foundation of our personal awareness. It defines our personal sense of who we are according to our personal like or dislike reactions to our experiences.

The impact of the underlying physical structure of our bodies on our personal sensations is also observed. We notice that we feel certain things in certain ways because of the way our body is made. We sensately experience our physical make up. Our eyes see things the way they do because of how our eyes are physically constructed. The hunger we feel is because of our body's underlying physical needs. What we physically feel as pleasurable or disagreeable are the reactions of the human body honed by many millennia.

There's a sense that we carry with us the experiences of our entire ancestry. We personally know the awareness of the root through our physical sensations. What the root chakra adds to our genital chakra is beyond our comprehension. Through our genital chakra, we know that we are a part of something far larger than ourselves. And we are aware of that presence in very intimate and personal terms.

At the same time the root chakra is felt to be something that we possess. We have a very personal connection to a transpersonal awareness, yet we personally hunger for what our individual body needs, despite the fact that the hunger itself is a mechanism that humanity has given us through the root chakra. A pleasurable sensation is ours personally, even if the capacity to have the experience has been given to us by humanity. We are still the ones who ultimately decide if we personally like or dislike an experience.

Saturn in Pisces; on the left experiencing side

We notice the impact of the root on how we sensately experience our outer environment. Our sensate reality is felt to be external from us, to be an outer thing that we experience. There's a heightened sense of resonance to our physical sensations as they reveal the underlying structures of the physical world we live in. The external source of our sensate experiences is felt to be deeply anchored due to the root's presence. There is a nebulous sense of an unknowable depth which is added to our physical sensate reality. This causes us to react to our world of sensate experience with greater sensitivity. It heightens the impact of the genital chakra's attraction or repulsion reactions. We take our physical sensations more seriously. We are also a bit wary. The mystery of exactly how and what we experience and know through physical sensation both intrigues and baffles us.

Our outer genital chakra serves as the foundation of our interactive experiential awareness. It defines our personal foundation of who we are according to our personal like or dislike reactions to our experiences. At the same time, the outer world is perceived as causing us to feel the way we do. The creative dynamic is felt to be external from us. We feel that our reactions aren't really chosen by us, but instead that they are our virtually automatic responses to something which happens to us. Our reaction is just another aspect of the impact of the outer world on us. We are extremely aware of the world around us, yet we feel a bit passive and reactive.

Saturn in the Solar Plexus Chakra

At the solar plexus an awareness of our social context modifies the instinctive drives of the root chakra and makes them less socially disruptive. The raw aspects of our nature are refined and socially redefined. We are aware of the role that the root plays in defining our society identity. Our basic physical desires and needs are placed into a larger personal and cultural context. Our sense of personal foundation, which is ultimately grounded in the root, is interpreted by our social group's perspective. The root's drives are modified by our culture's needs.

The root chakra is subservient to the solar plexus chakra. Our collective transpersonal foundation of existence is placed into a personal, concrete, socially structured context. At the same time, our root's awareness is seen as the basis of our social and cultural sense of identity. Society itself is seen as echoing the structures established at the root chakra.

The solar plexus chakra assimilates the awareness of the root into itself. Because the root is an unconscious part of our awareness, it's impact goes largely unnoticed and is assumed. So the solar plexus is indirectly aware of the impact which the root's instinctive drives and evolutionary momentum has on it. We automatically make this underlying collective reality part of our individual personal sense of social identity.

At the same time our personal social identity feels the presence of our underlying sense of collective awareness. We may feel personally inadequate within the larger social context. Or we may feel the root chakra supports us within the larger social context. It all depends on our reaction to what we consider to be our personal destiny, to our place in the world.

Saturn in Scorpio; on the right remembering side

Our inner sense of social identity becomes the lens through which we see the root chakra. The root's presence in the solar plexus brings a heightened awareness of the underlying structures and forces that underpin our inner sense of social identity. Our personal identity feels enlarged by the root's added weight. There's an underlying sense of our being the personal embodiment of the root's collective awareness. Our sense of personal identity is simultaneously enlarged and made more vulnerable. There's an increased personal sensitivity to the underlying structures that uphold our identity.

At the same time, a bit of the root's trust or mistrust mechanism is brought into the solar plexus chakra. This makes our inner sense of personal identity more skeptical and less spontaneous. The presence of the root chakra in the solar plexus makes our sense of social identity a bit more plodding and less fluid. The benefit is that our sense of who we are runs deep. It strengthens our own sense of personal authority because we feel that we embody more than just ourselves.

Our inner sense of social identity acts as the foundation of our awareness and we use our social identity as the final judge of who we should be and what we should do. Ultimately our world supports our inner sense of social identity.

Saturn in Aries; on the left experiencing side

We see the root chakra through the lens of our outer personal social identity. This sense of the underlying structure behind our own personal identity enriches our social awareness. Everyone we meet plays a part in a larger social machine. The collective identity serves as the foundation of our personal reality. It is basis of how we define ourselves.

Our sense of the collective social presence hampers the spontaneity of our outer social identity. When we assert ourselves we feel that we must answer to a much larger framework than just ourselves. This can either enable us to bend the collective structures and momentums to our own purposes, or inhibit us as we seek to conform to external demands. We are sensitive to the juxtaposition of our personal social identity and the context of our social identity. Our awareness of the impact of the larger culture on our personal identity is heightened. We are very aware of our outer social identity as the focal pivot point of our awareness. We agonize over exactly how we should merge our individual social identity with our surrounding cultural circumstances. Ideally, we see ourselves as an individual acting within the context of associated social currents. Less fortunately, we may find ourselves in conflict with the societal culture that we live within.

Saturn in the Heart Chakra

When the root feeds into the heart, the depth and scope of the root forces the heart to be more thorough. This makes the heart less impulsive. It seeks the underlying foundations behind our emotions. It looks for an emotional context that will endure. The heart will seek to know what is behind what it feels. This makes it difficult for us to float on the surface of our emotions. We may become emotionally cumbersome, either refusing to emotionally interact on superficial levels, or trying to force a depth of feelings on fleeting encounters. We try to use our emotions as an anchor, seeking to use them to connect us to a deep, stable sense of who we are.

The heart is the focal point of our self created, inner personal pattern. This makes the heart the personal counterpoint of the root's impersonal physical pattern. Oddly enough with Saturn in the heart we are aware of how our emotional state, or how we personally feel and the emotional pattern we create with those feelings, puts us in balance with the whole of humanity. Saturn makes our personal emotional reality the foundation our personal awareness.

Within the chakras the heart is the inner pivot point of our personal awareness. This makes the heart unique. It is the natural inner anchor of our sense of ourselves. This means that our heart controls much of our physical health. Because the heart is not linearly rational to the heart a physical illness often serves as an allegorical expression of how we emotionally feel. Our body becomes a means of expression. Because the heart has finally reached an awareness that transcends time and our physical death, the heart is able to use our body purely to tangibly express how it feels. Our physical state becomes pure emotional symbol.

Saturn at the heart may stabilize our emotional self expression and help sustain good health. Or Saturn may increase the sensitivity of the heart and the result may be poorer health as or body serves as a vehicle of emotional discontent.

Saturn will call on us to see the big picture emotionally. There is a need to broaden our emotional awareness so that we can look upon the struggles of humanity, both individually and collectively with compassion. With this placement of Saturn there is almost a need for the individual to love both themselves and the whole human race. There is also a need to love the actuality of our physical existence, despite it's vulnerabilities. This can lead us to feeling emotionally sustained by the whole human race. Failing that, we may become embittered by the emotional frailty of human existence with its constant stream of unfulfilled ideals, thwarted desires, and petty emotional hungers.

Saturn in Libra; on the right remembering side

The root chakra is seen through the perspective of the inner heart. The root brings depth and sensitivity to the awareness of the heart. The broad scope of the root also decreases the heart's spontaneity. When the emotional nature finally does move it is plodding and deliberate. The root chakra seems to well up from deep within us and move through us. The root chakra feels like something that we personally contain, understand and express through our emotional being. Because of the scale of the root, we feel that our personal emotional state embodies the feelings of all of humanity. We feel our emotions in universalized terms, even seeing an underlying depth to our more fleeting emotions. There's a sense of the heart as being not only our personal core but the core of all of humanity. We feel emotionally connected to all of humanity through the heart chakra..

The inner heart chakra becomes the foundation of our internal awareness. We feel that we are fated to endure our own inner emotional state. The outer world is internalized and it becomes a vessel which symbolically expresses our inner emotional reality.

Saturn in Taurus; on the left experiencing side

The root chakra is seen through the perspective of the outer heart chakra. We feel a connection the whole of humanity through our personal emotional interactions. Because it is on the experiencing side, we perceive the root chakra as something that, while a part of us, is still essentially external to us. We are aware of the presence of the root as an external force, as something that happens to us. This lends a feeling that our outer emotional environment is our emotional fate. We believe that our emotional events happen to us, rather than with us.

Our emotional understanding of the outer world becomes the focal center of our personal awareness. It serves as the foundation of our awareness. We seek to build stable enduring emotional structures in our outer world. This requires us to find a deep shared connection that we can mutually build on. Trust must be generated so that the bond between us and our environment can grow strong. There is an initial hesitance to invest ourselves in an emotional connection, but once the decision to commit ourselves is made we can be very persistent.

Saturn in the Throat Chakra

Saturn brings the root's large-scale sense of structure to the throat. The inflexibility of the root contrasts with the abstract fluidity of the throat. The two of them together can be a difficult mix. The throat is agile, quick, fluid and changeable. Saturn is slow, careful and thorough. Ultimately, the root chakra carries more weight than any of the five middle chakras. This means that it is up to the throat to align itself with the reality of the root. Our thoughts and ideas cannot successfully contradict the root. Ultimately, the throat has to include the scope and depth of the root in its understanding. This can be difficult for the throat, which is not very good at accepting things which it doesn't understand.

This can place a tremendous sense of pressure on the throat. At its best, the throat can become extremely reality focused. The throat also acquires the depth and assurance of the root. At its worst, the throat feels overwhelmed and unable to satisfy the root's required broad sweep and the meticulous detail. This is partly due to the fact that the root always remains only partially known.

Ultimately, the root has an awareness that goes beyond the understanding of the throat. This means the throat can never be completely sure of what the root is up to. The throat doesn't deal well with being unsure. This unsettling inability to know something can make the throat somewhat frantic. This can cause tension between the root and the throat. At its best, the throat reacts in a dynamic and creative manner. At its worst, this tension freezes the throat and makes it unable to trust itself and what it knows.

With this placement there is a sensitivity to the deeper needs of the throat. Because the throat is very abstract it can get caught up in chasing its own fleeting notions. It can lose sight of everything except its own ideas and ideals. Saturn in the throat makes the mind more aware of the larger context of it's ideas. This gives the mind more substance. The mind becomes more deeply anchored and reliable. The ability of the mind to maintain a tight focus is enhanced. The impact of the mind on how we interpret reality is also more readily apparent.

A side effect may be that our own ideas may feel oppressive to us when Saturn is in the throat chakra. There may be a sense that ideas happen to us, rather than being our own creation. Despite our awareness of the impact our own ideas have on how we see things, the facts are felt as forcing us to conclude what is true. We may become unaware of the largely unconscious underpinnings of our thinking. Our mind may become a means of self deluding rationalization, rather than a means of honest inquiry.

Saturn in Virgo; on the right remembering side

The root chakra is seen through the lens of the throat chakra. The throat chakra assimilates the root chakra's awareness into its own awareness. The root chakra makes the throat chakra more aware of a need to have depth and thoroughness in its thinking. Because it is on the inner side of the throat chakra, the root chakra feels like it is an intrinsic part of ourselves. We believe that we are perceiving another, deeper aspect of who we are.

The root brings what we feel is our personal destiny into our thinking. The ideas that we use to understand and shape our lives are part of our personal fate. Our inner throat chakra's thinking is the foundational anchor of our personal awareness. Our thinking becomes a bit more plodding but it also has increased scope. There's a greater sensitivity to how underlying structures affect the relationships our mind visualizes. Our mind realizes that it needs to look beneath the surface to fully understand things. We trust our mind to be reliable. We believe that what we think is our own ideas and we trust our own thinking.

Saturn in Gemini; on the left experiencing side

Here the throat chakra sees the awareness of the root chakra as something that is slightly remote from our thinking. Due to the outer placement within the throat chakra we are sensitive to how the underlying structures and momentums of humanity affect our thinking, both personally and collectively. There is a strong awareness of the collective nature of the mind's concepts and the social momentum of ideas. Our mind understands how the concepts within our outer culture's awareness are created and maintained. We see the community of shared ideas as a foundation for our personal awareness. We try to personalized and build on the concepts that society already uses.

At the same time we feel that our own intellectual assumptions, which surround us as completely as the air that we breathe, are largely a group creation which we are fated to live within. Our understanding of the world is shaped by ideas that we feel are pushed onto us, either by our culture or by the cold harsh facts of life. Our intellectual environment feels external and somewhat intractable.

Saturn in the Brow Chakra

With this placement the awareness of the root chakra is placed into the context of the brow. Our preconscious intuitive sense of the will of the world around us is impacted by the transpersonal perspective of the root chakra. This makes us aware of the overall flow of human momentum, which we then try to see in terms of our own personal goals. We see how we may be able to personally hitch a ride on the wave of a larger human momentum.

We try to intuit how the world around us is structured and how we can fit in. We are able to perceive the intent that underlies the situations that we find ourselves in. We make a judgement as to whether or not this intention can fit our own purposes as well.

Saturn in Leo; on the right remembering side

The depth of the root is added to the brow chakra. It is difficult to be consciously aware of the interaction of these two chakras. The root chakra's unconscious awareness feeds our preconscious intuitive awareness. Because both chakras are not fully conscious, the added awareness of the root to the brow may cause us to feel that we 'just know' something, but we are unsure of exactly what. We feel that we have intuitive insights about the underlying dynamics of a situation, yet we are unable to clearly see what to actually do. We may find ourselves hypnotized by what we can imagine happening on a grand scale, even as the details that would allow us to act elude us.

The brow chakra's style of using piercing intuition to grasp a situation provides the anchor of our personal awareness. We may or may not trust our intuitive reactions reliability, but they still serve as the foundation of our awareness. We add the root's trust/mistrust response to our brow's like/dislike reactions.

Our intuition searches for the impact of humanity's large scale patterns and momentums on our own intentions. Our personal aspirations then try to build on the collective movement. With this placement, our desires may become grand and we may feel that is our destiny to do great things. This may lead us to think that our personal fulfillment serves humanity's destiny. We may think that our purely personal desires actually serve the human race and that our own intentions are really the human race's intentions. While this may actually be coincidentally true, we must be very careful whenever we feel that we are personally fulfilling the destiny of humanity.

If we are able to accurately intuit our place within both the brow and root chakra's contexts we will find that we flow with things easily. We do not need to use sheer force of will to accomplish our goals. Our intuitions of the potentials surrounding us helps us to act in ways that fulfill both our own goals and those of the people around us. We do not overwhelm the world, but instead we work fluidly with it. The world becomes our collaborator.

If we are out of sync we may find that the world feels antagonistic. We are unable to fluidly interact with our environment and we feel the need to press the outer world into submission. We believe that we achieve our goals through force, not cooperation, and life is a competitive conflict rather than a synergetic blending.

Saturn in the Crown Chakra

This places our transpersonal concrete awareness into the perspective of our transpersonal abstract awareness. The underlying tangible mechanisms of our existence are seen in the context of our ideals and abstract sense of order. The crown assimilates the root's tangible order into it's sense of intangible order. The crown operates through an acausal magnetic attraction principle, while the root operates on linear step-by-step causal process principle. We personally hardly notice the process for both chakras operate outside of our conscious awareness. The two are kind of like oil and water aside from the fact that they are both concerned with structure.

With this placement the crown is felt to be the ultimate foundation of our personal reality. There is a strong sense of purpose behind the both the tangible and intangible structures of our world. The crown brings it's sense of spiritual intimacy and purpose to what the root feels is an essentially impersonal, mechanistic universe. The momentums of humanity as a whole seem to be happening by design and serve a larger purpose.

Saturn in Cancer; on the right remembering side

With Saturn in the crown chakra our sense of human racial momentum becomes intertwined with our sense of divine, or cosmic, order. It is as if God in heaven is a tangible presence on which we feel we can personally rely. We end up using our abstract awareness as the foundation of our personal being. Our abstract ideals feel buttressed by the underlying physical structure of the world. Physical reality takes on a mystical quality as it is seen in the light of cosmic order.

The human race feels as if its motion is directed by the Will of God. We feel there is a Plan which is apparent through the multiple levels of order found within the physical world. The sense that there is an underlying Ideal Order becomes real to us.

We intuitively feel that Big Things are happening, which we either trust or mistrust. This can add a sense of fate to life. This crown chakra placement can enrich us by enabling us to see greater depth in our abstract connections. Or it can leave us feeling nagged by a personal sense of superficiality and the need to help enact the Big Picture, if only in our own lives.

While our sense of solid concrete foundations impacts our sense of abstract relationships, the tangible order is seen as the servant and result of abstract order. We see the world as ultimately stemming from the abstract ideals which are the ultimate basis of concrete reality.

Our unconscious sense of physical structure is enlarged by an intuitive sense of tightly interwoven abstract relationships. This can make both the crown and root chakras function feel even more automatic.

Jupiter: Genital, point of self experience; glyph- ♃

Jupiter rules the genital chakra and it's world of sensate experience. Jupiter, or Zeus, was the ruler of Olympus. His strength was so great that he was able to defeat all the other Olympian gods at the same time. He was generally considered to be a benevolent God who bestowed good fortune. Jupiter fits the genital chakra because most of the time people find their sensate experiences both powerful and pleasing.

In traditional astrology Jupiter symbolizes self embodiment and personal expansion. This reflects how we feel about our sensate awareness. We generally feel enlivened by our direct sensory interactions with the world. We enjoy touching and being touched. The stimulation of our physical sensory experiences adds to our awareness. Also, our sensate experiences become the basis of our expectations of our reality. Saturn is reality as an transpersonal physical foundation of personal existence, whereas Jupiter is reality as a directly personal, intimate sensate experience.

Our genital chakra's awareness places us into specific, tangible situations and experiences. Usually this is seen as a good thing, if only because our sensations give us a core confirmation of our personal existence. Even through we may not enjoy all of our physical experiences, we need the awareness, both of our world and of ourselves, that the genital chakra's sensate awareness gives us.

By chakric association, Jupiter rules our physical ensoulment through personal experience and its immediate psychological impact. Saturn is our personal anchorage in a transpersonal concrete interweaving of relationships. Jupiter takes the root's relationships and makes them personal, intimate, and actual. The general human racial support at the root chakra actually bares fruit in the individual through the genital chakra's world of day to day experience.

Jupiter in the Root Chakra

When we place our own sensations into the context of the awareness of the human race as a whole, we know that what we personally experience has already been felt over a vast stretch of time by a lot of other people. Our personal experiences are seen as yet another instance of the human race's experience. We feel like we share our personal experiences with the whole human race. We experience the human racial pattern as something that defines the very core of our being. We know that we experience things in certain ways because that is how the human race has led us to experience things. All of the physical products of our evolution are felt to define our sensate awareness at the genital chakra.

Our personal sensations may be seen as aspects of humanity's existence, not just our own personal existence. Our personal sensations may also be felt to serve humanity. By physically existing we personally provide one more focal point of human consciousness. Through us the human race also has more experiences which helps humanity to further refine it's awareness.

In a way, the human race itself becomes something we feel we personally experience. The problem of Jupiter in the root is that the individual may occasionally feel engulfed by the larger transpersonal structure. Everything that we feel seems to be determined by the human race rather than ourselves. It may be difficult to separate and maintain an individual sensate identity. There may be a blurring of the root's instinctive reactions with our own individual reactions.

Jupiter in Capricorn; on the right remembering side

Jupiter places the genital chakra into the context of the inner root chakra. This puts our personal physical experiential awareness into the transpersonal framework of our root's subjective awareness. We believe that we sensately feel the world the way we do because of how our own body feels. We also place our personal physical reactions, our sensate likes and dislikes, into the context of the root chakra's large-scale perspective. Because our sensate awareness is placed into a context that sees our individual experiences as a instances of the way our body has been designed to feel, our reactions to our sensate reality may seem mechanistic and predetermined. This gives our own sensate experiences a quality of inevitability. For example, the reason that we are hungry for a certain food and feel that it taste's good is because it contains the nutrients that we need. Pleasure and pain become purely pragmatic responses designed by the human race. Our personal like and dislike responses are the surface results of deeper needs.

Jupiter in Aquarius; on the left experiencing side

Jupiter places the genital chakra's awareness into the context of the root chakra. This puts our personal physical sensate experiences into the large-scale transpersonal perspective of the root's outer awareness. The personal immediacy of the genital chakra's awareness is made more impersonal. We see our own experiences as mere instances of the way all of humanity feels. Our personal experiences, which are our own particular moments of liking or disliking something, are seen in the context of humanity as a whole. This gives our personal sensate reality depth as we sense a connection to all of humanity.

We are also focused on how the outer environment shapes our personal reactions. We see how in sync with the momentum of the whole human race our personal responses are. We may react by assuming that what we personally feel is what everyone else feels under the same circumstances. Everyone else seems to like rock and roll music, perhaps we do, too. This can lead to an assumption that what we feel is normal.

The strength of this placement is that we believe that we feel how humanity feels. This helps us anchor our transient experiences in something larger and more stable than ourselves. We may believe ourselves to be aware of the cutting edge of human momentum. The problem that we have with the root is accurately perceiving the larger context.

Jupiter in the Genital Chakra

Our genital chakra's awareness is provides it's own context of understanding. This strengthens the impact of our physical reality. Our sensate experiences are seen as complete and our sensate awareness stands on its own. Physical sensate reality is intensified.

We also may find that we have to physically experience something in order to believe it or understand it.

With Jupiter on the genital level our experiences cannot be placed into another chakra's awareness. This means that what we sensately perceive is understood purely through our own reactions to our experiences. Normally we have little doubt about what we feel and our reactions to it, but we are still limited to isolated sensate experiences and our reactions to those experiences. Because we are unable to find a broader context, when we are unsure of how we feel we may try intensifying our sensate experience to get clarity.

We may be able to perceive things, including things that are very subtle, through our sensate awareness. Our physical reality, and our reactions to it, can become the embodiment of abstract (spiritual) principles and relationships.

At it's worst, our assessment of what's trustworthy can become limited to only what we can physically experience. At its best, our sensate reality becomes a means of experiencing many facets of our existence. Our experiences feel rich and rewarding.

Jupiter in Sagittarius; on the right remembering side

Through the emphasis of our internal sensate awareness we find that we experience ourselves as much as the external event. All our experiences and our reactions to them are seen as something that we personally have a role in creating. This makes us feel that we have control over our sensate awareness. The inner emphasis of our sensate awareness makes us aware of how our sensate experiences are an intrinsic part of us. The inner side of the genital chakra accentuates how we retain our reactions to sensate experiences. We remember and emphasize our likes and dislikes as well as information about our sensate experiences. Our preference for vanilla ice cream to chocolate ice cream becomes part of who we feel we are, not just our reaction the taste of the two different ice creams. We define ourselves through our sensate awareness.

With this placement our genital chakra provides its own context of understanding. This obscures the larger context of our specific sensate self experiences, even as it accentuates the genital chakra's overall impact in our awareness. Our sensate experiences are felt to be complete and self contained. This means that there is nothing to help moderate our reactions to our experiences. This can make our reactions a bit extreme and out of balance. We use the exaggerated response to augment our self awareness. Our reaction's intensity becomes more about self awareness than it is about feeling and responding to an objective experience.

Jupiter in Pisces; on the left experiencing side

With the outside emphasis of our sensate awareness our physical experiences are felt to happen to us. We focus on the otherness aspect of our external sensate experience. We feel that our genital chakra's sensate experiences are created by the external world. We merely end up reacting in inevitable ways to experiences and events that are outside of us. Our likes and dislikes are reflections of the world around us rather than reflections of us. We dislike having our hand burned by a fire because the fire hurts us. This reaction is seen not so much a personal choice as it is an inevitable response. Our sensate reactions are seen as defining the actuality of the outer world, rather than as defining ourselves.

With this placement our genital chakra provides its own context of understanding. This obscures the larger context of our specific sensate experiences, even as it accentuates the genital chakra's overall impact in our awareness. It also makes our reactions to external events more extreme. This is partly because our experience of the external world has a strong resonance. We react deeply to the world around us. Because the outer world seems to happen to us rather than with us, we may tend to feel victimized by the impact outer events have on us.

Jupiter in the Solar Plexus Chakra

With this placement our genital chakra's sensate awareness has a large impact on our social self definition. The simple like or dislike responses of the genital chakra becomes more complex at the solar plexus. We begin to see ourselves as having sets of personal responses that define who we are relative to other people. With Jupiter in the solar plexus chakra, our genital chakra's sensate awareness is given social as well as personal value. What we physically feel and prefer to experience becomes the foundation of our social identity.

Our social self definition is created by our physical experiences and our sensate likes and dislikes. The things that we have experienced and our reactions to those experiences, become something that we possess. The solar plexus creates a pattern of actions and tangible possessions which becomes part of our social self definition. Our personal actions and taste are held up to group scrutiny for social approval or disapproval.

We also interpret our personal physical reality through the lens of our surrounding culture's perspective. We look to our culture for a broader context to help us understand and define what we physically feel. Our culture provide a larger context which helps us to understand our experiences. In this way our personal sensate awareness also gains added social significance.

The experiences of our physical reality become part of the our social reality. The social dimension of the solar plexus chakra absorbs our personal sensate experiences into it. The social measure of our personal sensate experiences is heightened in our awareness. We are aware of how we are supposed to feel according to our culture, as well as how we actually do personally feel. We notice any divergences.

Our sensate experiences become a factor in our social world. Usually the cultural demands of a society are intended to aid social cohesion and to help it's individual members interact in ways that are not destructive to either themselves or the larger group. At the solar plexus our genital chakra's naive sensate awareness is given a socially defined moral code that is meant to moderate and guide it's feelings and conduct. What was a response born purely of the moment at the genital chakra becomes redefined as who we are in a social context. There is some tension between the individual and society as we are pressed to behave along culturally acceptable lines.

We are seen as being defined by our cultural environment. We are members of a certain social class and ethnic group. At the same time we are seen as possessing our sensate awareness and the particular physical reality that leads to our experiences. An athlete lives in a different sensate world than a physicist. Their experiences on a cultural level are very different, yet they may both be members of the same society.

Jupiter in Scorpio; on the right remembering side

Our genital chakra is seen through the lens of our solar plexus. Our physical experiences, coupled with our personal likes and dislikes, provide information that helps our solar plexus to determine who we are. The placement on the inner side of the solar plexus emphasizes our personal social self awareness as it is impacted by our own sensate experiences. Our physical experiences are seen to internally impact who we feel we are.

Here our sensate reality helps to create our inner sense of who we feel ourselves to be. Our personal interpretation of our sensate reality is pivotal in our self understanding. Our personal experiences form the raw data by which we define ourselves. This self-definition is open to reinterpretation whenever there are major changes in our understanding of our sensate experiences.

In the struggle for balance between the personal and the social definitions of who we are, we tend to hold ourselves slightly aloof from the crowd. We see ourselves as the more active component of our social self definition. We create the person that we are. Society is viewed as a collection of individuals, with the parts ultimately defining the whole. The individual is the primary unit of the group and the group is the sum of it's individual parts.

Jupiter in Aries; on the left experiencing side

Our genital chakra is seen through the lens of our solar plexus. The placement on the outside of the solar plexus emphasizes the impact of external social conditions on our awareness. We are particularly aware of how social forces affect our sense of who we are. Our personal sensate likes and dislikes are seen in the context of the tastes of our outer culture. We notice the differences between our personal likes and dislikes and the culture's prevailing tastes. We may not see a strong need to conform to cultural biases, but there is strong awareness of where society stands. Personal difference is allowed, but the group is felt to be the more powerful force.

Society is seen as an entity that stands apart from any individual's self-definition. The social reality is felt to be something more than merely a blending of its members. A cultural group is a free standing entity that defines it's members even more than it's members define it. Society is felt to be something that exists apart from it's individual members in much the same way that we feel that our body is something apart from the mere amalgamation of our individual cells.

The otherness of our social environment is emphasized. There is an awareness of the dynamics of the gap between the individual and society. The social realm is considered to be something that an individual can play with.

Jupiter in the Heart Chakra

With this placement our physical sensations are seen in the context of our emotional awareness. Specific situations and experiences take on added personal emotional significance. We take our sensate events and see them as suggestive symbols. Our sensate like or dislike reactions to events become tinted with emotional responses and symbolism.

The heart has a tendency to generalize and universalize its feelings, which it proceeds to do with our sensate awareness. This tends to blur the boundaries between our emotional and physical responses. Our emotional reactions overlay our physical sensate reactions. At the genital chakra we like or dislike things, and at the heart chakra we also either feel emotionally connected and attracted to something or disconnected and repulsed to it.

We use our genital chakra's awareness to help us define our emotional sense of self. Our realm of experience directly impacts our inner emotional being, or our soul. Our physical sensations are interpreted by the heart and made to fit our emotional sense of who we are. We simultaneously feel things on both sensate and emotional levels. This means that we turn our sensate experiences into suggestive symbols to which we then emotionally react.

Because the heart chakra creates meanings through the association of similarities which helps it to generalize its feelings, actual physical events can take on personal significance in ways that are bewildering at first glance. Our actual sensate experiences can also quickly become mere starting points for our own emotional reactions.

Jupiter in Libra; on the right remembering side

Our sensate awareness is seen through the perspective of the inner heart chakra. We use the heart's emotional perspective to understand the way we sensately feel. We add emotional depth and personal symbolic nuance to our genital chakra's simple initial like or dislike responses. Because it is on the inside of the heart we feel that we have control over our emotional responses to our genital chakra's experiences.

With the inner placement, our awareness focuses upon our own emotional reactions to our sensate awareness. Our sensate awareness provides the actualities which then become meaningful within our emotional awareness. In this way we create our inner sense of who we are, or our personal pattern of being. As Libra is the focal center point of our inner awareness, our sensate like and dislikes become a part of who we feel we are in our soul.

As the lowest rung in our abstract awareness, outer objects and sensations may become idealized and made into symbols that express our inner being. Because our inner emotions are primarily abstract, we tend to move through them fairly easily. We can change our emotional contexts quickly which may make us rather moody in our reactions to our sensate experiences.

Jupiter in Taurus; on the left experiencing side

Our genital chakra is seen through the perspective of the outer heart chakra. Our personal sensate likes and dislikes are felt to have an external quality. We believe our sensate experiences and the emotional reactions that they evoke are the result of external factors. We perceive our own emotional responses as a direct result of forces beyond our control. We are emotionally responding to the impact of an outer sensate situation or event.

We see our emotional responses as a way of understanding the outer world, more than as a means of understanding ourselves. Our outer physical sensate reality is felt to be the cause of our emotional state. We use our personal emotional responses to physical experiences to connect us to the outer world. Despite our heart's tendency to idealize and abstract, the outer world remains undeniably concrete and real even as we respond to it's emotional significance. The outer world's symbolisms feel externally created.

The outer heart is the highest chakric point of concrete focus of awareness. This external focus stabilizes our emotions. Because the heart invests itself in it's external environment, if the outer world is stable, so is it. We have difficulty seeing how we project our own emotions and symbolic meanings onto our outer world.

Jupiter in the Throat Chakra

With Jupiter in the throat chakra our sensate experiences are intellectually analyzed by our minds. Our sensate reality provides many of the facts, or the raw data, about which our mind thinks. We are very discriminating about the nature and quality of our sensations. We use our mind to try to understand why we have the sensate experiences we do and what they mean. We see subtle nuances and look for underlying relationships within our physical experiences. Our mind is also aware of the role our physical sensations play in what we think. Even our most abstract ideas may seen as ultimately being connected to our physical world.

Our actual physical sensations may not fit into any of our mind's preset notions. While our mind usually does have a set of pre-existing explanations for whatever we may feel, these explanations may not adequately explain what some of our sensate experiences imply. Our mind then looks at our sensations and seeks to adequately understand what they mean.

We will use reasoning to understand our sensate reality. When individual sensations move into the throat they become part of a matrix of previously analyzed sensations. Individual sensations are compared to other sensations that we personally have had or that we know about from other people.

Due to the abstract nature of the throat we are able to share our sensations. We can vicariously have other people's sensations. This means that we can learn from the experiences of others without having to actually go through them ourselves. This furthers our understanding of our sensate realm as we have a much wider pool of experiences to use for our understanding.

Our throat's abstract awareness also gives us a less involved perspective on our sensate experiences. For example, we may end up deciding that the reason we like the taste of strawberries so much is because of a need within our body for the nutrients contained in a strawberry. We biochemically need what is in the strawberry and therefore it tastes good to us. While that may be a good analysis of the underlying reason why a strawberry may appeal to us, it has almost nothing to do with the sensual pleasure that the taste of a strawberry gives us on a purely sensate level.

Jupiter in Virgo; on the right remembering side

The genital chakra is seen through the perspective of the inner throat chakra. Our personal likes and dislikes are understood through our mind. There's a somewhat self-contained quality to our thinking. Our physical experiences serve as information for our mind's analysis. The emphasis is on intellectually understanding our personal sensate experiences. We use our mind to compare and judge our experiences. Because it is on the inner subjective side we feel that the ideas which we use to analyze and judge our genital chakra's sensate experiences are our own.

With this placement there is great attention to detail. There is a discernment and an appreciation of the finer, subtler levels of experience. For example, a person with this placement may be able to taste the differences between fresh, old and dried ingredients in their food. These distinctions may be considered to be so significant that if the food that is not fresh, it may be judged inedible.

This capacity for penetrating discernment is seen as a personal trait that we have created and sustained through careful effort. We see ourselves as being able to notice, understand and enjoy extremely subtle levels of experience.

Jupiter in Gemini; on the left experiencing side

Our genital chakra is seen through the perspective of the outer throat chakra. Our sensate awareness acquires an external emphasis. We see our sensate reality as objectively real and distinct from ourselves. We believe in the objective nature of our sensate reality and we have an objective slant in our mental outlook as well. Both our experiences and the ideas that we use to interpret them are seen in a collective context. While our personal physical experiences provide the raw data for our mind's understanding, we look out to the outer world's ideas to help us understand our sensate experiences. We use the concepts circulating within our culture to help us grasp our own sensate reality.

This placement makes us aware of our culture's cutting edge interpretations of sensate experiences. We are able to judge the various ideas that are in cultural circulation fairly easily and ponder their merits. We can apply them to our own situation when they fit and ignore them when they don't. Because we are so attuned to the cultural nuances of various concepts, we may find it difficult to step outside of our culture and think for ourselves. Independent thought and innovation is difficult for us. We believe we think better in a group context, where ideas are bounced around. We think most effectively in a dynamic social environment.

Jupiter in the Brow Chakra

With the planet Jupiter in the brow chakra our genital chakra's awareness is put into the context of our intuitive understanding. Our pure sense of personal self fulfillment organizes and understands our genital chakra's sensate experiences. Physical events often become a springboard for intuitive insights. This can make a specific physical event suddenly feel extremely evocative. Something ordinary may become an intuitive doorway of extraordinary significance. As is always the problem with the brow chakra, the context of a leap in understanding is often difficult to know. Is this flash of insight symbolic or literal? Is our intuition telling us something that matters in an objective sense, or is what we're seeing only symbolically important to us? Our sensate awareness feeds our intuitive awareness.

As our genital chakra's sensate awareness is understood through the haze of our intuitive awareness there will be moments of great clarity, as well as moments of utter confusion. Such is the nature of the brow chakra. The actual experiences of the genital chakra become departure points for the brow chakra. The brow chakra takes something and extends it far beyond it's surface appearance. To the extent that we're able to ride the brow chakra's large-scale awareness, we can broaden the significance of our genital chakra's sensate experiences.

For example, we look a large flat stone in the mountainous wilderness and intuitively 'know' that the stone was used for human sacrifice a long time ago. We simply 'see' it. Our intuitive awareness has a far broader scope than our genital chakra. All our sensate chakra sees is a large flat stone. Our brow chakra's awareness takes the physical stone and places it into multiple highly abstract contexts including a much larger time frame. Again, the problem becomes verifying what we intuitively perceive. As the intuitively perceived human sacrifices happened in prehistoric times, there is no written record and the culture that did it has long since vanished. If we wish, we may check with local archaeologists, or perhaps even do our own research. Unfortunately, verifying our intuitions isn't always possible. We are often stuck with either believing our intuition, or sticking with the plain sensate facts.

Jupiter in Leo; on the right remembering side

The genital chakra is seen through the perspective of the inner brow chakra. Our sensate experiences, with its likes and dislikes, are understood and interpreted through the brow chakra. Our preconscious intuitive awareness is used to understand and interpret our physical attractions and repulsions. This intuitive awareness is deeply personal and feels like it is a part of who we are and is separate from the external world around us. Because it is on the right subjective side the brow chakra tends to see our sensate experiences as part of ourselves and interpret them as something that is largely within our own being.

We tend to be decisive and sure of what the underlying implications of things are. This enables us to feel confident in ourselves despite there being no visible reason. We consider ourselves to be lucky as things usually just fall into place for us.

Our intuition takes our physical awareness through deeper and deeper levels of understanding until our personal will's connection to the sensate object or experience is perceived. Our inner will's need for self expression intuitively places the actualities of our genital chakra's sensate awareness into a desired context.

Like the genital chakra, the brow also reacts to it's perceptions with a like or dislike response. With Jupiter in the brow we tend to react strongly. We really like something or we really dislike something almost immediately. We may not know why, but we definitely know how we feel. The problem is the haziness of seeing the external context of our intuitions.

Jupiter in the Crown Chakra

The facts of the conscious sensate awareness of the genital chakra are placed into the crown's preconscious awareness. Individual sensations are placed into a larger pattern of complex interrelationships. Our genital chakra's experiences are seen as evidence of a larger order. Because the crown deals with large patterns of relationship, our sensate experiences are placed into a very abstract grid. A side effect of this may be that our physical reality gets lost in the echoing ramifications of what it feels connected to. When the genital chakra moves into the crown chakra, our physical sensations become understood within a larger pattern. With this placement we see events as having great significance, if only symbolically. Physical experiences may become hugely meaningful. We may see God's presence in a blade of grass. The physical world is interpreted through the eyes of the 'really big picture'.

Just like the brow chakra, the problem at the crown is accurately understanding the actual significance of objects and events. The crown will tend to glorify minor things. It will find evidences of some larger meaning within extremely mundane events. This can lead to a either an enriched sense of our day to day world, or a diffusing sense of grandeur.

The triggering physical event could be as simple as driving a car and making a turn at a traffic light. The act of driving a car can be placed into the larger pattern of our culture's polluting the atmosphere, or it's technical inventiveness, or testimony to our culture's elevation of individuality. (We're riding alone in a car, not sharing a train with a lot of other people). Or we could see a larger order in how we all follow the of the rules of the highway.

The larger pattern which we choose to place driving into is provided by our own crown chakra. Despite it's transpersonal nature, the crown chakra is actually our most personal chakra. It is our own personal sense of order. Our awareness of communing with God. It is our own self transcendent awareness.

At the same time the crown chakra truly can be cosmic in its scope. This means that we may have a physical event which triggers insights into how it fits into a much larger pattern. Our physical genital chakra, which is very specific and consciously knowable, becomes fuel for an awareness that is beyond our conscious comprehension. Our sensate reality is understood, but at such a height and such a depth that it is difficult for us to know exactly what we know. Using the prior example from the brow chakra, when we see the large flat stone in the wilderness and intuitively know that it was used for human sacrifice long ago, we also 'know' that such sacrifices did not successfully bridge the gap between the human and divine. Simultaneously, we see how our own personal sacrifices may be misguided and may not necessarily create the results we desire. It may be a while before the implications of our flash of insight fully falls into place.

At the crown chakra coincidences feel very meaningful. Random events are easily placed into a pattern that gives them deep significance. Everything acquires meaning. At its best, daily life takes on a spiritual luminosity and mundane things connect us to larger realms which make us feel more connected to everything around us. At its worst, meaningless details acquire an aura of tremendous significance as we irrationally and ineptly chase after the Divine, using completely random and disconnected events as our inaccurate guide.

Jupiter in Cancer; on the right remembering side

Our genital chakra is placed into the context of the inner crown chakra. Our sensate experiences provide raw data for our crown chakra's understanding. This means that our personal sensate experiences become the details of the larger abstract ordering pattern that we use to understand our world.

Our sense of the big picture is used to understand and interpret our sensate experiences. Because the crown chakra is a transpersonal awareness, it feels external to us even as we enact it on the right personal side. Also, as a preconscious awareness we rarely notice the ordering pattern that we use to understand our genital chakra's awareness. The crown chakra seems to automatically decipher what our sensate experiences truly mean.

We attempt to see all of our experiences in a larger abstract context. This can lead to finding hidden cosmic significance in very mundane events. The Big Picture can always be found if we look hard enough. At the same time this sense of the big picture helps us feel supported by the cosmos and the universe feels more intimate.

The down side is some object or event may become so laden with greater significance that we end up protecting and defending it beyond all reason. Rather than being a symbol of an ideal, it is seen as the ideal itself. Although the concrete symbol can be destroyed, the abstract ideal cannot. Abstract ideals can only be destroyed when their fruits are found wanting and people choose to turn away from them.

Mars: Solar Plexus, point of self enactment; glyph- ♂

Mars was the god of war. The god of war enjoys the self assertiveness of conflict. Mars revels in his own strength and power. With the planet Mars we reach the solar plexus chakra. The solar plexus is where our sense of tangible identity is created and maintained. The solar plexus is the focal center of our outer awareness. This makes Mars the ruler of our tangible sense of self and our connection to the outer world. In classical astrology Mars is very assertive. This gives a hint as to what the solar plexus is about. The solar plexus feels like it is in a constant struggle to prove itself and to confirm its identity.

Of course, the destructiveness of conflict can be a downside. But so long as we ourselves aren't affected, it is tragic but acceptable. In many ways this is an apt summation of the solar plexus. It often feels like it is in conflict and it has to struggle to defend itself. It enjoys it's own sense of power. The solar plexus is the home of the phrase 'I will rule the world.'

The placement of Mars shows how we deal with our social identity. Mars is also connected to our general sense of culture. This includes what we personally think a society is and what it should do. These social ethics affects the rules of the highway, what kind of music we listen to, how we culturally define and enact romance, and so on.

In classic astrology Mars rules assertive behavior. Mars defines itself through what it does. Mars is not passive. If Mars wants something, it goes out and gets it. Mars has tangible goals within a tangible world. Mars uses our personal skills to create our social position. It strives for social power and prestige but it tends to define these things in tangible ways. An expensive car, a big house, beautiful or handsome spouse; possessions of social desirability are the ways that Mars uses to prove its worth.

Mars places our active sense of social identity and social awareness into our own personal chakric context. It shows where our focal point of outer awareness is within our own chakric consciousness.

Mars in the Root Chakra

Here our social awareness is placed into an unconscious sense of physical order. Our personal identity is seen in the context of an underlying unconscious transpersonal foundation.   The cultural atmosphere in which we live is seen as being shaped by impersonal forces.

This can lead to a nagging sense of fate. A pressure to personally do something great may be felt. Or there may be an underlying sense of potential greatness that could be grasped. This can become a goad to real accomplishment or it may become grandiose dreaming. It all depends on whether or not our personal identity can deal with the demands of the larger social context.

At the same time our own personal concerns may be viewed as petty and insignificant. Some of the concerns of the solar plexus are seen as overwrought and trivial. This can help us balance our sense of self importance. In the broad sweep of time that the root perceives most of our daily personal concerns aren't seen as all that big a deal.

Our sense of personal identity becomes more serious and somber due to the perspective of the root chakra. The root chakra's larger perspective may also help the solar plexus to rebel against the more superficial aspects of social custom. This may lead to our marching to the beat of a less transitory drummer. Because the timescale of the root chakra is so large, our personal actions and sense of cultural reality are adjusted to fit the broader timescale. Longevity becomes a concern. We may have trouble doing things that we feel will not endure.

Mars in Capricorn; on the right remembering side

The solar plexus is placed into the context of the inner root chakra. Our social identity is seen in the perspective of our inner sense of foundational structure. We attempt to make our own social awareness fit into the large-scale root chakra's perspective. The day-to-day workings of our social reality is seen through the lens of our own personal sense of destiny. We feel that we are a part of the overall flow of humanity.

We have a sense of the larger social structure's impact on our own social identity. Yet we have no real quarrel with the larger social structure, as we feel that our place within it is ultimately under our own control. We feel like we have personal control of our own social identity through our place within the larger cultural structure. This feeds a belief that destiny is personal and that the individual is a partner in the creation of the larger foundations of society.

Mars in Aquarius; on the left experiencing side

The solar plexus is placed into the context of the outer root chakra. Our personal social identity is seen in the perspective of external collective social foundations. There is an emphasis on the impact of the momentums of the human race on our personal social self-awareness. This means that we feel that our personal identity has to fit into the larger movement of humanity. At the same time, society's collective destiny feels like something that happens to us, rather than something that is created by us. There's a sense of our being at the mercy of impersonal outer forces. Our personal sense of destiny seems directed by the destiny of collective events.

We may actively disagree with the larger social structure, partly because we feel that our place within it is ultimately beyond our control. At it's best we demand a fair and just society that is built on solid foundations. At it's worst our complaints about the oppressive structures of society are purely a matter of self interest.

Mars in the Genital Chakra

With Mars in the genital chakra we seek to physically enact and experience our sense of personal identity. This gives our physical experiences an added social significance. It also gives our sensate experiences an added personal importance. Our sensate experiences help us to enact our sense of social identity. Our social identity is reflected through our reactions to our sensations and our choices of sensate experiences to have. Our sensate awareness is used to describe who we are to ourselves and to other people.

With Mars on the genital level we bring our cultural perspective into our physical experiences. If we feel we are a rebel, then we will try to experience things that are slightly wild, daring and rebellious. This could be a defiance of social rules and our engaging in risky behaviors. Or we may refuse to follow normal social etiquette. If we have no quarrel with our culture then we might try to experience our culture's perspective. We may wear the latest fashions, go to popular concerts, or sporting events as we follow the lead of the crowd.

Ultimately there is a need to tangibly experience both ourselves and our culture. Our sense of personal social identity is seen through our physical experiences.

Because the solar plexus is higher than the genital chakra, the solar plexus imposes assumptions which define how we should feel at the genital chakra. We create, and then follow, a set of culturally based assumptions that determine how we should feel about an experience before we actually have the experience. At the same time the genital chakra's sensate awareness interprets and redefines the solar plexus chakra's assumptions.

Problems arise if our self-definition that tells us that we do not like chocolate ice cream and yet our sensate experience of chocolate ice cream is extremely pleasurable.   The experience contradicts the assumptions of the solar plexus.   This can cause tension between our actual reactions and our social identity's demands.

Because the solar plexus has a broader frame of reference than the genital chakra, the lower genital chakra will try to believe what the solar plexus chakra says is true. It may even convince itself that it doesn't like the taste of that sneakily deceptive stuff, chocolate ice cream. But, while the genital chakra is naive, it usually does live in its experience.   Ultimately, if it really does like the taste of chocolate ice cream it will find it difficult to pretend to dislike it just to appease the solar plexus.

This doesn't mean that the solar plexus won't influence the opinions of the genital chakra. Because of the solar plexus's broader frame of reference it might tell the genital chakra "Even though chocolate ice-cream tastes good, it still isn't heathy for us to eat." Also, by deciding what experiences we will like as well, as what they mean, the solar plexus controls the experiences that we seek. This enables the solar plexus to narrow the actual experiences of the genital chakra according to it's desires which helps to reinforce what it considers to be true. In rare cases the solar plexus may actually shape the genital chakra's reaction to an experience so completely that our sensate experience follows the presumptions of the solar plexus rather than the actual sensate event. We see what we believe we should see, feel what we think we should feel.

When we try to enact the solar plexus's premises there will be some mistaken assumptions.   This is the problem of the involutionary process. Principles and ideals don't always accurately translate into reality. Some details are also going to be overlooked or denied.   Facts that disrupt prior assumptions will appear.   Also, because we are following our expectations, our experiences may not be quite as rich and full as they could be. But they will be safer.

Assuming the solar plexus doesn't contradict the actual experience of the genital chakra, there shouldn't be too many problems.

Mars in Sagittarius; on the right remembering side

The solar plexus's awareness is placed into the context of the inner genital chakra.   We try to shape how we react to our experiences according to our social identity. Our social identity is enacted by how we choose to internally respond to our sensate experiences. Our sensate experiences are felt to be something that we personally possess and create. There's a bit of a 'which came first, the chicken or the egg' quality. Our social perspective seeks to express itself through our tangible experiences. But our reactions to our tangible experiences are caused by us. Sometimes this means that we will try to seek out experiences that fit our sense of social identity and our culture's biases. In order to save face we may try to turn our own actual embarrassing reactions to our experiences into what we try to call the real us. There can be tension between who we want to be and who we are.

At it's best, we use our social identity to help us choose the best experiences we can allow ourselves to have. Both our own social identity and those of the people around us are respected while we all share the world of tangible experience. At it's worst, our social identity constrains us to a narrow set of experiences and an equally narrow set of interpretations of their meaning. Who we really are is suppressed.

Mars in Pisces; on the left experiencing side

The solar plexus's awareness is placed into the context of the outer genital chakra. We use our solar plexus's perspective to help us know how we feel about our sensate experiences. Our social identity is enacted through what we sensately choose to experience and how we react to the world around us. Even as we try to shape how we react according to our social self-definition., our sensate experiences seem to happen to us, rather than being something that we create and control. This means that we are reduced to liking or, disliking, accepting or denying the importance of an experience.

Our experiences, and our reactions to them, are seen as reflecting who we are on a cultural level. As we believe that our personal reactions reflect our society's values, our objective sensate awareness also becomes a means for us to see how our culture feels. We see the outer world of sensate experiences as a means of understanding our culture. At it's best, we basically agree with the assumptions of our culture and find guidance in it's beliefs. At it's worst. we disagree with the prevailing cultural attitudes and find ourselves in conflict with our culture.

Mars in the Solar Plexus Chakra

With Mars in the solar plexus chakra our sense of social identity doesn't place its awareness into the context of any other chakra. Therefore, the solar plexus becomes self-contained and our outer ego becomes self defining. It alone tells itself who and what it is. Within our chakric awareness there is no inhibiting factor. This allows our sense of social identity great fluidity and tenacity. The problem is that our outer ego doesn't have a context, or counterpoint by which to see itself. This makes for tremendous confidence on the one hand and a nagging sense of insecurity on the other.

Indeed, our self awareness may be a bit hazy due to lack of contrasting context. In order to become more visible to ourselves, we may act in an exaggerated manner. The need to define ourselves may cause us to be overly dramatic. This can lead to strong self assertiveness as the our social identity bluntly acts in order to see who and what it is.

At the same time there may be a sort of fascination with ourselves. We may simply enjoy watching ourselves be ourselves. The ego, being its own boss, may let itself get away with everything. This can lead to a strong self-absorption. It is like someone who is always keeping an eye on themselves in the mirror as they mingle with the other guests at a party. This can be disconcerting to the other guests who would like some of the attention to also be focused on them. But ultimately we all need to see ourselves in order to know who we are. With this placement we the need is even stronger and so we are more assertive and self enacting than most people are. We explore ourselves as we explore our world.

As there's an underlying curiosity about who we really are, there's also a strong concern with self creation. This can become a restless need to do things. At the same time there is also an underlying insecurity about whether or not we really are here. So we may keep on trying to provide evidence of the reality of our own existence. This can lead to significant achievements as a person seeks to prove their existence to themselves. It can also lead to despair as we feel that all our actions are hollow and in vain. We can become callous and cynical.

The ego can act to assert itself quite vigorously. It is capable of cruelty, as well as kindness. With this placement there is a tendency to manipulate the world around us. Sometimes this becomes a need to control either ourselves or our outer world. Sometimes our need to control involves deception, either of ourselves or of others. Reality is felt to be somewhat flexible and we try to shape it to suit our needs. While the solar plexus is capable of cunning, it is incapable of very complex thought. Yet it's schemes can be fairly intricate.

Mars in Scorpio; on the right remembering side

The solar plexus provides its own internal context of understanding. Our sense of social identity is felt to be something that we personally create. Who we are, and who we feel we should be, is considered to be under our own control. This means that we feel that we determine our own personal identity through our pattern of likes and dislikes and that we only choose to accept those cultural values that fit into our personal social identity. This means that our self-definition is somewhat autonomous and intractable.

Our social identity is considered to be self-created and there is a part of us that is always held aloof and separate from the external world. We feel like we are slightly beyond the reach of outer reality. The world doesn't define us. We define ourselves.

Mars in Aries; on the left experiencing side

The solar plexus provides its own outer context of understanding. Our self-awareness is seen in through the lens of our outer social identity. Who we are is considered to be a part of the larger social reality that we live in. There is a mutual interaction that defines both ourselves and our world. Our personal identity is the result of a give-and-take between ourselves and the world around us. There is a dynamic tension between how we define ourselves and the definition given to us by the world around us.

At the same time, our social identity is relatively direct and unselfconscious. There's a naturalness to who we feel we are, along with an expectation that the world around us will allow us to be and do whatever we require. We adjust and move through the external world just as naturally as a person in a pool displaces and moves through the water they swim in.

Mars in the Heart Chakra

Here the awareness of the solar plexus moves up to the heart. This means that our social awareness is seen in the context of our emotional perspective. This places the solar plexus chakra, which is the focal point of our outer reality, into the heart which is the focal point of our inner reality. Our social awareness augments our personal sense of emotional being.

The solar plexus's awareness becomes information for the heart's emotional awareness. We end up emotionally judging and interpreting the culture in which we live. For the heart this process of emotional interpretation is clothed in symbolism. Our culture is understood according to our inner desires and fears as seen through various personal symbols.

With this placement there is a tendency to create personally meaningful symbols within our outer cultural reality. There is also a tendency to romanticize elements of our cultural reality. Because the heart generalizes and universalizes how it feels, it will make our relationship to our culture's preferences seem broader and richer than they may factually be. Our social reality becomes a screen for our projection of personally evocative emotions and symbols.

Details of the culture, such as who wears makeup and under what circumstances, will become symbolically significant. Cultural symbols will also acquire personal significance. This can be an inner emotional attachment to the kind of vehicle we drive, the neighborhood we live in, the clothes we prefer to wear, and so on. All of these external signs of cultural values become absorbed and turned into symbols within our inner being. The outer cultural values are seen as substantiating our inner being.

The larger time frame of the heart allows it to see the awareness of the solar plexus in a more complex fashion. The solar plexus's concerns about our social position and its tentative belief in our personal durability is placed into the more enduring time frame of the heart. In some ways this is reassuring to the solar plexus. Although they both deal with establishing a sense of connection and belonging, we respond to the emotional symbols of the heart very differently than we do to the cultural symbols of the solar plexus. At the solar plexus our self definition is more sharply individual, even though we see ourselves as part of a group. At the heart our emotions generalize our self definition. We blur our sense of individual distinctiveness as we believe that how we feel is how everyone else would feel under the same circumstances.

Mars in Libra; on the right remembering side

When the solar plexus moves up to the inner heart, the more abstract and idealized emotional perspective of the heart provides the context of our social awareness. There's a tendency to see our social selves through rose tinted glasses. Because our heart's perspective is on the inside we feel that we have some control over our emotional assimilation of our solar plexus's awareness. At the same time, how our social reality impacts our emotional well-being becomes a concern. We internalize our social reality and turn our cultural values into personal symbols. We use our emotional reactions to social issues as a means of inner self definition.

While our social reality provides some facts, our personal emotional associations reshape those facts into emotionally charged personal symbols. At it's best our social reality is made more personally meaningful. We feel emotionally connected to our social environment. At it's worst, we may overly idealize our social surroundings. Our emotionally tinted glasses may make it difficult for us to deal with either our own social identity or our cultural surroundings realistically. We react to our emotional attitudes rather than to the world around us. We are emotionally out of sync with our environment.

Mars in Taurus; on the left experiencing side

Our outer emotional awareness provides the context of our social awareness. Our solar plexus awareness provides the facts, while our heart provides the context. At the same time, we tend to connect our emotions to external objects or situations. Because it is on the outer side, our emotional reactions to our social environment seems to happen to us.

We emotionally react to what happens to our solar plexus. These emotional reactions seems like the inevitable result of external events. The world forces us to feel to feel the way we do. There is a tendency to try to idealize our solar plexus's awareness, but the idealization remains external in its focus. Our emotions help us know who we are in terms of the outer world. Because our emotional state is felt to be so intimately connected to our outer connections, we feel that by changing our outer social circumstances we can change our emotional state.

At it's best, we enrich our social reality with added emotional meaning. The outer world feels richer and more connected to us. We feel that we are in harmony with our social reality. At it's worst, the social environment as an objective fact becomes emotionally oppressive. We end up feeling emotionally coerced.

Mars in the Throat Chakra

When the throat provides the context of the solar plexus's awareness, our mind is concerned with understanding our social awareness. The throat uses it's abstract conceptual awareness to analyze the far more tangible realm of the solar plexus. The throat and the solar plexus are actually similar in style. They both stand slightly aloof from the actualities that they seek to understand. The solar plexus tries to order and fathom the genital chakra's experiences. The throat tries to understand pretty much everything.

The throat and the solar plexus are also both very competitive. The throat is protective of its understanding, just as the solar plexus is protective of its social position. The solar plexus is protective of the objects and social affinities it uses to define itself. The throat is protective of the ideas which it also uses to define its reality. Just as the solar plexus is very aware of it's relative position, the throat is also very aware of its place in the larger scheme.

Both the throat and the solar plexus are able to remain slightly aloof from the realities which they deal with. They are also both the home of a distinctive sense of "I." The throat is the inner sense of "I," while the solar plexus is the outer sense of "I." The main difference is that the mind can use its abstract logical understanding to know things in a much broader framework than the solar plexus can. Yet their similarity of style makes it easy for the throat to understand the solar plexus.

When the solar plexus moves up to throat it, it influences what the throat thinks about. But the throat retains it's highly logical rational mode of understanding. The throat does not become just an abstract solar plexus. Still, we do become concerned with the impact our social environment has on how we think. This can make the throat more ware and self-conscious.

Mars in Virgo; on the right remembering side

The awareness of the solar plexus is seen in the context of the inner throat chakra. Our personal social identity and our cultural factors are intellectually analyzed and understood. We subject our social situation to the ideals our own inner understanding. The throat chakra inspects the interconnections of the solar plexus, looking for what it can change. The inner perspective gives us a sense of our being in control of the ideas which we use to understand our social reality. We also feel that through our intellectual understanding we can manipulate our relatively passive social reality. The reshaping of our social identity according to our own higher standards becomes our goal.

Being on the right inner side makes our social situation feel like it is something that is under our control. We use our ideas to define what society means, if only to us. This enables us to feel slightly detached from the social realm. We feel as if we are looking down on the concerns of the solar plexus, we observe and analyze. By changing our concepts, we feel we change our social reality,

Mars in Gemini; on the left experiencing side

The awareness of the solar plexus is seen in the context of the outer throat chakra. Our social awareness is analyzed and understood through the intellectual concepts of the throat chakra. The external perspective means that we tend to use the ideas that are in social circulation around us to help our understanding. At the same time, we also tend to see both our intellectual and social circumstances as something external to us, as something which happens around us and to us, rather than as being something that is basically within us.

As we use our mind to understand and define our social reality we find that our intellectual understanding helps us to manipulate our social situation. It enables us to know what parts of our environment we need to change in order to shift our social reality. Because we are externally focused we are concerned with the social dynamics involved. We try to understand what the impact of what we think and do has on other people.

Mars in the Brow Chakra

With this upward move, the solar plexus chakra places its awareness into a preconscious, intuitive context. The brow chakra takes the facts of the solar plexus and uses it's intuition to elaborate on them. The brow then makes choices based on intuitive perceptions that are beyond the understanding of the solar plexus. Our tangible social reality becomes the starting point. Our inner, abstract (or spiritual) will integrates our social reality with the purposes of inner self.

This makes the brow chakra aware of how the solar plexus fits into the fluid swirl of possibilities that the brow perceives. This is a study in contrasts, because to the brow everything is fluid and filled with possibility, while the solar plexus lives in a much more structured and inflexible environment.

The solar plexus's impact focuses the brow chakra on our social reality. The brow chakra then uses its intuition to "see" the nuances and ramifications of the choices available to the solar plexus. Because the brow sees far more than the solar plexus's self-definition, the brow may not be all that gentle with the solar plexus. This may confuse and upset our social awareness.

The brow uses its like or dislike reactions to make choices in the realm of the solar plexus. Because the brow is a preconscious intuitive awareness these judgements, and the reasons behind them, may not make sense to the solar plexus. The brow is abstract and arational, whereas the solar plexus is tangible and ploddingly semi-logical, so it is difficult for the solar plexus to understand the reasons behind the brow chakra's decisions. Because the brow chakra is essentially dealing with a form of perception, there may not even be any reasons that can be given for it's choices. The brow is extremely individualistic and it directly perceives things and so it simply knows what it knows. In contrast, the solar plexus uses more of a herd mentality to understand things.

Mars in Leo; on the right remembering side

With this placement the awareness of the solar plexus is placed into the context of the brow chakra. The brow chakra with its intuitive understanding deals with the issues and concerns of our solar plexus. There will be flashes of intuitive insight as to what to do about our social situation that we cannot quite understand. At the same time we feel confident in our intuition's knowledge.

We have a fairly broad sense of the context of our social identity. We use our own personal sense of who we are at a rather deep level to help us shape who we wish to be on a social level.

Problems may occur when our solar plexus is unable to trust our intuitive awareness. Because the brow is so much higher, larger and more abstract than the solar plexus, our brow chakra's attitude toward the solar plexus may be aloof and condescending. Even if this is true, it is a difficult pill for the solar plexus to swallow. The solar plexus has to suspend it's disbelief and go along for the ride.

Mars in the Crown Chakra

When Mars moves the solar plexus to the crown chakra, it takes a very self-conscious social awareness and places it into a highly abstract preconscious context. The scope of the solar plexus is extremely limited compared to the crown. The crown deals with abstract patterns and "the Big Picture." This enables the crown chakra to understand the awareness of the solar plexus very easily. At the same time, if the solar plexus's feels safe it becomes more flexible when placed into the crown. It becomes a bit more fluid. Even so, the solar plexus isn't able to see the large scale patterns that control our social interactions the way that the crown chakra does. While the crown is able to understand the solar plexus, the solar plexus is bewildered by the crown's awareness.

Mars in the crown is concerned with how our personal social reality fits into the larger configuration of our life. This can lead to both self-aggrandizement and self belittlement. We might believe that we really are the center of the universe, which the solar plexus already tends to feel is true. The crown tends to extreme idealism and seeks perfect order and harmony. While this sense of perfect harmony is relatively easy to see on the very abstract levels that the crown perceives, a sense of everything being in perfect harmonious order is extremely difficult for the solar plexus to see within the day to day conflicts that continuously surround it.

Because the crown sees things on such a large scale, when it chooses to change things on the solar plexus level, the solar plexus is often completely baffled. This happens merely by taking the awareness of the solar plexus and putting it into a completely different, novel context. This changes what the solar plexus thought it knew completely and the solar plexus usually doesn't handle such changes very well. Meanwhile, to the crown chakra everything has become much more accurately described. Ultimately, due to the huge difference in scale, the solar plexus ends up having to trust the crown chakra. Considering the control issues that the solar plexus has, this is not an easy thing for it to do.

When the solar plexus moves to the crown, the issues of the solar plexus become more important to the crown chakra. The crown chakra becomes more concerned with our personal time and space identity. This can help anchor the crown chakra a bit more in 'reality'. The crown chakra becomes more directly aware of the tangible situation that the solar plexus lives in.

When the crown takes the reality of the solar plexus and abstracts it - or "spiritualizes" it - the tangible world's abundance of desires may get lost in the swirl of larger, grander things. So long as our actual physical identity is transcended and placed into a larger, richer context instead of brutally shoved aside, this is fine. Also, so long as the solar plexus is able to keep its balance within the huge scale of the crown chakra, everything will be all right. Ultimately the "ego" of the solar plexus isn't so much destroyed by the crown's personally transcendent perspective as it is awestruck by it. Then, when the solar plexus realizes it is in a much larger context than it can even begin to fathom, it quite naturally and peacefully steps aside.

Mars in Cancer; on the right remembering side

When the awareness of the solar plexus is placed into the vast perspective of the crown chakra we end up feeling somewhat detached from our more concrete personal concerns. The crown uses it's abstract awareness to see the larger context of our social reality. There is also a desire to change our social circumstances in keeping with our abstract ideals. Despite our seeing the injustices that happen to us and all around us, we may decide that in the larger scheme of things many of our solar plexus's concerns are relatively unimportant.

With this placement we presume that there is some sort of larger abstract pattern behind our day to day lives. There is a sense of a bigger picture lying behind our social reality and that we need to discover what it is so that we can help it unfold. We may even feel that our social reality is being supported by the divine. We may seek guidance in various ways (through prayer, meaningful coincidences, and so on) to help us navigate our way in our day to day lives.

At the same time there is an uneasy feeling that who we are may not really matter in the "Big Picture". The vastness of the whole is beyond our ability to comprehend, so how can we deal with it? We have the feeling that we are out of our personal depth. We are a small ship floating on a vast ocean.

Therefore when we attempt to place our social reality within a larger context we look for an abstract pattern that unites all the divergent parts of our social reality. We try to order the chaos and thereby discover what we truly are and what we should do.

Venus: Heart, point of self fulfillment; glyph- ♀

With the heart chakra and Venus we reach the midpoint of our inner chakric awareness. In classic astrology Venus, as the goddess of love, rules the emotions. At the heart we emotionally invest ourselves in our inner and outer worlds. We place our inner ideals onto outer objects. Our inner desires and attitudes are projected outward onto the world around us. When we emotionally connect our inner being with our outer reality, external objects take on personally symbolic meaning.

Venus was the goddess of love and beauty. Venus is appropriate to the heart because like Venus the heart also idealizes and romanticizes. Also, Venus created a magnetic attraction that drew what she desired to her. Like Venus, the heart is also magnetic. The heart uses attraction to draw to itself what it desires. This is in strong contrast to the solar plexus (Mars) which actively reaches out and attempts to grab what it wants. The heart (Venus) passively pulls what it desires to itself.

Because the heart is passive it requires the active response of the object of it's desire in order for it's wishes to be fulfilled. The heart can only bait the trap. The desired object must do something in order to actually get caught. In reality, none of our chakra's is an island and the standard distinctions of active and passive are a bit misleading. The heart is quite assertive in it's own way.

As well as drawing, at the heart we are also drawn ourselves. What our inner wishes desire may not be realistic, but that really doesn't matter to the heart. Our hopes and dreams are what matters. The heart takes the tangible outer world and connects it to our abstract inner world. Our ideals become our notions of what would be the perfect tangible reality. At the same time, our inner ideals exist in a place above and beyond tangible reality. Our emotional being's attachments are the substance of our soul.

Venus is associated with the libido, or an internal psychic energy that unites us to the world around us. This is most easily seen through the spell of sexual attraction. In a sense, the heart chakra creates a glue which uses our emotional ideals, desires and feelings as a binding agent. It is through our inner desires and ideals that we are drawn out of ourselves and we voluntarily enter into the external world.

The heart helps us to give an outer tangible form to who we are internally. Our relationships to what we desire affects how we feel. If we feel our desires are unattainable, that happiness isn't possible, then we may become ill.

The context of our emotions is shown by Venus. Where the planet Venus is placed tells us how we will see with our emotions. If our emotional state is not dealt with adequately, we may become withdrawn and emotionally out of balance, or perhaps even physically ill. Our emotions are the key to our physical well being. It is through the heart that we ensoul ourselves in the flesh.

The heart sees our outer physical state as a symbol of how we emotionally feel. The heart is grounded enough in the abstract realms to believe that there is personal continuity after death. So, to the heart all aspects of our being serves as a symbolically expressive canvas. When viewed from a purely pragmatic, 'realistic' perspective the heart's perspective of tangible reality as a form of pure inner self expression can make the heart's actions appear quite irrational.

The chakric placement of the planet Venus shows the context of our emotional awareness. It reveals the chakra through which we will most directly seek to understand and express our emotional reality.

Venus in the Root Chakra

The heart is interpreted through the lens of our sense of physical structures and destiny. Our emotional being is submerged in the tides of fate. We may feel that our personal desires are thwarted by our circumstances. At the root, our heart is felt to be subject to broad transpersonal momentums. These large scale movements can both fulfill our desires and frustrate them at the same time. Our emotional awareness becomes connected to our personal destiny which is placed into te context of the general human condition by our own personal momentums.

The root is a very serious chakra. It is concerned with durability. It does not do things that are lighthearted and pleasurable only for a passing moment. This is in contrast to the heart chakra which is moody, changeable and much more involved with the whimsical nature of the moment. When Venus is in the root the light and playful quality of the heart is hampered by the ponderousness of the root. Normally the heart moves fairly quickly, but the root obstructs it's fluidity. While the heart has some concern for the consequences of it's desires, it usually just wants what it wants. The root is very aware of consequences. When Venus is in the root, the heart is overshadowed by the all the things that must first be taken care of before it's desires can be properly addressed.

For example, for the root romantic love has to be more than just a passing means of self-expression. It needs to be connected in some way to our destiny. This greatly narrows the circumstances where romantic love is considered appropriate. How long a desired situation will last, the overall impact it has on other people and so on, becomes the measure of a romantic liaison's value.

With this placement the problem isn't so much becoming more spontaneous (although it may feel that way at times), as it is anchoring our emotional connections. Only when the root feels that it is actually fulfilling its destiny will it allow itself to become playful. This means that when Venus is in the root the heart needs be invested in something with a fairly large scope. The root demands that we feel emotionally connected to something deep. This doesn't necessarily mean doing great things ourselves, but of our feeling personally connected to something that helps us to flow with the broad sweep of our deeper being.

The root placement of Venus will make us less concerned with our more superficial desires. The root will also stabilize the heart's tendency toward mood swings. Because of the large scope of the root's time frame, many of our more momentary desires will be disregarded as being trivial. At the same time some of our deeper desires may take on a fated quality. For example "I would still be with the love of my life if only this stupid war hadn't torn us apart. I wonder if I'll ever see them again?" fits this chakric placement.

Venus in Capricorn; on the right remembering side

With Venus on the inner directed side of the root chakra, we find ourselves seeking enduring emotional foundations. The transpersonal awareness of the root demands that we emotionally invest ourselves in enduring things. Usually this means that we've connected our emotional being to something larger than ourselves. Because it is on the inner side we feel that the cultural and physical foundations that the root connects us to are emotionally a part of us. Because Capricorn is on the inside of the root chakra we feel that we are personally involved in the creation of the foundational structures of the root chakra. We see how the needs and actions of many individuals help to create the group structures that we all use. We also see this group activity as being helpful to us in our own personal fulfillment.

When we run into what we consider to be our destiny, or fate, it feels like something that we have somehow helped to create. If we feel that we are suffering our fate, then at least it is our karma, or what we've made for ourselves. The inner side of the root gives us a sense of our being an active participant in the affairs of the root.

This personal quality helps us to feel a sense of emotional fulfillment when we deal with the foundational structures of the root. For example, when we go to court we are content with the structure and aspirations of the judicial system. While the fact that our court's may be corrupted by money and political pressures doesn't meet our heart's ideals of justice, but the social structure is still impressive with all it's judges, lawyers, and law enforcement divisions which are seen as necessary and basically useful.

Venus in Aquarius; on the left experiencing side

With Venus on the outer directed side of the root chakra, the heart chakra sees itself in the context of the root chakra's external large-scale momentums and structures. The heart chakra places the highly personal whimsicalness of the heart into the somber and serious context of the root. Although the heart seeks ideal forms of expression, the actual objects that the heart attaches its ideals to tend to be fleeting, at least from the root's perspective. The root makes us align ourselves with the deeper aspects of humanity.

This leads to our having a sense of an outer personal emotional destiny. Our personal fate is connected to the momentums of the larger group. We have a tendency to feel that our destiny is an impersonal force that overtakes us. We may feel empowered by what we see as our large scale destiny or we may feel victimized by it. In either case, our destiny feels like it is the creation of something external to us.

This impersonal external quality thwarts our sense of emotional fulfillment when we deal with the foundational structures of the root. For example, when we go to court we tend to feel angered by the structure of the judicial system with all it's judges, lawyers, and law enforcement divisions acting without any real awareness of us as an actual individual person. We don't see the court as serving justice, but as mechanically enacting it's own heartless procedures and rules, assuming it isn't merely corrupt.

Venus in the Genital Chakra

When Venus moves the heart down into the genital chakra, our emotional attitudes are transferred to our sensate awareness. The higher chakra provides the general principles that orders the awareness of the lower chakra, therefore the heart feeling's influences our genital chakra's reaction to its sensate experiences. These feelings do not create the actual experiences of the genital chakra, but they tint our reactions. The heart also tries to influence the genital chakra's choices of as to which experiences to have as it seeks to have our sensate experiences embody the feelings of the heart. In this way the genital chakra expresses the heart.

If the heart feels fulfilled by love songs, then the genital chakra will seek them. The genital chakra will see the music as sounds and rhythms, as something that it directly experiences. The heart will see the music as a symbolic representation of it's own feelings. To carry this example further, a problem can arise when the heart likes music that the genital chakra doesn't like. The higher heart chakra may attempt to tell the lower genital chakra that the genital chakra actually does like the music. This confuses the genital chakra. Also the genital chakra is unable to understand the emotional reasons as to why the heart likes the music. To the heart, the music may remind them of a person they once loved. The genital chakra is more direct in its sensate experience causes it to merely react to the rhythms and sounds.

While the heart adds it's emotional nuances to the experiences that the genital chakra has, the genital chakra still remains fairly naive. If chocolate doughnuts have bad symbolic associations to the heart, then the genital chakra may not enjoy eating them as much as it would have. Suppose that an old romantic interest loved chocolate donuts and the breakup was very painful. Now whenever we see or eat a chocolate donut it reminds us of them and it hurts us emotionally. To the genital chakra the chocolate donut stills tastes the same, but it reminds the heart of something it'd like to forget. Meanwhile, to the genital chakra a chocolate doughnut is still just good tasting food, not the emotionally charged symbol that it is to the heart.

With Venus in the genital chakra, some of the drama of the heart will seep into the experiences of the genital chakra. Our experiences will feel more intense. We will more readily really love or hate a sensate experience, rather that merely like it or dislike it.

Venus in Sagittarius; on the right remembering side

With Venus in Sagittarius we find that the emotionally symbolic meanings of the heart are expressed and felt through our physical experiences. Because the heart sees things as primarily having symbolic significance, our physical experiences become the vehicles of our own inner symbolism. Our sensate experiences feel like they resonate within us. They reveal as much about us as they reveal about our external world. Through our sensate experiences we emotionally reaffirm ourselves.

Sensate reality becomes a way of discovering who we are, rather than just the experience of the outside world. Sensation becomes a foil for our inner sense of symbolic meaning. A stormy sky is seen as expressing our own sense of inner turmoil, rather than merely being a random meteorological event. Our actual sensate experiences may be obscured by our own beliefs about their emotional significance. With this placement our reactions to our sensate experiences matter to us more than the experience itself.

Because it in on the inner side we feel that the symbols and emotional meanings of our experiences are something that we create. This means that by choosing the right sensate experiences we believe that we have control over what we emotionally feel. This control may be in the experiences we choose. Or it may only be in how we interpret our experiences. But we emphasize our emotional command of our sensate situation.

Venus in Pisces; on the left experiencing side

With Venus in Pisces we find symbolic meaning in our experiences within the objective world around us. There is a sense of emotional depth permeating our outer experiences. This gives our genital chakra's sensate experiences a more personalized meaning. Our sensate experiences become poetic as they reveal things that we emotionally connect ourselves to in our outer world. Events don't just happened, they symbolically express something about the world. A stormy sky is seen as symbolically describing the mood of the outer situation. It may be seen as expressing an underlying conflict between heaven and earth. Our sensate experiences are felt to symbolically describe the emotions of the forces active within our environment.

Because this placement is on the outside, the experiences and emotions that they evoke feel like they happen to us. We are not discovering ourselves, we are discovering the outer world. The emotional symbols that we see and the feelings that they cause reflect external events. The creative dynamic behind these events belongs to the outer world. We get swept up in our external sensate experiences. We feel like we are along for the ride.

Because we are focused on the external nature of our sensate experience, the impact of our heart on our sensate experiences is less obvious than it is on the inner side. But by moving down to the genital chakra the heart does help to shape our sensate reality. This can be a romanticized fascination with a particular object or experience. Or perhaps a tendency to emphasize one emotional mood above all others. The point is that we are so busy being wrapped up in our emotionally charged sensate reactions that we don't see how we may be producing them.

Because we are quietly projecting our own emotions and symbols onto things, we don't feel in control of the process. Ultimately, we believe that our emotional reactions are provoked by our sensate experiences. We presume that anyone else would naturally react the same way we do.

Because of this placement there is a strong emphasis on the our emotional responses to our sensate experiences. There is a tendency to bask in our emotional responses. To draw out how they make us feel and revel in the pleasure or suffering that the world 'forces' onto us.

Venus in the Solar Plexus Chakra

The heart is placed into the context of our social awareness. This adds a strong tint of personal symbolism to our sense of social identity. Our emotional awareness is seen through the lens of our social perspective.

The heart, with its swirl of emotional associations and desires is added to the solar plexus with it's swirl of social issues. Our social awareness is pressed into embodying our emotional awareness. For example, when the heart hears a song that used to be 'our song' all the personal symbolic associations we have with the relationship become intertwined with the song. At the same time the music is a cultural symbol that we associate with the social events of the music's era. While the heart may think 'this used to be our song' as it hears a song and remembers a pleasant romantic involvement, the same song may remind the solar plexus how 'Those were really rough times. Money was scarce. Everyone was barely scrapping by.'

Because the heart is higher than the solar plexus, the solar plexus will not fully understand the reasons for the heart's feelings about certain things. Why something has the symbolic significance to the heart that is does is beyond the grasp of the solar plexus. The heart may associate eating hot oatmeal for breakfast with being nourished by our mother. Meanwhile the solar plexus may associate eating hot oatmeal for breakfast with being poor. This difference in meaning can become a problem. For the heart, the personal emotional meaning is more significant. (The oatmeal as a symbol of maternal love and nurture.) For the solar plexus the dimension social is more significant. (The oatmeal as a symbol of the crushing poverty of our childhood.)

The romanticism of the heart will transform the tangible facts of the solar plexus into something more ideal. Meanwhile, the solar plexus also has its own preferences for what the facts should mean. Each of these chakras has a tendency to dress things up to suit their wishes. When we combine these two chakras the danger of slipping away from reality into fantasy is heightened. The heart adds its need for personal meaning to the solar plexus's need for social position. Due to its idealistic nature the heart will add its inner ideals to the solar plexus's social yearnings. It may be difficult for us to stick to the facts.

The heart uses romantic idealizations to connect our inner being to the outer world. The heart is very possessive of it's symbolic meanings. This combination can make for a very jealous nature as the solar plexus acts to protect the heart's emotional investments.

The heart is very possessive. Especially when the symbolic object feels necessary for us to maintain our emotional cohesion. This happens when we have a strong emotional investment in someone or something. ("I can't live without you.")

The solar plexus is also extremely possessive. The solar plexus will fight to protect its territory. Due to the placement of the heart into the solar plexus, the solar plexus sees the heart's emotional connections as something that it possesses.

The two chakras have very different definitions of love. For the heart, love can be an abstract inner sense of connection. This means that the heart can release it's tangible ties to what it loves as an act of self sacrifice and still internally feel emotionally connected. The solar plexus is much more tangible. The solar plexus usually tries to physically possess what it loves. Unlike the heart, the solar plexus will rarely willingly let go of anything.

Venus in Scorpio; on the right remembering side

With this placement our emotions are seen in the context of our inner social awareness. Our emotional state becomes part of our social identity. Our social self-definition is influenced by the heart's associations and feelings. This creates an arational self-concept.

Our sense of personal identity is based more on our internal self-definition than it is our external physical circumstances. We use our overall emotional tone to help create our social self image. Because Venus is on the inner side we feel that we create our own social identity according to our emotional nature.

Because this is on the internal side of the solar plexus, the emotional connections are felt to be created by us. We see how our emotional state helps to create our social reality. Our social circumstances are shaped by how we feel. Therefore we believe that in order to change our social circumstances we must first change our emotional state. We believe that an inner change in our emotional awareness will be mirrored by a change in our external social situation.

As the heart moves down into the solar plexus we tend to romanticize both our desires and our social position. This may create some problems when our emotional self image conflicts with our social reality. This may cause us to try to redefine our social reality so that it will align with our emotional self image. Also we may deceive ourselves about our motives or the impact of our emotions on our social acts. Because we wish to feel good about ourselves we may not admit to some of our more blatantly irrational or self serving motivations.

This placement allows us some latitude in our emotional expression. We are less likely to conform to society's emotional constraints because we are in touch with how we actually feel. But our emotions may cause us to behave inappropriately on a social level at times. We may also be a bit defensive about our feelings. Because we use our emotions to define ourselves socially, we may stubbornly cling to internal feelings that conflict with our outer circumstances. We believe cannot give up how we feel without giving up a part of ourselves. Our solar plexus may end up blindly defending our emotionally held attitudes and beliefs.

Venus in Aries; on the left experiencing side

With this placement our emotions are seen in the context of our outer social identity. Our outer social awareness is impacted by our heart's associative process. Our emotional state becomes part of our external social self definition. This produces a social reality that feels intimately connected to us.

Because this is on the external side of the solar plexus, our emotions are seen as directly responding to the impact of the external world. Our emotions are seen as a result of our circumstances, not as the creator of them. Therefore if we wish to change our emotional state we believe that we must first change our outer social circumstances.

We are largely unaware of the impact that our emotionally tinted world view has on our social awareness. While our emotional tone to helps to define our overall social reality, we believe that we are merely reacting to the way the world actually is. We do not see how our emotions may be pulling the strings behind the scenes and so causing things to happen to us, or to feel a certain way.

We tend to romanticize our social reality in ways that make it conform to how we emotionally feel. This could be our always seeing the silver lining. Or we could always see how bad things are. Our outer circumstances are tinted by our emotions.

This placement means that we are less likely to conform to society's emotional constraints because our own feelings will come first. Problems may arise when our emotional tone does not comply with our outer social reality. Because we use our emotions to define ourselves socially, we may stubbornly cling to feelings that conflict with our outer circumstances. We believe that we cannot give up our feelings without giving up ourselves and so our emotions may cause us to behave inappropriately.

Venus in the Heart Chakra

With Venus in the heart chakra our emotional awareness does not move to another chakra. Our emotions become more isolated and self-contained. We think that we feel the way we do emotionally because that's the just the way it is. When our emotional reactions get going, they seem to move all by themselves. We end up emotionally reacting to our emotional reactions. We have to wait for our heart's process to come to rest all by itself. On the positive side, this gives our emotions a great deal of depth. On the negative side it makes it more difficult for us to place our emotions into a context. They seem to float on their own.

Our emotions will try to provide their own context. But this is like saying that you love someone because you love them. Due to the lack of context we know that we feel something but we do not fully know why we feel that something. The heart also ends up feeling its emotions without any sense of control over them. We may come to believe that our emotions simply happen. Our emotions are like the ocean: lots of varying surface turbulence, lots of undercurrents, and varying depths. The heart can only test these emotions by their power, by how deeply and completely we feel them.

The heart uses symbolic meanings to understand things. The heart chakra tries to use a string of associations, or a string of symbols, to try to increase its understanding of how it feels. So the heart may follow a line of symbolic associations until it comes up with what it feels is the ultimate cause of its emotional state. The process is similar to using one dream to interpret another dream. It may work, but it is very difficult to be sure of what things mean.

Suppose that we really love the taste of a chocolate milkshake we're eating because it reminds us of our childhood. So we go to the old neighborhood, where we remember an old jacket we used to wear. Then we go to a thrift store looking for our old jacket, where we find a shirt that reminds us of someone we knew... and so on. Eventually we may gain additional insight into of our love of milkshakes, but it will take a long time and most of what we discover will not be very helpful. More information doesn't necessarily make for greater understanding.

Paradoxically, because our emotions are so self-contained, they become more important to us. Our emotions stand out. They are purely themselves. This emotional intensity helps us know what we feel. Unfortunately, understanding our emotions will require a conscious effort to think about the context of our feelings. We will have to move beyond our natural tendency to feel our emotions and then feel them more deeply, and then even more intensely, and so on. We will have to look at the circumstances behind what we are feeling and try to see the impact the context has on our emotions. But in order to do this we will have to step outside of our natural emotional process, which is difficult to do.

Venus in Libra; on the right remembering side

With Venus on the inner side of the heart chakra our emotional state is felt to act on it's own. We believe that our emotions are the natural result of who we are. This gives our some autonomy to our emotional state. It also means that nothing counterbalances any of our emotional excesses. Once our emotions get rolling, it is hard for us to get them to stop. This can trap us in a narrow emotional niche. We get caught up in a particular set of feelings and their associated internal symbols and we have trouble breaking out of them. When we experience our emotional responses, we will replay the experience again and again in an attempt to dig deeper into the experience in order to understand it more fully.   While this will make our feelings more intense, unfortunately it may not increase our understanding.

There's an underlying sense that we are the creator of our own emotions. Because we see our emotions as something internal, we closely identify with our own emotional state.   They are our emotions. We made them and we feel them. We feel that we are the creators of our emotional awareness which gives us a sense of ultimate control over how we feel despite the tendency of our emotions to spiral off on themselves.

This means that we tend to emotionally react to our emotional reactions. Part of why this happens is that we enjoy the intensity of our emotions and the power of our feelings.   Our emotions are seen as being a deep self affirmation, as proof of who we are. Our heart's emotions are felt to be reflections of us, rather than mere reactions to our external world.

This means that our outer circumstances may serve as a screen on which we project our own emotional symbols and feelings. Occasionally our outer circumstances may get lost in the press of our inner emotions. This may mean that our inner emotional reality is out of sync with our outer circumstances.

Venus in Taurus; on the left experiencing side

With Venus on the outer side of the heart chakra we find that outer events and experiences provide their own context of emotional meaning.   We trust how we react to the world around us.   This enables us to be deeply involved with how external objects and events make us feel.

We are somewhat emotionally naive. We see ourselves as primarily reacting to our circumstances. We believe that the outer world generates our inner emotional state. Because our emotions feel like they're created by our external circumstances, our emotions feel like they have been thrust onto us. This can lead to our feeling victimized by our own emotional state.

When objects become emotionally charged with symbolic meanings it is because that is simply the way they are. While these symbols are actually our own creation, we are unaware of our role in making them.   Since our emotions are unable to step outside themselves for a fresh perspective, we have difficulty understanding the impact of the context of our emotions.

We believe that if we become emotionally frustrated then it is due to our outer circumstances. This means that we believe that in order to change our emotional state we must change our outer circumstances. If this doesn't work, then we are stuck. We are unable to see how our inner emotional pattern both chooses and interprets our outer circumstances.

Venus in the Throat Chakra

Venus places the heart chakra's emotional awareness into the throat chakra's perspective. The mind is used to understand the emotions. The associations and reactions of the heart chakra, which are based on personal ideals, are seen in light of the throat chakra's more nuanced conceptual structures. The intellect's reasoning process is used to analyze our heart's feelings and associations. This gives us a better grasp on why we have the emotional reactions that we have. The mind enables us to move beyond the limitations of the heart's symbolic association process.

When our mind receives the awareness of the heart it takes on some of the heart's concerns. Our thinking focuses on our emotional reality while maintaining an intellectual detachment. Although we think about our emotions, we do not necessarily get caught up in them. Our emotions are analyzed in multiple ways, not just in ever lengthening strings of symbolic associations or increasing emotional intesity. As we understand our heart's awareness we see how we can change our emotions by changing either our sense of what things mean, or our circumstances. As our intellectual understanding of our emotional symbol system grows, so does our ability to deal with our emotions. We are able to shift our emotional paradigm.

At the same time, the heart adds its sensibilities to the throat. The heart gives our throat a greater aesthetic awareness. Our throat more deeply appreciates the simple elegance of a nice concept. The mind remains analytical, but it is softened a bit and is less detached.

Venus in Virgo; on the right remembering side

Here our emotions are placed into the inner subjective side of our mind. We use our mind to understand our emotions. Ultimately, our emotions become data for the mind. We logically analyze our emotions and seek the underlying causes of the heart's awareness. We become slightly detached from our emotional state while we rationally investigate how our emotions work.

This placement of Venus can enable us to acquire a fairly detailed understanding of our emotions. Because the right side of the chakras is concerned with sustaining our inner sense of who we are, our intellectual understanding of our emotions helps refine our sense of self. Because of the nature of the throat, these emotional self definitions can become extremely detailed. This can make our inner sense of self hinge on some minor emotional details. It can also allow us to understand why some minor detail has such a strong emotional impact on us. We believe that we must change ourselves if we wish to change how we feel emotionally.

Ultimately, we may find the intellectual process of understanding our emotions as intriguing as the emotions themselves. We strive to create a full, detailed understanding. We feel that the concepts that we use to understand our emotions are primarily our own creation. We also tend to see our heart's awareness as being somewhat personal and unique. Our understanding of our emotions is felt to be our own creation right down to the last necessary detail.

Venus in Gemini; on the left experiencing side

With Venus on the objective side we place our emotions into an externally focused intellectual context. Our emotional state is seen as interacting with our environment. We notice how our external situation shapes our emotions. Our external world shapes our emotions and then our emotions help shape our external world. We use our intellect to analyze and understand the various external relationships that are involved. The ideas that we use to analyze our emotions are taken from our intellectual environment.

Because our mind is able to detach itself from our emotional state, our emotions are viewed primarily as data. Our minds are able to analyze our various emotional situations without becoming enmeshed in them. This provides us with some sense of emotional freedom. It also enables us to look at situations in greater depth. Details become more significant as we refine our analysis. Often fairly complex situations will be reduced to a few important relationships. By understanding these relationships we feel that we can control both the outer situation and our own emotions. Although our emotions are felt as being inside us, our emotions tell us about the world we live in. We believe that we must change our circumstances if we wish to change how we feel emotionally.

We are aware of how similar our emotions are to the emotions of others. We tend to think that how we feel is how everyone else feels, too. The shared ideas that we use to understand our emotions helps us to feel closer to other people. Our emotional understanding creates yet another bridge between us and others.

Venus in the Brow Chakra

When Venus moves up to the brow chakra, our emotional awareness is placed into our intuitive perspective. When our emotions are added to the brow's awareness, our intuition rides on our emotional awareness. Our emotional symbols are placed into the brow's intuitive context. This makes the brow more concerned with how potential situations may emotionally affect us. The brow also tries to intuitively understand why we emotionally feel the way we do.

The brow is the steering wheel of our personal reality. Its choices set our course. With Venus in the brow our emotions influence the brow's choices. Yet, because the brow is concerned with things that are far more complex than the heart can understand, the heart may never fully understand the reasons behind the brow's choices.

The brow is primarily concerned with visualizing potentials and making choices on the basis of what it "sees" as probable. This places our emotions into a context that changes their significance. Comprehending our emotions helps diffuse their pressures. The vastness of the brow makes our emotional concerns less important. Oddly, by putting our emotions into our largest purely personal context they are actually more likely to be fulfilled.

Ultimately, the brow chooses and brings the heart along with it. But despite appearances, the brow's choices do not contradict the heart, but seek to fulfill it. The brow will tend to emphasize the abstract qualities of the heart more than it's concrete aspects. The heart is seen mostly as set of symbols, ideals and wishes, which become part of the reasons for the choices that the brow makes.

The main source of conflict is the brow's lean to the abstract. Due the abstract nature of the brow, it will focus on our heart's emotional symbols as abstract connections. Yet the heart can get extremely concrete and be very specific in what it desires. This can make the heart want a particular person who it feels fulfills it's romantic ideals. The brow may see that this particular person isn't going to work out romantically (for reasons that are beyond the understanding of the heart) and so the brow looks for someone else. This may not sit well with the heart which has a strong attraction to that one person. Unless the heart can learn to trust the brow, there may be serious resentment and discord.

Venus in Leo; on the right remembering side

When the heart chakra is placed in the context of the brow we only have an intuitive awareness of the larger context of our emotions. Intuitively, we are emotionally attracted to a situation, or we are repulsed by it. The lack of an external counterpoint makes our intuitive awareness lack clarity. Our main conscious awareness is reduced to having a hunch that we should do something or that we should not do it. We may have an intuitive sense that a great deal more is going on than we consciously comprehend. The problem becomes trusting our intuitive awareness. In order to trust our intuition it has to be a strong enough presence in our awareness that it feels real. We need to learn to tell when our intuition is truly speaking to us and when we are just telling ourselves what we want to hear. Not easy to do when our emotional desires are involved.

Of themselves our emotions are unable to do little more than tell us what we want. We use the brow's intuitive understanding to help us guide our emotional understanding. Usually this means that we vaguely feel that a situation is emotionally good or bad for us. There are scattered moments of clarity and understanding, but most of the time all we have are vague hunches. This makes it difficult for us to feel confident in our intuitions, although often we have little more to go on. When we are able to synchronize our emotional desires with our intuitive awareness this placement gives us tremendous emotional agility and fulfillment.

Venus in the Crown Chakra

When Venus is in the crown our emotions are placed into the context of our larger abstract pattern. This means our personal desires are placed in the context of something larger than just ourselves. Exactly what this context is depends on the desire and its circumstances. If we desire to drive down the street, then the larger context is our culture's rules of the highway. If we desire to fulfill our personal reason for living, then the context of our aspirations depends on our personal cosmology. We might see ourselves as fulfilling God's plan, or nature's plan, or humanity's needs.

The crown chakra adds our emotional awareness to its concerns. It uses our sense of abstract order to understand why we emotionally feel as we do. Our emotional awareness is placed into a preconscious intuitive awareness of purpose, or of a "divine plan" that then interprets our emotions.

The vast scope of the crown's abstract order reorients our personal emotional matrix. Our tendency toward emotional self absorption gives way to a less purely self focused outflank. Our personal symbols with their associated meanings and desires are put into a larger transpersonal context. The crown chakra's mystical, all-inclusive perspective transmutes the personal awareness of the heart chakra. The crown chakra uses our emotional awareness as information but is not particularly swayed by it. In the crown chakra's perspective the concerns of the heart are just one more piece of the puzzle. These concerns are not ignored, but they are not the foundation of our choices at the crown.

As our emotions become more abstracted they become more diffused in their focus. A bird's song may become the joyous singing of creation. We may end up feeling that we love everything. God is love. Or we may feel that God is a god of justice and righteous anger. We see the firm just hand of divine retribution in an tragic turn of fate. Actually, what we are really seeing is ourselves. Our own emotional nature is projected onto the larger abstract pattern by which we order our world.

The preconscious nature of the crown makes it difficult for us to understand the exactly what context our emotions are placed within. The crown sees a multitude of tightly integrated patterns of connection that we are unable to fully comprehend what we see. Our personal individual emotional connections are superseded by an amazing sense that everything is interwoven. Connection is seen to be the nature of the universe and exactly where our emotions fit in becomes hazy.

Venus in Cancer; on the right remembering side

When the heart chakra is placed into the crown we place our emotions into a large scale abstract context that can only be intuitively perceived. The crown seeks an integrating pattern that explains our emotions. This means that the crown tries to see our emotions within a transpersonal matrix that explains how we feel.

With Venus in the crown chakra the way that our emotions are ordered and understood can become more important than the actual emotions themselves. We find ourselves believing that an emotional state of affairs is either right or wrong for abstract ideal based reasons, rather than the purely personal ideal reasons at the heart chakra. Personal desire is trumped by abstract ideals.

Perhaps on looking at the rapid changes in our emotional state we may come to believe that our emotions are intrinsically capricious and on feeling our emotional pains and disappointments we go 'What else can you expect from our emotions?' Or we may take the same emotional pains and disappointments and try to see how to use them to transcend the limitations of our personal desires. This may mean that we believe that 'this moment of emotional pain will pass and it is a small price to pay for the latter benefits'. The crown may place our emotions into a context whose transpersonal concerns may deny the value of what we personally desire. The crown's concern with the Big Picture of our emotional situation enables it to interpret how we feel in a way that the emotions themselves cannot. Hopefully this knowledge comforts us.

Mercury: Throat, point of self expression; glyph- ☿

Mercury was the messenger of the Olympian gods. In classic astrology, Mercury rules communication and the mind. This fits the throat chakra quite well. Mercury and the throat define the world through abstractions that represent tangible things. The mind then takes it's symbols and manipulates various relationships between these symbols. These abstractions can be symbols such as words or numbers, or they can be concepts about how various things relate together.

The throat is the abstract mirror of the solar plexus. The solar plexus tangibly manipulates reality. Similarly, the throat intangibly manipulates reality. While the solar plexus is self-aware, it does not have the same degree of the ability to 'watch itself watching itself' that the throat has. In a sense, the throat is an "I" that sees itself.

Mercury does not use the same methods to get what it wants as Venus or Mars. Venus is magnetic, drawing to itself what it wants and it is passively assertive. Mars moves toward what it wants and is actively assertive. Mercury is much more subtle. Mercury thinks about a situation and does something here to make what it wants to have happen over there.

When classic astrology assigns a gender to these three planets Venus is female, Mars is male, and Mercury is sexually androgynous - it is both male and female. This implies some of the mind's qualities. The world of ideas, logic and reasoning acts in a manner that is both receptive and assertive. The mind listens to other ideas. It also speaks and gives voice to its own ideas. The mind requires either external (talking) or internal (thinking) communication and analysis to work effectively. The symbols that the mind uses to manipulate its ideas requires much the same kind of cultural agreement and cohesion that we find at the solar plexus. In a sense, both the solar plexus and the throat and manipulate culturally created and sustained realities.

Because the throat is one of the higher chakras, and it is the highest dichotomized conscious awareness that we have, it often acts in an involutionary manner. Usually, the throat's awareness moves down into a lower chakra. This means that the throat will often provide the abstract principles which direct the awareness of a lower chakra.

In ancient Greek mythology Mercury (or, as the Greeks called him, Hermes) was not associated with wisdom. Athena, who sprang out of the forehead of Zeus, was the goddess of wisdom. Our minds are intelligent and capable of understanding extraordinary things, but the intellect of itself is not wise in the broadest sense of the word. Our intellect has the same egocentric problems that the solar plexus has and they are both highly competitive. At the throat we like to think of ourselves as smarter than other people. Wisdom avoids such arrogance. The throat doesn't.

Mercury in the Root Chakra

Mercury rules the throat, which is our highest chakra that is active both internally and externally. (Although the root is active on both sides, it remains an unconscious awareness.) Normally in an involutionary motion the higher chakra would pattern the experience of the lower chakra. But because the root deals with transpersonal concrete structures, the root chakra actually has a larger scope of awareness than the throat. This can make us think that our ideas have to be able to match the depth of the root's awareness. Or we may feel that our concepts are engulfed by the needs and momentums of all humanity. Adding to our intellectual discomfort is that because the root chakra's awareness is unconscious, we cannot really see the process. Our mind merely knows that its concepts have been placed into the larger perspective of the root chakra. This nebulous quality makes our mind a bit tentative as we realize that we have to think in terms of the underlying structures that we stand upon.

Our thinking feels as though it needs to withstand the test of time. We try to deal with deep issues that are greater than just ourselves and that are beyond our purely personal interest. Because these deeper issues connect to unconscious threads of awareness, our mind sometimes feels as it is walking down a dark path and it occasionally steps off into thin air. It is difficult for our mind to relax and trust the root. At the same time, our mind is sharpened and prodded by the root. At best, our thinking may become honed by the call to deepen our understanding. We have an increased awareness due to placing our ideas into a transpersonal context of awareness.

At worst, we may mistrust our own judgments. Our thinking may become somewhat strained, fearful and timid as we feel unable to comprehend and cope with the extreme detail and depth which the root chakra routinely integrates.

Mercury in Capricorn; on the right remembering side

When our throat chakra is placed in the context of the root chakra on the inner personal side we see how our concepts impact our underlying foundations. These individual personal ideas about how things are structured become the ultimate foundation of larger social systems, such as the court system, that is supposed to provide justice in our community, or the economic system of our society.

We look at the foundations which underlie a situation to determine just how stable the situation is. Poor foundations lead to shaky structures. Strong foundations lead to strong structures. Our ideas are seen in terms of their strength and durability.

We also become aware of the structural underpinnings of our own psyche. Our mind lends its own particular perspective the foundational structures of our life. At the same time there is a sense that our minds are influenced by our surrounding physical and social structures. We feel that as an individual we are part of the powerful collective social and physical forces that the root chakra deals with. Therefore we see ourselves as a partner with the large scale transpersonal structures that the root perceives. We feel that we personally, due to our individual needs, are the ultimate underlying force behind the larger structures. We feel that it is individuals like us who have collectively created the large scale foundational structures that we all live upon.

Mercury in Aquarius; on the left experiencing side

When the throat chakra is placed in the context of our outer root chakra we become more concerned with how our ideas affect external transpersonal structures within our objective environment. Our underlying ideas about the external structures at the throat becomes a concern of the root. This is includes things such as the effects that the kind of government a culture lives under has on our thinking. For example, an authoritarian government, such as a dictatorship, has a very different intellectual climate than a representative democracy. A dictatorship presents different conceptual opportunities and constraints to its populace than a government that uses popular referendum to determine it's social policy. With this placement our ideas are seen within the context of their impact on external foundational structures.

The mind's perspective is interpreted by the root. Because it is on the outside we feel that we are dealing with forces that are outside of us and greater than us. We feel that our personal impact is similar to that which a drop of water has on an ocean. This means that even though we have definite ideas about how things should be, we feel that our singular efforts to effect change probably will not make much of a difference. We feel that our personal intellect is at the mercy of collective forces. We also believe that the way that we think is ultimately shaped by external collective forces, such as our environmental circumstances or our human biological structure.

Mercury in the Genital Chakra

With Mercury in the genital chakra our abstract thinking is placed into the context of our sensory awareness. With this placement we have an intellectual understanding of our sensations along side our immediate sensate responses. Because the genital chakra is naive and incapable of understanding complex relationships, the full awareness of the throat isn't grasped by the genital chakra. Still, the throat is able to make the genital chakra aware of some of the nuances behind its sensate perceptions.

In adding it's somewhat remote abstract intellectual understanding to the directly involved sensate experiences of the genital chakra the throat assumes what our experiences will be like. We then tend to bend our perceptions and reactions to fit our throat's expectations.

With the throat in the genital chakra we seek to place the abstract ideas of the throat into specific concrete situations. This takes the mind's concepts and looks at how they fit into a particular situation. The throat's ideas about how something should sensately feel modifies the actuality of a specific sensate experience.

For example, suppose that we want to learn how to ride a bicycle. First we read a textbook on how to ride a bike. This gives us an abstract (throat) understanding of bike riding. When we try to ride an actual bicycle, we have to translate the ideas in the book into our actual experience of riding a bike. We have to take the expectations created by the book's abstractions and fit them to our actual experiences. We may find that the textbook gave us a vague, perhaps even slightly misleading, sense of what is actually involved in riding a bike. The better the book, the more accurately the abstract ideas it presents will enable us to anticipate the actual concrete realities we will experience when we ride a real bicycle.

The throat can project its own awareness onto our sensate experiences. In this way the throat seeks to mold the particular experiences that it wants us to have on the genital level. For example, intellectually we know that we like the taste of a particular chocolate cookie so much that if we have one, we always wind up eating way too many of them. Our mind may tell us not to eat even one of those cookies despite the fact that our genital chakra loves the taste. The conflicting desires can generate tension.

Our mind can also tint our sensations. For example, in our mind we are afraid of the ocean which makes our physical sensate experience of swimming in the ocean feel unpleasant. As our mind dwells upon how large the ocean is and on the dangers that could be lurking in it, our body has trouble focusing on it's sensate experience of the water and the feeling of the motion of the waves. We are too afraid to allow ourselves to simply experience the sounds, smells and feel of the ocean. The physical sensations are still there but our mind is preoccupied with it's own imagined fears. We never get a chance to recognize our actual physical pleasure in the sensate experience of the sun and surf.

At best, our abstract awareness adds to the possibilities of the genital chakra. Our environment and it's experiences are better anticipated and understood. At worst, our abstract awareness overshadows and hampers our genital chakra's ability to accurately anticipate and deal with it's sensate experiences. We attempt to force our genital chakra's reality to conform to our mind's assumptions even when these ideas are wrong.

Mercury in Sagittarius; on the right remembering side

With Mercury on the subjective remembering side there is a tendency for us to take our actual sensate experiences and shape them according to our personal ideas. Our mind acts as a buffer between what we think we want to feel and what we actually feel. Our mind's notions seek to influence our actual sensate reactions. This can hamper our ability to directly interact with our sensate experiences. It may also help us avoid some bad experiences.

Because it is on the inner side of the genital chakra we feel that our sensate experiences as well as our reactions to them are under our own intellectual control. Our sensate awareness is something that we create through our own choice of sensate experiences and through how we define our reactions to those experiences. Because it is on the inner side our sensate experiences and our reactions to them are seen as part of the substance of our own inner being. We tend to shape either our actual experiences or our reactions to them to fit with the internal self-image that we have at the throat chakra. Because we emphasize impact of our assumptions on our sensate experiences we tend to blur the line between our inner reactions and our outer sensate reality.

At best, our intellectual assumptions are accurate and helpful as we move through our world of sensate experience. At worst, our intellectual assumptions are actually at odds with our sensate experience and undermine the tangible reality that we are actually living in.

Mercury in Pisces; on the left experiencing side

There is an intellectual curiosity about what we sensately experience and how we react to those experiences. There is a heightened intellectual investment in our day-to-day world of sensate experience. The genital chakra's sensate world is where we seek to prove our ideas. We also use our mind to tell ourselves what our genital awareness is either actually experiencing or what it probably will experience. This can be a bit of a problem when how we actually sensately feel differs from how we intellectually expect to feel. If our thinking is sound and it fits the facts, there is little problem. It is when our ideas do not fit that it becomes a problem. We may try to force our assumptions onto our external situation. If there is no way that our assumptions can be made to work we may still try to tell ourselves that our assumptions are accurate under the proper circumstances.

Because it is on the outer side of the genital chakra we feel that our sensate awareness is created by forces external to us. We believe that we our mind helps us in our direct sensate experiential interaction with an external objective reality. Our objective sensate reality is seen as something that is distinct separate from ourselves. While we have a strong sense the boundary between ourselves and the world around us, we tend to think that our sensate reactions are caused by our outer circumstances. We believe that it is our environment that causes our reaction. The active dynamic is seen as being external to us.

At best, our mind to uses our intellect to help us clearly understand all the factors involved in our sensate awareness. This helps us to see our attractions and repulsions and so we make better choices. At worst, our mind tries to ignore any experiences that do not be fit into our prior notions. Such experiences are intellectually explained away. We find ourselves out of sync with our actual sensate environment. We dol not allow ourselves to move beyond our mind's inadequate notions.

Mercury in the Solar Plexus Chakra

The throat chakra is seen through the perspective of the solar plexus chakra. This places our ideas into the context of our social awareness. Our cultural reality is used to implement our mind's concepts. This may constrict our cultural reality to what we already think. It can make it so that we will not allow ourselves to notice things that we think are socially unacceptable. This can either help to censure our ideas so that we don't become culturally eccentric or it can press us into a position of social intellectual rebellion. For example, the Renaissance astronomer Copernicus made discoveries that conflicted with the traditional ideas of his culture. His concepts, despite their intellectual and physical soundness were socially unacceptable. So, he was unwilling to publicly state his discoveries during his own lifetime. He refused to release his observations about the nature of the solar system until after his death in order to avoid the storm of controversy he felt they would arouse.

With this placement our thinking becomes an underlying part of how we create our social awareness. How and what we think becomes a part of our social identity. Because the throat has a larger perspective than the solar plexus, much of the awareness of the throat is beyond the understanding of the solar plexus. Ideally, the solar plexus is able to be open to the ideas of the throat without feeling that its world view is being undermined.

On the more positive side, the solar plexus chakra's filtering of the throat chakra can make sure that we don't say, or do, something that would be harmful to others. This can be mere politeness, such as telling someone you like their haircut when you don't really care for it.

With this placement the throat may use the solar plexus for its own purposes. There may be an underlying tension when the solar plexus cannot avoid the disruptive implications of the throat's awareness. With Mercury in the solar plexus the throat has the final word in determining what is "socially real." We may try to ignore ideas that do not conform to our social identity. Because the throat's awareness is beyond the grasp of the solar plexus, the solar plexus is unsure of itself in it's dealings with the throat. We may try to cover up our confusion with notions of relying on "common sense". Our solar plexus may also try to dismiss the throat's ideas as nonsensical egghead foolishness. Unfortunately, because our solar plexus cannot follow the logic structures of the throat it can only either trust and accept, or mistrust and reject, the throat's ideas. Either way, our ideas help to shape our social identity.

Mercury in Scorpio; on the right remembering side

With this inner placement of the throat chakra in the solar plexus chakra we find our mind is used to serve our sense of personal identity. Our mind helps to shape and substantiate our cultural self-image. At the same time we also use our concepts to shape our image of our cultural environment . This is fine so long as our intellectual concepts do not damage our cultural reality. When as our ideas are socially acceptable (or when we remain quiet if they aren't) there will probably be little problem. If our intellectual notions are too far outside the norm then a conflict may develop.

Our social identity is something that we feel is more a matter of who we are inside, rather than who we are outside. We allow ourselves a large amount internal intellectual freedom even as we may outwardly seem to conform to strict social conceptual standards. We assume that we can use our minds to personally create and modify our inner social self definition. We use ideas to help us understand and modify our social identity as we see fit.

We may find ourselves stubbornly refusing to go along with the conventional wisdom. We may argue with our culture in order to prove to ourselves that we really are a unique individual. We may honestly feel that we are smarter than society as a whole.

Mercury in Aries; on the left experiencing side

Our intellect helps shapes our cultural expectations and assumptions. This impacts how we interact socially and our own personal sense of identity. We use our concepts to try to shape our social reality and our external social identity. We use our cultural reality as a place to test our ideas. So long as our concepts are not so eccentric that the people we interact with find us scary, we should be alright. If our ideas are too outside the norm then we might find ourselves marginalized. At its worst this can become destructive, undermining either our own sense of personal identity or the personal identity of those around us.

Our social identity is something that we feel is externally determined. We assume that we can use our mind to help us understand how we can modify our personal external social identity into what we desire. We are intellectually aggressive and feel that other people should listen to our ideas. We use our mind to help us build and maintain our social position. We feel that our thinking should be practical and have a social purpose.

Mercury in the Heart Chakra

Here the mind adds its awareness to our emotional perspective. Sometimes the result is that the throat chakra is used by the heart to help to provide a rationale for the way we want to feel. Our thinking gets sucked into our emotional agenda. The higher perspective of the mind becomes a means of emotional self justification, rather than an aid in our emotional inquiry.

At the same time our thinking actually does have some underlying impact on how we emotionally feel. Our mind, with its ideas about the way things are, tints our emotional awareness. The general principles of the mind, become assumptions that underlie how we emotionally feel. In actuality, we may not really feel the way our mind expects us to. For example, rather than be upset when someone tries to publicly embarrass us, we might laugh at ourselves along with everyone else because the joke actually was funny.

The larger, more rational, perspective of the throat is placed in service to the heart. The throat chakra's skills are used to help the heart figure out how to get what it wants. This enables the heart to see the context of it's desires more completely and also to manipulate both itself and its outer environment more effectively.

Normally the heart moves back and forth between the tangible and the intangible aspects of it's awareness. With the throat in the heart chakra the heart tends to emphasize the abstract side of its awareness. The heart becomes more idealized and less caught up in the concrete specifics of its desires.

Without realizing it, the heart also shapes itself to fit our ideas. The judgements of the throat modify the feelings of the heart. If we think that romantic love is irrational foolishness, then the heart will suppress its romantic urges. If we think that romantic love is the reason for life and a grand folly, then we will act on romantic urges in impulsive and implausible ways. The key concept is that the heart enacts our ideas about romantic love without questioning the validity of the ideas that it assumes and enacts.

Mercury in Libra; on the right remembering side

With this placement we intellectualize our emotions, giving ourselves the reasons for how we either actually feel, or think we should feel. We also use our mind to tell our emotions what they actually are. Our mind anticipates how it thinks we will emotionally feel in various situations and shapes our emotional responses accordingly. These ideas may be accurate or inaccurate, depending on our assumptions. While there is an intellectual curiosity about our emotions, our emotions are seen as a proving ground for our ideas about our emotions, which we then use to manipulate our own emotional state.

We use our mind to help us govern our emotional awareness. We feel that our emotions are ultimately something that we personally create and are under our own control. Our heart is felt to pivot on our own inner dynamic and our feelings as seen more as reflections of who are rather than as reflections of our outer world. Our emotions are primarily a part of us and only secondarily a part of the outer world. We believe that in order to change how we feel emotionally we must first change our perspective. By changing ourselves, we change our world.

Mercury in Taurus; on the left experiencing side

With this placement we use our intellect's overall conceptual understanding to help shape our external emotional reality. Because we are dealing with our emotional reactions to external objects and events our mind attempts to use our ideas to understand the symbolic meanings of our external environment. While there is a tendency for our mind to project it's ideas onto our external emotional reality, ultimately we believe we are reacting to the emotional actuality of the outer world.

We may unknowingly use our mind's concepts to understand and control our external emotional circumstances. Because our emotions seen as products of our environment, rather than of ourselves, we believe that in order to change our emotional state we must try change our outer circumstances. In order to change how we feel, we must first change what we feel. By changing our world, we change ourselves.

Mercury In the Throat Chakra

Here the mind provides it's own context of awareness. Because our mind doesn't move on to another chakra our thinking becomes a stopping point. This creates a tendency to think about what we're thinking about. We also think about our mental process, or we think about how we think. At best, this describes an intellect that can step back and take a look itself. There's a tendency for the mind to fixate on itself, analyzing and reanalyzing its own contents or processes. As it does this it either loses sight of what it was originally thinking about, or it takes its original concerns and magnifies them beyond all proportion. This placement can get a bit convoluted. If we actually are worried about something, we might end up worrying about the fact that we are worried.

Our thinking with this placement can also become extremely detail oriented. A lot details are added together and become the basis of our judgments. The mind also can become very judgmental with this placement. We trust our logic and therefore believe that we are right. With Mercury in the throat we can become very sure of ourselves and argumentative. We can easily slip into arrogance, because we think we are so smart.

Because of its tendency toward abstract idealizations, our mind may strive for what it considers perfection. It may even become relentless in it's pursuit of it's own ideals. This can lead to an extremely exacting temperament. Because perfection is virtually impossible to achieve or sustain, this can lead to anxiety.

Here the mind provides it's own context of awareness. At its best, the mind is unfettered and quite free. With this placement our thinking is often is clear and concise. We know what we're thinking about and we know why. Our mind helps us to understand things more clearly. We trust our intellect. At its worst, our mind answers to nothing, not even it's own logic structures. Our perspective can easily slip out of balance. If our mind decides to become obsessed with something, there's nothing that can stop it.

Mercury in Virgo; on the right remembering side

This placement heightens our mind's self-awareness. Because the mind focuses upon itself we tend to define things through our intellect. This can lead to a competitive sparring over ideas as we try to prove how smart we are. Therefore with this placement our verbal skills are also emphasized.

There is a concern with our ideas and the way that we use them. We are concerned with the accuracy and quality of our ideas. We test various concepts and make judgments about their worth.

We tend to be rather judgmental, analyzing the relative qualities and properties of things. We have strong preferences. We are fairly discerning about the subtle details which we use to analyze things. We are exacting in the details of life. This means that what most people may consider minor details actually can matter a great deal to us.   We notice and enjoy subtle nuances. This can be in the taste of foods, or in the impact of an idea.

Being on the inside we believe that we are what we think and that we have control over our own ideas. The ideas and concepts that we use are felt to ours as well.

Because it is on the subjective side, our mind becomes a foundation of our self-definition. We use our mind to buttress our inner personal identity and we enjoy ideas. At best, this can become intellectual confidence. At worst, this can become intellectual one-upmanship and ideas may become a weapon.

Mercury in Gemini; on the left experiencing side

This placement heightens our awareness of the social nature of the mind and it's ideas. We see how ideas connect people. Ideas are seen as a strong means of connection to the external world. There is an interest in the social nature of ideas as something that people mutually share and sustain. Concepts also shape our personal world as they provide a means for understanding ourselves. We use ideas to both manipulate our external environment and to connect to it. We join social groups and causes according to our sympathy with their ideas.

There is a tendency to jump on the intellectual bandwagon. This can make us less discriminating about the social ideas that we may agree with. Yet there is a real pleasure in the discovery, sharing and weighing of ideas. We enjoy discussion and exploration.

Ideally we are able use ideas to connect ourselves to other people. As we exchange ideas with others we become more aware of our both ourselves and our environment. Negatively, we may use ideas as a means of division and exploitation. We may use the infectiousness of ideas to exploit and control other people.

Mercury in the Brow Chakra

This planetary placement moves the throat chakra up into the brow. The concerns of the throat become emphasized in the awareness of the brow. This means that the throat influences what the brow looks at. The brow assimilates our intellectual awareness and then uses its own intuitive perspective to understand and deal with the concerns of the throat.

Our intuition will seek to solve the problems of the throat. Because the brow has a larger perspective than the throat, some of the concerns of the throat may be ignored because they are not considered to be a real problem. Because the brow is concerned with making choices between various potentials, it isn't as curious as the throat. It picks up some of the throat's desire to know things purely for the sake of knowing them, but ultimately the brow is much more concerned with finding a direct perception that helps make those choices that lead to our personal fulfillment.

The throat, with its rational methods, often uses a method of logical inference.   Ultimately the brow is a form of perception that discerns relationships that are imperceptible to the throat chakra. This means that the brow's perceptual insights can occasionally lead to some sudden, radical changes in our thinking. The brow takes our conscious awareness at the throat and moves beyond it's known boundaries. This frees the throat from some of its preconceptions and allows it to escape its tendency to get into a linear logical rut. It also can make the throat unsure of the stability of it's own conceptual foundations. This makes the throat more aware of the need to deepen the underlying perspectives on which it's concepts are based.

Mercury in Leo; on the right remembering side

This placement puts the mind into the context of our brow's intuitive awareness.   Our ideas becomes a springboard for our intuitive understanding. Our thoughts serves as a foundation for our intuitive leaps of understanding. This process is a bit difficult for the mind to follow because the mind's linear methods of logical thinking is what our intuitive understanding ultimately leaps beyond. All that the mind knows is that we've suddenly come up with a 'that's it!' idea.

This chakric perspective makes our minds more fluid. Our thinking is refined and improved by our intuitive insights as we use our mind to try to fill in the gaps in our conceptual understanding that are revealed by our brow's direct perception.   With this placement we blur the line between intellectual understanding and intuitive insight. We tend to presume that intuitive insights will arrive when we need them and we simply believe that they are part of how the mind works.

Mercury in the Crown Chakra

The throat chakra's awareness is placed into the crown chakra. Our intellectual awareness provides information which is molded by the crown's larger abstract pattern perspective.   The crown's perspective sees patterns and underlying relationships that the are implied by the more linear conceptual understanding of the mind. Where the mind sees separate unrelated parts, the crown chakra sees an interwoven whole.

With this placement the concerns of the throat are emphasized within the crown. The crown chakra uses its intuitive awareness to deal with the throat's issues. At the same time, the throat, with its reliance on intellect and detail, affects the way the crown functions. The crown's awareness of integrated patterns remains far beyond the throat's step by step rational methodology, yet the crown searches for the missing parts of the mind's logic structures. This can lead flashes of insight that redefine our ideas.

While the crown remains true to itself and is assured of its own awareness, it is also willing to accept the linear logic of the throat. Again, because the mind has moved up into a realm that is larger than its' capacity to perceive, it is difficult for the mind to fluidly move about in the crown chakra. Meanwhile, the crown simply takes the awareness of the throat and reorders it in multiple ways according to various abstract patterns of order.

Mercury in Cancer; on the right remembering side

Here we rearrange our ideas according to transpersonal abstract patterns of relationship. Seemingly separate ideas are interwoven and organized into sets of relationships. These can be fairly concrete, such as the underlying concepts behind a game such as chess. Things like the way the pieces should move and their initial placement on the board. Or they can be extremely abstract, such as the underlying reasons behind our existence. This placement sees ideas as being relatively tangible. The mind, as it is perceived by the crown, is considered to be very pliable and able to be placed into multiple contexts of understanding.

Here we look for the overarching abstract structure that guides our understanding of how our mind's ideas interconnect. Our intellectual understanding is seen as a sort of starting point in the 'real' world, yet the creative dynamic within the situation resides within the crown and it's dynamic sense of the multiple layers of tangible relationships.

Sun: Brow, point of intrinsic self; glyph- ☉

Apollo was the Greek god who carried the sun across the heavens in his chariot every day. He was also the god of prophecy, or what will become true. Apollo brought illumination in mundane and spiritual realms. In personal terms the Sun lights and intuitively guides each of us on our life's individual path.

The Sun is the bedrock of our personal individual being. It is our purest point of pure self. It is where we are ourselves as a pure intention to be. In classical astrology the Sun symbolizes our sheer personal will to be. It reveals our inner spiritual drive to be ourselves. A side effect of being ourselves is that we shape our outer world so that it reflects the inner reality of our self. The sun views the world in much the same way that an artist views their canvas and paints, as a medium of expression. The tangible world is the Sun's means of ensoulment and self refinement.

The perceptions of the Sun are highly intuitive. The Sun sees the world both as it is and as what it could become. This enables the Sun to look out at the world and make choices about which possibilities we want based upon who we intrinsically are. The Sun is how we connect our inner self to our outer tangible world.

The Sun is the abstract counterpart of Jupiter. The Sun reacts to what it 'sees' intuitively with the same "like or dislike" response that Jupiter has. Both planets represent personal ensoulment, just in differing ways. Because the Sun rules a highly abstract preconscious awareness, usually the activity of the Sun goes unnoticed. Most of the time the Sun runs on autopilot. Our Sun's intuition makes choices that shape both ourselves and our world without our even consciously noticing them.

The Sun focuses on individual choice as the primary shaper of our world. The Sun sees the Will, or inner intent, of both ourselves and of everything around us. This helps us to weave our own way through the swirl of pure intention which is continually being enacted by everything all around us at the same time that we are enacting our own inner intentions.

Sun in the Root Chakra

With the Sun in the root chakra our personal preconscious will to be flows into our unconscious awareness of the physical structures that underlie our existence. Our intuition is placed into the transpersonal context of humanity's physical structure. Our personal intuition is subservient to the root's transpersonal concrete awareness. Our brow's intuition is made to work through the root chakra's tangible structures.

With this placement we are concerned with our personal large-scale destiny and what we may be able to accomplish. There's the possibility of a sense of personal grandiosity, or on the flip side, of a sense of being personally inadequate in dealing with what we see as an overwhelmingly large, fated situation. In either case, our intuitions are placed into a large scale, collective context.

With this placement there's a need for our personal will to maintain its integrity in the face of the root's transpersonal pressures. There is also a need for us to place ourselves into a structure that we trust. Because the root is vast and unconscious, we may feel enveloped by the root chakra. While the brow chakra is our largest purely personal awareness, it still has a smaller perspective than the root. It is similar to swimming in the ocean. We can only see so far into the water before everything becomes murky and vague, yet we know that the water extends on much farther than we can see.

Sun in Capricorn; on the right remembering side

This places our will to be into an internal awareness of the underlying structures of our personal existence. We are aware of the impact that large scale tangible structures have on our personal potentials. We feel that we can use these structures to reach our own goals. Accepting the physical and social structures that are already in place as they are, we tend to try to see how to make them beneficial to our lives. We do not seek to replace or modify them in any great way. The world as it stands is seen as basically functioning adequately. We feel that we are able to use the world's foundational structures as we choose.

We believe that we are participating in the ongoing of the momentum of humanity. We can choose to ride the flow to the movement of the human race if we wish. If changes are felt to be necessary, we feel that we should modify ourselves first, rather than the structure of our outer environment.

Sun in Aquarius; on the left experiencing side

This placement puts our personal will to be into the context of an external transpersonal structure. We believe that we are participants in the collective momentum of humanity. There is a sense that we can help push humanity along its ordained path. We also have a sense that we are also being pulled along by the momentum of humanity.

Our personal sense of the underlying structures on the left experiencing side is that they more fluid than how we see them on the right remembering side. We also tend to believe that the outer environment isn't operating quite fairly and it should change. We seek to modify our outer circumstances first, ourselves second. We also feel that the individual has the capacity to reform our outer transpersonal structures. We have a restless idealism. The problem becomes discerning what can or cannot be changed within our environment, as well as how to change what can be changed.

Sun in the Genital Chakra

Our personal intuitive awareness is seen through the lens of our genital chakra. Both the brow and the genital chakras use an attraction-repulsion response mechanism as their basis for making choices regarding an outer stimulus. Because the brow and the genital chakras operate in very similar ways, there is an easy rapport between them. With this placement the genital chakra provides the context for our intuitive awareness. The sensate reality is what is being dealt with, so the brow chakra adds intuitive support to the genital chakra. The genital chakra uses the brow's preconscious intuitions to help it decide what to do.

For example, you are at a party and you meet someone that you find attractive. You talk and flirt a little bit and you really like them, but for some reason right when things reach the point when it could become serious, you choose not to. You're not really sure why you shut down the interaction, but you did. As the night progresses you notice that they are getting very drunk. You ask a friend of yours about them. Your friend shrugs and tells you that they heard that they have a problem with alcohol. You realize that the intuitive part of you was right and you consider yourself lucky as you don't want to be involved with a drunk.

When the Sun is in the genital chakra our intuitions focus on the genital chakra's fairly immediate, tangible world. Our intuition is more aware of our immediate surroundings and what they could be. The brow chakra is more engaged with the details of tangible reality than it normally would be. This means that our intuition may occasionally get stuck in minor details. At it's best, the brow enables the genital chakra to feel some of the more subtle aspects of it's environment helping it to make better choices. At its worst, the brow brings in so much intuitive information that it hinders the genital chakra's ability to clearly see what it sensately feels and obscures what it knows making it indecisive.

Sun in Sagittarius; on the right remembering side

This placement puts our personal will to be into the context of our own sensate experiences. Our intuitive awareness adds depth and dimension to our sensate awareness, altering the shape of our personal reality, which changes our choices. We use our intuitive understanding to choose sensate experiences that resonate with our inner sense of ourselves. We are quick to make a decision about whether or not something is appropriate to who we are or not. Because it is on the subjective side, our experiences are internalized and analyzed until what they mean both to us and about us is understood.

We also feel an intuitive sense of control over our sensate reality. There is an intuitive sense of whether or not we will like a potential experience, as well as an underlying sense of a situation's larger impact on our lives. We feel that our inner being has the active dynamic. Ultimately, what we are really doing is using the brow to help shape both our sensate reactions and choices in order to create a sensate reality that reflects our inner self definition.

Sun in Pisces; on the left experiencing side

This placement puts our personal will to be into the context of our external sense of personal sensate experience. The brow chakra's intuitive awareness is brought to our perceptions of our tangible sensate world. Our brow's awareness adds depth and breadth to our sensate experiences. This gives our external environment added personal resonance. This enlarges our personal sense of the potential impact that an experience may have on us. When we sensately experience something we feel we are touching a world that is vast and stretches out beyond our full comprehension. Occasionally, we may feel overwhelmed by our sensate experiences and become engulfed by our intuitive awareness of their broader significance. Ideally, we use our intuitions to help us to deeply understand what something is. Then this helps us to decide whether or not to be a part of it. We may get so wrapped up in our ever deepening intuitive perceptions that we hesitate to act or react. Or we may find ourselves being sweep along by events that feel unstoppably vast and at the same time a deep part of us.

Sun in the Solar Plexus Chakra

With this placement our highly abstract intuition is seen in the context of our tangible social reality. Our inner being and our social reality are connected. The Sun's sense of pure inner desire impacts our personal sense of social identity. Our preconscious abstract sense of self helps to shape our conscious sense of identity. This gives our sense of who we are greater depth. The concerns of the solar plexus also overshadow the concerns of the brow. Our intuitions are more concerned with helping us to establish our social identity. Because the solar plexus has a more limited perspective than the brow many of the choices made by the brow are only vaguely understood. The solar plexus finds itself having to make a bit of a leap of faith. It all comes down to self trust.

Meanwhile, at the solar plexus we tend to accept our culture's beliefs about the nature of intuition even as we are using our intuition. This can create some internal contradictions. Our culture may not accept the brow's intuition as something that is trustworthy and so our tendency may be to mistrust our inner intuitive awareness. Or our social reality may mistrust deeply personal motives and seek to suppress what it sees as a disruptive individualism. This may create tension within our psyche.

At its best, our social identity is deepened and more in sync with both our outer environment and with our own inner being. At its worst, our personal goals and the intuitive awareness that seeks to enact them is stilted by the narrowness of our cultural identity.

Sun in Scorpio; on the right remembering side

Here our intuitive self creation is placed into the context our inner sense of social identity. Our social position has a large impact on who we feel we are. At the same time bring how we internally define ourselves and our goals (the intangible aspects of our self) into our social reality. (These are things like honor and self respect.) We strive to produce an outer social identity that we expresses who we really are internally. The dynamic tension is between our inner sense of who we are and our sense of our outer social reality. Because this placement is on the inner side we feel that our social position is our own personal creation. There is also a sense of the world as being our personal stage. Our inner intuition is used to help us to choose the outer objects and experiences that we feel best describes who we are.   At the very least, we will try to refine our social reality so that it fits our inner self image.

Despite the strong sense of our self as being reflected in the mirror of society, there is a naive simplicity to our social reality. The complexity of various competing social forces doesn't concern us, except when they get in the way of our own self assertion. Most of the time we simply do something because we want to.

Sun in Aries; on the left experiencing side

Here our intuitive sense of self creation is placed into the context of our external sense of social identity. We use our inner being to define our goals in the tangible world that defines our social reality. While we strive to produce an external social reality that is in sync with our inner sense of identity, we feel that ultimately our social identity is largely the result of external factors over which we have little control. For example, we may focus on how the culture in which live impacts who we are. This awareness of the impact of our environment heightens our perception of our circumstances. Because we feel defined by external factors there is a drive to manipulate and change our external situation. By changing our social setting, we believe that we change who we are. Our intuitions helps us to decide which outer changes to make and what direction to take. Our brow seeks to guide our social awareness. At the same time our outer social reality is aware of the brow's concerns.

Our social sense of self is buttressed by our inner intuitive awareness as we pick and choose our way through our external social environment. There are occasional moments of stress when our inner personal values and our outer social realities clash. Usually our personal values win out and we may find ourselves stubbornly asserting ourselves, even in the face of social censure. Despite our reliance on the outer world as the measuring stick by which we define ourselves, ultimately we believe that must be who we are, no matter where that leads us.

Sun in the Heart Chakra

Our abstract sense of self is placed into the context of our emotions. At the heart we connect our inner and outer sense of being and we also connect our concrete and abstract sense of being. With this placement our emotions are the context of our intuitions, which makes it so that we have a tendency to see our intuitions as a metaphor. Our desires become symbolic as our inner being's meaning is placed into the context of our emotional reality.

Our inner will to be (or spirit) serves our personal sense of meaning as defined by our emotional being (or soul). This means that our emotions use our intuitive awareness to help them express and fulfill themselves. Our heart's awareness is used by the brow's broader awareness to help it enact it's wishes and desires.

Because the heart is both abstract and concrete, the abstract source of the brow's awareness is not very difficult for the heart to understand. This enables the heart to trusts its own desires even more than it would've on its own. This can allow the heart to become more entwined with its wishes and dreams than it otherwise would be. The expanded vistas of the brow give it's flights of fancy a larger sense of scope.

This addition of an extremely abstract awareness to an already highly symbolic personal reality can reduce our need to dwell in the tangible, or real world a great deal. We focus on the inner personal meaning of objects and events instead of their outer impersonal impact.

At its best, the heart is helped by the brow's intuition to pick and choose its way through various situations to so that it can fulfill its emotional reality. At its worst, the heart's tendency to become abstract and removed from tangible reality is accentuated and the heart may become lost in fantasy and wishful thinking.

Sun in Libra; on the right remembering side

This placement adds an intuitive depth to our inner emotional awareness. There is a large internal investment in events which become symbolic metaphors for who we are and the world we live in. Ultimately our internal emotional state is the proving ground for the fulfillment of our personal desires. Because a lot of the emotional activity takes place within us, we are able to quickly and fluidly change the external objects that serve as the symbols of our inner desires. While what we desire remains fairly stable, the external objects which are seen as fulfilling those desires may change. We emphasize the abstract qualities of our desires.

This inner side placement puts our sense of emotional control into our own hands. The external objects which fulfill our internal desires come and go according to the flow of external circumstances. But our internal desires are seen to be our own creation, something that we can shape according to our own wishes. Our inner emotional desires and how they connect us to the outer world are felt to basically under our personal control. This gives a slightly dispassionate quality to our external emotional awareness. We feel that the objects we covet are instrumenting our desires. Our emotional pleasure or pain is felt to be the result of our own desires rather than our circumstances. If we want to change our emotional state we should simply change our inner desires.

Sun in Taurus; on the left experiencing side

This placement adds an intuitive depth to our outer emotional awareness. There is a strong inner attachment to our outer environment. We use our sense of intuition to help us connect to the people and things around us that fulfill our desires. These external objects become the actual means of our symbolic emotional self-fulfillment.

Because we feel that the outer environment has the active dynamic in our emotional reality, we feel emotionally reactive. This makes us less emotionally fluid and mobile. We are unable to change the objects of our desires very easily. Emotionally we become a bit more plodding and deliberate as we seek to maintain the connection of our inner emotional state with our outer circumstances. We are unaware of how we project our inner emotional desires out onto our environment. We believe that we are emotionally reacting to the caprice of outer circumstances.

We feel that the objects we desire cause our desires. Our desires happen to us. Our emotional pleasure or pain is felt to be the result of our environment and largely beyond our control. If we are unhappy it is because we have aligned ourselves with the wrong person, or the wrong circumstances. In order for us to change our emotional state we feel that we have to change our external emotional connections.

Sun in the Throat Chakra

Here our personal will to be is placed into the perspective of the mind. With this placement our intuition is seen through the lens of our intellect. This can lead to the sudden intuitive solving of a problem that our intellect has been struggling with. For example, one of the scientists who helped discover DNA couldn't quite understand it's molecular structure. The story goes that he had a dream one night of two strings wrapped around each other, in a double helix, and he realized this was the structure of DNA. His intuition had spoken to his intellect through a dream.

When the brow's awareness moves into the throat there will often be such enlightening moments. Because the brow's field of awareness is greater than the throat chakra's, when the throat finally does understand the perspective of the brow it seems to come in a single illuminating burst of insight when the throat suddenly understands what the brow sees. Awkwardly, such understanding tends to be an all or nothing proposition.

Although the brow and the throat are both abstract, they use such different methods in their understanding that they are extremely dissimilar.   The throat uses concepts to analyze relationships. The throat places things into categories according to various attributes. It may group things according to their color, or it can use their size, or it can use their place, and so on. The brow is more experiential. It 'feels' and 'sees' relationships which it both understands and that it either likes or dislikes. This means that sometimes when the throat grasps the understanding of the brow it also receives some of the brow's reaction.

At its best, the brow gives the throat intuitive leaps in understanding, especially when the throat is literally at its wit's end and most willing to accept the intuitive perspective. At its worst, the throat will mistrust knowledge that it does not understand. Because the awareness of the brow is beyond the throat's capacity to comprehend, the throat may have a crisis of confidence. The throat may end up mistrusting the brow's perception and our psyche may feel divided against itself.

Sun in Virgo; on the right remembering side

This placement adds an intuitive dimension to our inner intellectual awareness. Our sense of inner purpose finds an outlet through our mind. We use our intellect as a means of knowing who we are on a deep internal level. We implement ourselves through the mind and its intellectual awareness. We use the mind to define ourselves, seeing ourselves in our ideas and our intellectual capacities. This means that we enjoy analyzing things and enjoy the act of thinking itself. At moments of heightened intellectual focus we have intuitive flashes of insight that help us understand both what we are thinking about and how we think.

Because it is on the inner side we tend to see the impact of our intuition on our mind as our own personal creation. There is a strong idealism which makes us feel a disconnect between how we intuit things could be and how we think they actually are. Ultimately we feel that our mind, and the intuitive support that we've come to expect for it, is under our own personal control.

Sun in Gemini; on the left experiencing side

This placement adds an intuitive dimension to our outer intellectual awareness. There is a strong personal investment in the intellectual constructs that we use to organize our external reality. We see how ideas shape our external circumstances and social interactions. We intuitively relate to other people through ideas. We enjoy sharing thoughts and ideas. We intuitively share concepts which mutually support ourselves and the larger conceptual whole we are part of.

We feel that through our ideas our inner purpose becomes connected to the outer world around us. We have flashes of insight as to how a set of outer circumstances works. We are intuitively aware of relationships that are beyond the grasp of our intellectual understanding. This enables us to anticipate unforeseen situations. Ultimately we feel that the mind, along with its intuitive support, is a shared external process that we can participate in, but which we do not personally control. We are essentially reactive and we use our intuition to find situations and ideas that we can personally use to enact our sense of who we are.

Sun in the Brow Chakra

This placement gives the brow the freedom to act on its own terms. Here our intuition answers only to itself and it is seen as directly as possible. This gives us fairly direct access to our intuitions. Yet because the brow's awareness is preconscious, it requires a bit of a leap of faith on our part. We cannot know how we know something or even exactly what we know, we can merely trust or mistrust our intuitive awareness. This means that when we are out of sync with our inner self we may have difficulty knowing what to do. We have trouble placing what we know into a context. This makes it difficult for us to get back on track.

The brow usually has only a partial understanding of what it knows. We either trust this knowledge, or we don't. When mistrust dominates the brow's awareness our intuition is rendered useless. Yet even if we utterly trust our intuition, it's meaning still is unclear. We aren't sure of the full context of what we see.

Additionally, the realm of the brow is totally abstract and so fluid that what is truth at one moment may become folly at another. The problem is discerning exactly what level of relationship the brow is perceiving. Our more superficial surface reality can be very changeable. The surface levels of our being - things like what we want to eat tonight - can change quickly and easily because the relationships are not very deeply rooted in our self definition. In contrast, the deeper levels of our being change slowly because they are part of who we are. We use the relationships that they hold in place to create and define ourselves.

At their best our intuitions flow easily and we are able to connect our inner being with our outer world. We are able to anticipate situations fairly well and this allows us to make choices that are reasonable and appropriate. At its worst our inner and outer being are disconnected and our intuitions are absent or vague, making it difficult for us to make choices that connect to our inner being with our outer circumstances.

Sun in Leo; on the right remembering side

With this placement our intuitions serve as their own context. The brow chakra's perspective is completely self-contained. This helps us to act with decisive self-assurance. We feel certain of who we are and where we are going. When we are confident, our intuition is very self-assured and flowing.

If we lose our self-confidence our intuition may falter and we may have trouble knowing what to do. With this placement there is no second point of reference to help us understand our intrinsic will to be. When we lose our intuitive bearings we have to discern if an intuitive insight is a true unbiased perception or a self created projection. If it is a perception, then we need to try to understand the context of what we are seeing. If it is a personal projection, then we need to understand why we are creating this particular illusion. Usually, our projections tell us what we want to hear. They are useless in making choices, but they can describe what we want. This may actually help us to 'see' how to become what we truly seek to be.

Sun in the Crown Chakra

Our intuitive awareness is seen through the lens of the crown chakra's highly abstract sense of pattern. Our personal will to be is placed into the context of our sense of transpersonal order. This gives our intuitive understanding an even greater sense of depth and resonance.

Our intuitions are used to help us perceive the crown chakra's realm of underlying abstract order. Still, despite all of its abstract spiritual qualities, the brow is still an individually directed awareness. Yet with this placement the brow becomes aware that the world is far larger than just our personal possibilities. With the Sun in the crown chakra our intuitions step beyond the confines of our purely personal being.

Our intuitions are used to help us fulfill ourselves within a larger transpersonal pattern. This can lead to a tremendous sense of idealism. This idealism can be totally impractical or it may lead to something that we actually can attain. Either way, the intuitions of the brow help us to ensoul ourselves in a larger than ourselves, transpersonal context. What we seek to ensoul stops being purely about us. We feel an obligation to the larger whole.

At its best, we are able to intuit how our personal will fits into a larger pattern. The fulfillment of our personal will is guided by the broader perspective of the crown chakra. Our personal being ends up being refined by the crown's perspective. Our own Will and the Will of the Larger Pattern are felt to work in sync together in mutual respect.

At its worst, the crown chakra's perspective may make our personal world seem inadequate and unreal rather than a true expression of who we are. The larger context may be felt to stand in the way of our personal fulfillment. Or our personal will may feel engulfed and trivialized by the larger pattern. The crown chakra's ideals may seem so lofty that trying to enact them seems impossible. Either way, a rift is created between the personal and the transpersonal, between the whole and the part. We are left feeling fragmented, unfulfilled and unable to act.

Sun in Cancer; on the right remembering side

This placement gives us an intuitive sense of ourselves as a part of a larger context. Often we feel a sense of intrinsic connection with the larger pattern that we are operating within. This can give us a sense of confidence and that all is right with ourselves and the world.

There is a concern with how our personal will to be ourselves fits within a larger context. There is also an underlying sense of having a large-scale purpose. This purpose is often somewhat nebulous because it is difficult for us to put ourselves into the larger abstract perspective. We try to intuitively see the larger order that we are operating within. This can lead to our occasionally feeling that we just know what to do, know what's going on.

At it's best, our intuitive insights allow us to easily fit ourselves into the larger context. We are able to accurately visualize probable outcomes on a large scale. We see our place within the larger pattern and are able to take our place with minimal confusion. At it's worst, we try to use our intuitive insights to bend the larger situation to our personal will. While we may be able to exploit the whole for our own personal gain for a while, eventually the whole will move to protect itself from such exploitation. Over time we may become increasingly isolated, finding ourselves feeling cut off from our own spiritual source.

Moon: Crown, point of self aspiration; glyph- ☽

In ancient Greek mythology Artemis was the goddess of the moon. She was virgin huntress who was served by maidens that were also virginal. Apollo, the Sun god (who was no virgin) was her twin brother. Their being twins helps to describe the closeness of the Sun and the Moon. It also describes the closeness of the brow and the crown chakras.

The top two planets are called "the lights" in astrology. The Sun, of course, is a flaming ball which burns in the heavens with tremendous light. The Moon, the second brightest object in the sky is so close to us that it reflects the sun's light to us in the night sky.

This implies that the Sun is the primary force. In purely personal terms it is. Both of the top two chakras deal with realms that are most uniquely individual. The higher we go up the chakras the more individual and personal the chakras become, until we reach the crown and we enter a very individualized transpersonal awareness. The moon connects our individual light (the personal Sun) to something that transcends our individuality and is above and beyond us. Paradoxically, the moon is also our most personal planet and the crown is our most personal chakra.

The moon is a very complex symbol. The moon connects us to a spiritual world that is far larger than ourselves. This realm is the source of our inner spiritual being. Occultly, the moon is seen as connecting us to a reservoir of collective psychic energy from which we each individually draw.

Symbolically, the moon acquires some of the qualities of the crown chakra. The moon connects us to transpersonal abstract patterns. The crown chakra, and the Moon, connects us to a vast realm of infinite interwoven connections within our world of personal actuality. It is the intangible counterpoint of Saturn's concrete transpersonal order. Both the top and the bottom chakras are our personal anchors in realms that are above and below us.

The moon also yields a sense of inner limitation which is born out of our abstract patterns of relationship. Yet, because the relationships of the Moon are so abstract, they are more pliable than the tangible actualities of Saturn. Although the Moon feels less restrictive than Saturn, the Moon is still quite demanding. With the Moon our limitations are initially less keenly felt for we see infinite depth and potential. The moment we choose a particular potential, the infinite becomes increasingly finite and specific. Formless possibility quickly gives way to the demands of a particular actuality. A resonant sense of depth often remains with us.

It is through the moon that we find the substance that we use to ensoul ourselves. We use the Moon to clothe our spirit in this particular body, at this particular time, for these particular reasons. We take the impersonal formless infinite, which starts off virgin, unformed and untouched, and we make it personal, actual, and particular. Yet we know that at it's core reality stretches out far beyond our purely individual being.

Moon in the Root Chakra

This placement puts our awareness of our transpersonal abstract patterns into the context of our transpersonal concrete awareness. Both chakras are beyond our conscious access and so they generally operate behind the scenes. Both of these chakras are equal to each other in the sense that they are always in balance.

With this placement the crown's idealism is seen through the lens of the root's pragmatism. Some of the excesses of the crown are blunted by the root's tangible focus. At the same time, the crown's fluidity impacts the root's tendency toward unchanging stability. The crown has enough depth and scope that it is able to get the root chakra to change. The normal tentative trial and error process of the root chakra is aided by the crown chakra's broad grasp of abstract relationships. The root takes in the possibilities visualized by the crown and moves toward them. Because of the complexity of the root's physical reality these changes usually still happen slowly, even with the hastening influence of the crown.

At its best, the crown's propensity for idealistic utopianism is stabilized in the world of physical actuality. Our abstract sense of pattern is connected to the tangible world and we feel supported in a very deep way. We're able to see our destiny as something that is both intimate and far larger than just ourselves. We feel connected to the Big Picture and we move fluidly within a large scale context. At its worst, our personal idealism feels overwhelmed by the sheer weight and inertia of the structure of physical reality. It is as if God demands something impossible of us and then will not help us do it. Our life feels like a trap.

Moon in Capricorn; on the right remembering side

Here our preconscious sense of abstract pattern is placed into the context of our inner unconscious awareness of concrete structure. There is an intrinsic trust in structure, especially as they affect the underpinnings of our own personal reality. At the same time it is difficult for us to grasp what the underlying structure actually is. In some ways we make a leap of faith that allows us to believe that the world we live in has an underlying structure and purpose. It is as if we feel the presence of the Divine through an internal sense of deep physical order.

Because the right-hand side is inner and subjective, our personal abstract ideals feel anchored within our own being's awareness of physical order. The sense of the union of abstract and concrete structure feels like it exists within us. We then take this inner sense of order and project it out onto our outer environment. Although the underlying order is transpersonal, we feel that we personally are a partner in it's creation.

Even as we are idealistic about how the world is structured, our ideals are only considered meaningful if they actually work in the real world. We have a practical idealism. At the same time we feel that the physical world we live in has a magical quality. We feel we are rooted in a magical world whose physical structure and existence innately expresses the spiritual.

Moon in Aquarius; on the left experiencing side

Here our preconscious sense of abstract pattern is placed into our unconscious awareness of external concrete structure. Our personal ideals are seen in the context of our outer environment's structure. Sometimes it is difficult for us to see how our own abstract patterns and ideals are being enacted in the underlying structure of the world around us. We believe that they are. It is as if we feel the presence of the Divine through the underlying order of our outer environment. When we look at nature's order we believe are seeing God.

Because it is on the left-hand side, our crown's abstract ideals are seen as being shaped by the reality of external structures. On the outer side the initiative feels like it belongs to our environment. The personal idealism of the crown runs into the matter-of-fact transpersonal nature of the root. As our abstract ideals run into the actuality of the outer world it feels like our ideals must give way. Sometimes this helps us to search for a greater understanding of the workings of our environment. Sometimes we feel frustrated by our structures and seek to change them.

Moon in the Genital Chakra

With the Moon in the genital chakra we enrich the meaning of our tangible experiences. Also, it is through our sensate experiences that we seek to embody the ideals of the crown chakra. We place the crown's abstract cosmic awareness into a particular physical context. It is through our sensate reality that we recognize the spiritual. In a way, we believe we know God through our experience of the physical world.

This gives our physical sensations added resonance. The tangible is used to describe the intangible. We use the physical world to know and understand the spiritual one. This adds a quality of transcendence to our actual physical sensations. Our connection with the divine, or group mind, or oversoul, is felt to be tangibly experienced. This can also make our imaginations very vivid. The crown's awareness of interrelationships flows easily into our sense of the tangible world. This can blur the boundaries between an actual object and it's multiple levels of interconnection. An actual experience carries the echoing presence of a larger context.

At its best, the physical world has greater meaning. We see individual events as part of a larger pattern. The physical world is not seen as a series of random objects and events, but everything seems intimately connected to everything else. We have a sense of underlying purpose and meaning.   At its worst, our sensate experiences are overwhelmed by hidden meanings. The simplicity and directness of tangible reality is lost as we try to use the physical world as a vehicle for our own sense of higher purpose.   Another problem could occur when our the crown chakra's ideals change our actual physical experiences into the way they 'should' feel, rather than allowing them to merely be what they are.

Moon in Sagittarius; on the right remembering side

Here our abstract ideals are placed in the context of our inner genital chakra's awareness. The world of physical sensation is felt to be connected to a realm of abstract order. We use the actualities of our sensate experiences to know and understand a ltranspersonal order. It is through our personal physical sensations that we know larger pattern. This added significance blurs our sensations even as it deepens the meaning of our experiences.

Our sensate reality becomes our way of experiencing our abstract ideals. We believe the pattern of our reactions to our sensate experiences matter more than the actual events.   Our reactions affirm our own existence. Because it is on the internal right-hand side we feel that we are in control of our sensate awareness. We use the crown to shape and define our sensate experiences.   Ultimately, we feel that we are the active dynamic behind our experiences, while the actual events are merely things that we've chosen to have happen.   We shape our sensate experiences and reactions to help express and define who we are.

Moon in Pisces; on the left experiencing side

Here our abstract ideals are connected to our sensate experience of our outer environment. We are aware of a larger abstract pattern being enacted through our genital chakra's sensate awareness. It is through the physical immediacy of our experiences that we touch what we feel is the Divine. This gives our physical reality a great deal of depth and resonance. We can feel that there is more going on in our sensate experiences than what is superficially apparent.   The physical world is felt to have multiple layers of relationships which are present at any given moment, in any given object or event.

Because it is on the external left-hand side we feel like we are basically passive participants within our sensate experiences. The outer world has the creative dynamic. Even our responses to our sensate experiences are often felt to be the inevitable results of a higher pattern. We are unaware of our own role in how we create both our experiences and our reactions to them. We feel that we are experiencing to the world as it is, not creating the world through our interaction with it. Meanwhile it is own crown chakra's sense of pattern that we unconsciously use to shape our sensate reality.

Moon in the Solar Plexus Chakra

The crown chakra's abstract ideals are seen in the context of the solar plexus. Our social awareness has the crown chakra's awareness of transpersonal order added to it. In a way, we see God through our social reality. We can see the larger patterns of the crown through how our social surroundings function. This may lead us to idealize our cultural milieu.

At the same time we are aware of what our social reality actually is. Often the reality contrasts sharply with the ideal. We may find then ourselves with a cynical attitude, quarreling with our social environment. This can be an attempt to bring our culture into alignment with our ideals. We may argue in the face of long odds against what we feel are unjust social rules. We may honestly believe that our criticisms of others are for their own good. We may attempt to get others to see how their actions can fit into a more idealized pattern. Because we're dealing with the solar plexus, we may be somewhat confrontational.

We may also devolve into a world of social fantasy. We may imagine that we have a higher social position than we actually possess. We may see our culture as better than it really is. Our aspirations toward the ideal may sabotage the accuracy of our perceptions. An example would be the way that Hitler's Nazi Party saw itself. Hitler and the Nazi's clothed themselves in lofty ideals and ambitions, which they used to rationalize their atrocious acts. They used their ideals to hide from themselves the actuality of what they we doing to their fellow human beings.

At its best, we see how personal social actions and attitudes fit into a larger abstract cultural pattern. Seeing God in the way society functions helps us to strive to embody our social ideals. We seek to attain a better grasp of our social connections. Social reality becomes a means of personal fulfillment rather than coercion. At its worst, abstract social ideals are forced upon ourselves and others. We are callous and unfeeling as we criticize those around us. Our ideals become weapons which are used to hurt other people, rather than a source of shared aspiration.

Moon in Scorpio; on the right remembering side

Here our abstract ideals are connected to our inner sense of personal identity. We see ourselves as enacting ideals that are larger than ourselves. This heightens our personal sense of identity and purpose. We feel that we have a role to play which is given to us by the larger scheme of things. We feel intimately connected to the world around us and feel protective of the abstractions that help give us our social identity.

Because it is on the inner side, our ideals are seen as part of our sense of self. We also feel that we personally create and sustain these ideals. This means that we feel that our social identity is self-contained. Our abstract awareness of the Big Picture increases our own sense of personal identity. Even as we feel intimately connected to our social reality, we have a sense of being slightly removed from our social environment as we strive to serve what we see as higher principles. This can lead to our cutting through social blockages and dysfunctions. This can also lead to our trying to impose our ideals on others. We are also very protective of our spiritual values.

Moon in Aries; on the left experiencing side

Here our abstract ideals are connected to our external sense of personal identity. We see the social realm around us as ultimately being guided by transpersonal order. This can make us feel that we are living by a higher set of rules than our prevailing culture, and so 'their' rules do not apply to us. This can lead to an adventurous social self assertiveness. It may also lead to an attitude of smug social superiority.

Or we may see our culture as shaped by rules which we must all follow, as these rules ultimately stem from a higher source. The collective social pattern provides an ideal that is a guide for the individual. We must all individually strive to take our proper place in the larger social collective pattern.

Because is on the outer side, these social rules and ideals are felt to be outside of us. Even though social reality is felt to be something that we are intimately involved with, we feel that it is an external force in our lives. This makes us believe we are essentially reacting to the larger social group and it's overshadowing abstract principles. We only have a few choices: comply, disobey, pretend to comply, or seek to modify our culture's values. Whatever we choose to do at any given moment, we are always aware of the our culture's rules and where we stand in relation to them.

Moon in the Heart Chakra

Here we place our abstract sense of order into the context of our emotional awareness. Our emotions are shaped by our spiritual ideals. This can leads us to feel that any particular emotion is just a part of a larger matrix. We look for the larger context of any particular emotional feeling. There's also a tendency to idealize our emotions. Negative emotions are seen as expressions of a larger discontent. If we remove the source of discontent, then we remove the negativity.

This can help us to find a stable emotional bedrock. The problem is that we may create a list of emotional 'shoulds' and 'shouldn't's'. Rather than help us to understand our emotions more fully, the crown chakra may lead to our becoming rather judgmental. How we feel is pressed to conform to our idealized notions.

There may also be a tendency to use our ideals as an escape mechanism rather than as a source of aspiration. We may create a sense of ourselves and the world around us that isn't necessarily accurate. We might then retreat into fantasy to protect ourselves emotionally.

At its best, we feel the presence of divinity through our emotions. The statement 'God is love' fits this planetary chakric placement well. We feel that there's an underlying pervasive emotional bond which exists between ourselves and everything around us. Through this rapport we attain a greater trust in ourselves and in the world around us. The larger context also helps us to place our own emotional frailties into a larger, gentler context. At its worst, our emotions may use a larger context to justify our emotions. We may become emotionally self-indulgent. Our emotions may swell and become grandiose. We could become isolated, believing that we have a unique a connection to the abstract ideals of the crown. Rather than connect us, our emotional ideals separate us and become a means for us to look down on others. We feel personally blessed and favored by God.

Moon in Libra; on the right remembering side

Here our inner heart chakra receives and manifests the awareness of the crown chakra. This adds a sense of higher divine presence to our emotional connections and our own inner emotional state. We tend to idealize our emotional state and see it as a way of connecting ourselves to the divine. We use our ideals to help shape our sense of ourselves and our emotional responses. This can lead to an unwillingness to feel unpleasant emotions because that does not fit our ideals. We tend to self censure our emotions.

Because is on the inside, our emotional state is something that we feel exists within us and is largely under our own control. We do not just emotionally react, we create and control our selves through our emotional reactions and ideals.

We use our own sense of transpersonal order to help shore up our personal emotional state. By trusting what we know in our hearts our emotions help us connect to the Big Picture. This placement makes us believe that our soul represents a larger pattern and that through our emotional being we can know the transcendent. We believe our emotions run deep and enable us to both feel and express the presence of the divine.

Moon in Taurus; on the left experiencing side

Here our outer heart chakra receives and interprets the crown chakra's awareness. This adds a deep of sense significance to the things that we feel emotionally connected to. It adds a transpersonal depth to our emotional bonds. We see this connection as something that is created externally to us by the presence of the divine. This may lead us to idealize our emotional reality. It also increases our trust in our own emotional responses.

Because the activity is on the outside, our emotional reality feels like it happens to us. The active dynamic is felt to be in the hands of the outer world. We basically react, using our crown chakra's sense of pattern to guide us. Our emotional responses feel like they're the direct result of large scale external factors. This doesn't necessarily mean that we are the victims of our emotions. Rather that our emotions are partly responding to a larger whole which we feel all around us. This can enable us to have a clear awareness of exactly how we feel about things - assuming that we don't become enmeshed in our crown's idealizations. Ultimately we feel like we are acting in response to an outer stimulus. It is the outer stimulus that calls forth our emotional response.

Moon in the Throat Chakra

With this placement our sense of abstract structure is placed into the throat chakra's intellectual awareness. The crown chakra's pervasive awareness of interrelationship influences the way our mind thinks. Even though the throat chakra cannot perceive the relationships the crown sees, the crown, and therefore the throat, presumes that some kind of abstract order at work. The crown chakra provides an integrating pattern for the throat's ideas.

The throat may make a leap of faith and decide to trust the crown's sense of order. Or the throat may find itself attempting to rationally prove what the crown intuitively believes is true. If the throat attempts to prove to itself what the crown perceives, it may find this task very difficult. Because the crown's understanding is beyond the throat's comprehension, the throat may find itself incapable of creating an adequate rational explanation. This may cause the throat to become anxious.

If the throat can establish a degree of trust, then assimilating the crown chakra's awareness will not be disruptive. It will use the crown chakra's greater awareness to help it understand things more clearly. Occasionally, the throat will be able to use the crown's awareness to fill in some blank areas in it's understanding. The throat may use 'labeling parts' as a method of understanding. The crown doesn't label parts because it sees wholes. This makes it more difficult for the throat to gain access to the crown's understanding. When the throat is unable to breakdown a whole into parts and then name those parts, it feels it's knowledge is incomplete.

At its best, the crown chakra aids the throat's understanding and enables it to move about in a world that is larger than the throat would normally see. Our mind is able to accept the limitations of it's understanding and yet still stretch it's normal boundaries. The crown chakra's sense of interwoven relationship aids the throat in developing a more complete intellectual framework of understanding. At its worst, our rational mind is undermined by assuming the crown's sense of order. Our thinking becomes lazy and intolerant. We may feel that our crown chakra's notions have been divinely inspired, making rational inquiry unnecessary (and unwanted). We may become zealous in protecting our crown's convictions, refusing to see the possible truth behind anything that might contradict our crown chakra's beliefs. Or perhaps our mind is unable to trust the crown chakra. It may become anxious due to it's inability to fully comprehend the crown's awareness. By striving to figure out how the notions held by the crown actually work, the throat may become increasingly confused and frustrated .

Moon in Virgo; on the right remembering side

Here our throat chakra receives our crown chakra's awareness. We use our mind to enact what we see as the divine order. We are aware of abstract patterns of relationship and tend to look for them with our minds. We also use our mind to analyze and understand our own abstract foundations. There is an overshadowing sense of precision to the way world is ordered. We feel a strong compulsion to understand that order. If we feel that something is outside this often vague sense of ideal correctness, it may cause us to become anxious or upset.

Because it is on the inside, the concepts we have about the higher abstract order feel like they're created by us and are a part of us. At the same time, we see our notions of ideal order as stemming from what is true in an absolute sense. This can make us rather judgmental, or as we prefer to see it, very discriminating. We feel that the concepts that we use to understand the crown's perception of order are our own and something which we have made happen.

There is a tendency for us to become anxious as we try to enact our ideals in our own personal realm as well as in the world around us. We worry about our own inadequacies in light of the ideals we believe we must uphold.

Moon in Gemini; on the left experiencing side

Here our throat chakra receives our crown chakra's abstract awareness of pattern. We use the mind to perceive and enact what we see as a divinely created external order. We use our minds to try to understand and share this order. Because it is on the outside, we feel that the order already exists and we merely have to uncover it. There is an added social element to our quest. We observe what other people think. We ideas that mutually aid our understanding. We use our mind to connect ourselves to both the crown's Big Picture and to the world around us.

There's a sense of ourselves as an intellectual voyager who intuitively uses an abstract paradigm to perceive various kinds of order. We trust the realm of the mind and see it as reflecting this higher order. We take the awareness of the crown chakra see how it provides an explanation for how things are. Because is on the outside, our concepts feel like they are objective entities that exist in their own right. We feel that we have uncovered a truth rather than created it. At the same time, we are the one who decides which ideas are good, which ideas are bad, and which ones are irrelevant. We are aware of the impact of the crown's concepts of order on the social groups that we interact with. We choose to belong to those groups that fit our own ideals.

As we try to enact our ideals in our own outer world we tend to become anxious. We worry about the world's inadequacies in light of the ideals we perceive, seek to share and which we try to uphold.

Moon in the Brow Chakra

With this planetary placement there is a tendency to see God through the vastness of the world's possibilities. The comment 'With God all things are possible.' fits this placement quite well. The world feels miraculous. This can lead to a belief that the higher pattern actually supports our personal desires. Our goals, as seen through the brow chakra, are seen as spiritual and blessed by God. Unfortunately, we may find ourselves trying to bend the larger pattern to serve our own purposes. If we are truly being spiritual then we will try to see how our wishes fit into the whole, rather than seeking how to make the whole conform to our personal desires.

With the awareness of the crown chakra placed into the brow chakra an abstract sense of interconnectedness influences our own will to be. Subtle abstract relationships are seen in the context of our own personal aspirations. Our personal aspirations are modified by the crown chakra's ideals. At the same time our personal intuition is used to select the underlying abstract pattern that most closely fits our own spiritual will and self expression. Our personal sense of purpose may become larger and more spiritual in scope. Or we may simply have an inflated sense of the importance of our desires and aspirations as we feel that what we want fulfills the larger pattern.

When we intuitively trust our crown's sense of order we are able to decisively choose what to do. When we mistrust our crown's sense of order, we will be hesitant and unwilling to commit ourselves to a course of action. In order for us to be able to be decisive we have to believe that we are acting in accord with the crown's higher pattern.

At its best, this placement will enable us to fluidly move in and out of situations as we achieve what we desire. We understand our larger context and see how larger situation and our own goals can work together. We fulfill desires that include the bigger picture, not just ourselves. At its worst, we will feel that the larger context can be bent to our personal will and that the real purpose of the world is the fulfillment of our own desires. While this is true on one level (due to spirit's extremely cooperative nature) the end result of following this concept is a soul eroding spiritual isolation. We become trapped in a world in which all we see is ourselves.

Moon in Leo; on the right remembering side

Here our preconscious sense of abstract pattern and relationship is placed in the context of our personal intuitive awareness of our own possibilities. Therefore we have an underlying sense that the Divine supports us in our desire to enact who we are in the world around us. Because our brow chakra only functions on the inner side it difficult for us to understand the outer context of our possibilities. Exactly how the outer world's larger order relates to our preconscious will to be is beyond our grasp.

We end up just assuming that things will work out. The opportunities which we require will be presented to us as we need them. Normally we have a genuine expectation of a benevolent universe providing us with what we need. We presume that if we keep our eyes open and are internally aware of the larger whole things will fall into place for us. That's just the way things work.

At the same time there can be a sense of frustration when things do not go smoothly and events don't just fall into place. Because we have no conscious frame of reference it is difficult for us to know what to do when things aren't flowing well for us. We might even come to expect things to go badly. We may believe that we are being punished because we have in some way stepped off our True Path. A sense of being out of sync pervades us.

At it's best, we are in tune with our larger purpose which in turn is in sync with our personal purpose and things do just flow into place. We actually are lucky. At it's worst, we are working against our own larger purpose, as well as our outer environment, and so things feel like they are a constant struggle. We are unlucky as we feel disconnected from ourselves and the world around us.

Moon in the Crown Chakra

This placement has the crown chakra standing alone. The crown's awareness is not placed into the context of any other chakra. This can lead to an intuitive sense of how things interconnect that is fairly strong and fluid. Because our awareness acts on it's own it can gather a momentum that is rather detached from anything other than itself. The problem becomes placing our awareness into an effective context. Our intuitions of abstract order have no external reference point and so they can become self-revolving. We may try to dig deeper into our ideals as a way of reassuring ourselves. This can lead to our becoming both more intense and more out of touch. Which then leads to digging even deeper... we act in a way that is circular and self feeding. Eventually there will either be an intuitive breakthrough, or a completely frustrated, confused melodrama.

With this planetary placement the divine is known through a sense of psychic rapport with the extreme orderliness of the world. God is considered to be the Great Architect. The abstract patterns of the crown chakra may seem to float far above and beyond tangible existence. While we may feel able to understand the way things should work in an ideal universe, that universe may feel distant from the normal reality of time and space.

Ideal order, while intuitively felt, is also often barely understood. When we trust our intuitive understanding, everything works together the way it is 'supposed' to work. We feel that everything is being watched over by a transpersonal intelligence and all is well. When we mistrust our intuitive understanding of the integrating pattern, we feel that whatever ideal order there may be has little impact on the real world. It is as if God has withdrawn from the world that God created.

Because the crown is preconscious, with this placement we normally have little conscious awareness of the activity of the crown chakra. On occasion we may be overwhelmed by a sense of the extreme order of the universe. We may see everything as actually existing in the abstract ideal and not in the tangible world. If spirit becomes more real that matter, the underlying integration of the abstract and the concrete may be lost. Without the physical world to express them our abstract patterns of relationship become meaningless. Without spiritual enrichment the physical world becomes dull and drab.

At its best, this placement enables us to feel an intimate personal connection with the spiritual. Life feels animated by an inner abstract presence. We feel that ultimately everything will be all right, although the exact details as to how may seem to remain beyond our field of vision. At its worst, spirit feels absent from the world. There is no underlying cohesion to things. Aspects of our world float all by themselves as a bunch of isolated islands. Anarchy is loosed upon a world that interacts without mutual purpose and is devoid of rhyme or reason.

Moon in Cancer; on the right remembering side

Here the crown chakra provides it's own frame of reference. We feel personally anchored by an abstract sense of order. This means that we assume the presence of the larger framework that we are operating within. We also believe, without thinking about it, that on some deep hidden level that the world is a highly ordered place. It is difficult for us to see this underlying assumption. The preconscious nature of the crown chakra, along with its transpersonal nature, makes it difficult for us to consciously grasp its beliefs and mechanisms. Usually we just assume that our spiritual beliefs and ideals are reasonable and true.

At it's best, the world of spirit and matter are intimately connected. We are able to act with the confidence that we live in a world that sustains us within an enveloping larger purpose. Everything is intimately interwoven, bound together in mutually sustaining activities and purposes. We have flashes of intuitive insight which both direct and anchor us within a guiding ideal. At it's worst, we feel that spirit and matter are at odds and struggle against each other. We may strive to be either spiritual or material and create tremendous personal tension in the attempt to separate the two. An unbridgeable rift is seen between the ideal and the real. We long to be something that we feel we cannot be and feel saddened by our situation. The world is felt to betray us by being either a purely tangible machine that is devoid of any spiritual meaning, or else by being a material prison that keeps us from our true spiritual home.

APPENDIXES

Brief Chakric Meanings

Root: transpersonal physical structure (trust or mistrust)
Genital: sensate experience (like or dislike)
Solar Plexus: social identity, outer self (dominant or submissive)
Heart: emotional core, soul (connected or disconnected)
Throat: mental awareness, inner self (true or untrue)
Brow: intuitive awareness of potentials (fulfilling or stifling)
Crown: transpersonal abstract structure (fits or doesn't fit)

Brief Planetary Meanings

Saturn: point of personal foundation, destiny
Jupiter: point of personal awareness, experience
Mars: point of personal activity, enactment
Venus: point of personal fruition, fulfillment
Mercury: point of personal reflection, knowledge
Sun: point of personal affirmation, ensoulment
Moon: point of personal integration, understanding

Brief House Meanings

1st   Identity, persona, outer self, body, subjective experience, situational subjective self anchorage, self as physical focus in time and space

2nd   Possessions, wealth, money, resources, tangible fulfillment, situational self buttressing, ownership, material outreach of social position

3rd   Environment, habits, day to day activities and circumstances, writing, communication, siblings, short journeys, lower mind, situational percepts

4th   Home, self realization, immortality, abstract identity, subjective perspective, remote parent, final products, spiritual roots, inner self

5th   Self expression, play, love affairs, courtship, sports, gambling and speculation, pleasures, children, offspring of any sort, situational self extension

6th   Duty, service, work, adaptation and adjustment, illness and maladjustment, situational sustainment by self

7th   Partnerships, marriage, opportunity, one to one relations, romance, objective experience, situational objective anchorage

8th   Heritage, legacy, inheritance, sex as physical act, death literally or figuratively, change, t r a n s f o r m a t i o n, regeneration, transcendental self discovery, situational objective support

9th   Higher mind, intuition, cognition, philosophy, religion, prophecy, long journeys, inspiration, self as consciousness, conceptions, mind as sustainment of identity

10th   Honor, social position, authority, recognition, business, ambition, closer parent, objective perspective, situational flowering, social identity being

11th   Objectives, friendship, ideals, aspirations, advice given and received, goals, drive, s o c i a l o r g a n i z a t i o n s, o b j e c t i v e extension of partnerships, wishes and dreams

12th   Sustainment, hidden relationships, unconscious mind, karma, self undoing, intangible aid and grounding, confinement, spiritual resources, situational sustainment of self

Seven Vehicle Structure and Substructure (derived from Marc Edmund Jones)

MACROCOSMIC VEHICLE

		Virgo	Sagittarius
			Libra
			Scorpio
		Leo	Capricorn
		Cancer	Aquarius
		Gemini	Pisces
		Taurus	Aries

CAUSAL VEHICLE

		Libra	Capricorn
			Scorpio
			Sagittarius
		Virgo	Aquarius
		Leo	Pisces
		Cancer	Aries
		Gemini	Taurus

MENTAL VEHICLE

	Virgo		Sagittarius
	Libra		Capricorn
Leo	Scorpio	Scorpio	Aquarius
Cancer	Sagittarius	Libra	Pisces
Gemini	Capricorn	Virgo	Aries
Taurus	Aquarius	Leo	Taurus
Aries	Pisces	Cancer	Gemini

ASTRAL VEHICLE

	Leo		Capricorn
	Virgo		Aquarius
Cancer	Libra	Sagittarius	Pisces
Gemini	Scorpio	Scorpio	Aries
Taurus	Sagittarius	Libra	Taurus
Aries	Capricorn	Virgo	Gemini
Pisces	Aquarius	Leo	Cancer

ETHERIC VEHICLE

	Cancer		Aquarius
	Leo		Pisces
Gemini	Virgo	Capricorn	Aries
Taurus	Libra	Sagittarius	Taurus
Aries	Scorpio	Scorpio	Gemini
Pisces	Sagittarius	Libra	Cancer
Aquarius	Capricorn	Virgo	Leo

ORGANIC VEHICLE

	Gemini		Pisces
	Cancer		Aries
Taurus	Leo	Aquarius	Taurus
Aries	Virgo	Capricorn	Gemini
Pisces	Libra	Sagittarius	Cancer
Aquarius	Scorpio	Scorpio	Leo
Capricorn	Sagittarius	Libra	Virgo

MICROCOSMIC VEHICLE

	Taurus		Aries
	Gemini		Taurus
Aries	Cancer	Pisces	Gemini
Pisces	Leo	Aquarius	Cancer
Aquarius	Virgo	Capricorn	Leo
Capricorn	Libra	Sagittarius	Virgo
Sagittarius	Scorpio	Scorpio	Libra

expression	sustainment	expression	sustainment
of	OF	OF	OF
expression	expression	sustainment	sustainment

Classic Color Assignments of the Chakras

Crown	Purple
Brow	Magenta
Throat	Blue
Heart	Green
Solar Plexus	Yellow
Genital	Orange
Root	Red

There is a great deal of interest in the color of the chakras and the aura. We need to understand that the chakras are interactive and they connect us with our environment. In different situations some chakras are active while others are passive. This means that the color and the intensity of our aura changes depending on our circumstances. If we are in a competitive social situation the solar plexus chakra would be most active. In a spiritual situation the brow and crown chakra may dominate. If we are reading or engaging in an intellectual activity the throat will become the primary chakra. We can only use a chakric diagram to find which chakra or chakras would normally be dominant in a person's awareness. This enables us to roughly guess what color a person's aura would be most of the time.

This means that we would expect a person who is primarily active at the heart chakra to have a green tint predominant in their aura. If their throat chakra is dominant then we would expect their aura to be mostly blue. If there is no dominant chakra then their aura's color would depend on their situation. The color would depend on which chakra is the most actively involved. Change the situation and primarily active chakra may change and the auric color would also change.

Chakric Diagram Worksheet

For_____ Birth Date _____

Time____:____ Am/Pm Time Zone ___ Location_____

Outer Sign	Chakra & Planet	Inner Sign
	Crown ☽ ♋	
	Brow ☉ ♌	
♊	Throat ☿ ♍	
♉	Heart ♀ ♎	
♈	Solar Plexus ♂ ♏	
♓	Genital ♃ ♐	
♒	Root ♄ ♑	

Chakric Motion

Up
Down
None

Cultural Motion

♀ Solar Plexus
♆ Genital
♅ Root

Sources

My personal experiences with the chakras are the core of this piece . My chakras spontaneously became apparent to me one summer and it took me quite a while to realize the full scope of what I was experiencing. The more formal concepts within this study come from a variety of sources:

• Chakric: while I found Ledbetter's and the Theosophical Society's perspective a bit stodgily Victorian and anchored in a somewhat dampening morality, it was westernized enough so that it's perspective was more approachable to me than the purely Hindu or Buddhist models. For example, I have found the root to be far more than a fight or flight mechanism. Also, while I have experienced the activity of my own chakric awareness within each of the three nadis, I am unwilling to argue the subtle differences between systems.

• Kundalini: there are many books and articles on the kundalini available in English. The kundalini, in my experience, does not live up to the magical hype that I've read about. So, either some accounts are exaggerated, or my experience of the kundalini is incomplete. Probably a bit of both. This is not to discount the extremely animated sense of depth, connection and vitality that the kundalini brings to one's awareness. I've found it to have strong visual effects, revealing swirls of energy, a deep sense of clarity, as well as causing difficulty focusing on mundane. I guess it could be seen as the crown chakra buried within the root chakra.

• Astrological: while the methods of bringing the chakras to life in the chakric astrology system presented here are my own, the core astrological structure is found in the "Theosophical Astrology" lesson set written by Marc Edmund Jones in the 1930's for the Sabian Assembly (an esoteric organization which he founded that is still active). According to Marc Jones the Theosophical Astrology lesson set is based on an ancient Egyptian astrological system, while the more familiar house wheel based astrological system is Sumerian in origin. (I never saw any documentation of this, but I remember being told by a member of the Sabian Assembly that this is something Jones had once said in an off-the-cuff comment during a lecture.) Marc Jones stressed a 'torso' chakric emphasis - the genital to throat chakras - which he felt was where most people spend most of their time. He didn't use the system of planetary rulerships to connect the individual chakras (this is my major innovation), instead he was more focused on the overall spatial balance of the chakric diagram.

- The overall astrological work of Marc Jones is both broad in scope and very insightful. I highly recommend his astrological textbooks which can still be found with a little bit of searching, although his chakric astrology system is only found in the Sabian Assembly's Theosophical Astrology lesson set.

Contact the Author

I sincerely hope that you found the ideas in these pages useful and interesting. I regret that the writing isn't more fluid, but I had great difficulty organizing and distilling the ideas and was pleased to get them into a form that was evenly remotely coherent. (Hopefully I've achieved a bit better than that.)

If you wish contact me with any questions, observations, or requests for a personal chakric astrological delineation (sorry, but I will have to charge a fee for any readings due to the time involved), you can e-mail me at:

chakricastrologer@hotmail.com

Hopefully after reading this book you will find your self awareness enriched and the people around you a little less mysterious.

- Tom Sheeley

www.ingramcontent.com/pod-product-compliance
Lightning Source LLC
LaVergne TN
LVHW061222060426
835509LV00012B/1391